THE POLITICS OF MODERATION

An Interpretation of Plato's Republic

John F. Wilson

UNIVERSITY
PRESS OF
AMERICA

LANHAM • NEW YORK • LONDON

Library of Congress Cataloging in Publication Data

Wilson, John F., 1943-
   The politics of moderation.

   Includes bibliographical references and indexes.
   1. Plato. Republic. I. Plato. Republic. II. Title.
JC71.P6W48   1984   321'.07   84-10442
ISBN 0-8191-4017-1 (alk. paper)
ISBN 0-8191-4018-X (pbk. : alk. paper)

To Moxie,

In Loving Memory

ACKNOWLEDGEMENTS

Like everyone who does this work, my first and greatest debt is to Socrates and Plato. Of hardly less practical significance is our debt to all of those who have helped keep their thought and the texts alive.

I have two major intellectual debts. The first is to the late Professor Leo Strauss, of the University of Chicago and St. John's College. Through his seminal interpretative work on the Republic and other texts, Professor Strauss has restored the tradition of serious interpretation in political philosophy. The second is to Professor Henry S. Kariel, my colleague in the Political Science Department of the University of Hawaii at Manoa. Fifteen years of often spirited discussion of politics and political philosophy have left a deep impression on my thinking and on this book. Professor Kariel also provided sound practical advice.

I wish to thank Professor John G. Gunnell, in the Political Science Department of the State University of New York at Albany, who introduced me to Plato's political philosophy; my sometimes colleagues Professors Hilail Gildin and James N. Jordan, in the Philosophy Department of Queens College - C.U.N.Y., who kindly encouraged my work; Mr. Stuart Kiang, of the University of Hawaii Press, who made fundamentally helpful suggestions on an earlier draft of the manuscript; my colleagues Professors Benedict J. Kerkvliet and Neal A. Milner of the University of Hawaii at Manoa, who provided useful practical advice; and Ms. Helen Hudson, Production Editor of the University Press of America, for her prompt assistance on technical questions.

This work could not have been brought to completion without the efforts of Ms. Vivian Piilani Luning, Ms. Teryn Shea Aina, and especially Ms. Anne Witebsky. I am most grateful to them.

CONTENTS

Very slowly - over literally thousands of years -
there has come to exist a "standard" Republic, which
begins at the end of Book III, with the dutiful Guardians and the Noble Lie, and ends at the end of Book
VII, with the philosopher sailing off to the Isles of
the Blessed. This standard Republic, with some amazing
contradictions, inconsistencies, and discontinuities
ignored or gainsaid - the obvious one being between
dutiful Guardians and transcending philosophers - has
resulted in the conventional Platonism of caves, forms,
and philosopher-kings. This may be uplifting, in some
inspiriting sense, but it is not the book which the
discussants speak and/or which Plato wrote.

In The Politics of Moderation, one of my basic
purposes is to restore the wholeness of the Republic.
To this end, I place considerable emphasis on the
later books. The Republic is a dialogue. More, it is
some approximation of the practice of the dialectic.
Dialogues move: each response or objection is significant because some element or aspect of being human is
making a claim to be heard, considered, weighted, and
included. The dialectic presents, argues, and aims at
accommodating opposites or contenders. In the best
sense, it is political. All this being so, it is
logical to place more rather than less emphasis on the
later books, expecting that some resolution may occur
there. I will try to show that this resolution does
take place.

Not all problems in the Republic are equally
fundamental. The obvious subject of the work is justice. Since justice is problematic, politically but
especially philosophically, the fundamental problem of
the work is the relationship between justice and moderation. Cryptically, Socrates says at 433c that justice
is the "rival" to moderation (and to the other virtues,
but above all to moderation). The explication of this
rivalry is the plot of the Republic, a plot sometimes
fairly apparent, sometimes touched on lightly, and
sometimes hidden. My second basic purpose is to bring
that rivalry fully to the surface. Discussion of the
claims of the rivals also leads to the answer to the
basic practical question, how should one live? Justice
as integrity, and moderation as, let's say, blending-

ness present what appear as conflicting attitudes of
soul and ways of life. They seem to imply different
philosophical, personal, and political existences.
Beyond the deflecting of a Glaucon's eros or even the
complicating of an Adeimantus' austerity, the relationship between being just and being moderate is the serious problem of a serious man. At least, so I interpret
the Republic, and so I will attempt to persuade my
reader.

A word about my method. I try here to make no
assumptions about the meaning of what is being said:
within the limit of developing main argument lines, to
skip or skim over nothing without understanding it: to
be surprised or curious or puzzled when a statement is,
or seems to be, or is intended to be surprising or
curious or puzzling; to work my way through these difficulties, until I think that I understand and have
resolved them, and then to test my understanding
against the subsequent flow and developments of the
dialogue: to remember exactly what has been said or
proved or accepted: as the basic problems begin to
become evident to me, to note Glaucon's or Adeimantus'
characteristic lapses and inattentions, and to point
out their and Socrates' response (or nonresponse) to
them: and perhaps above all, to act as if nothing is
certain or authoritative or final unless it actually
turns out that way, and then to trust my thinking and
judgment that it is really so.

In attempting a careful and attentive reading, I
was helped fundamentally by Allan Bloom's painstaking
translation (Basic Books, 1968). To give only one
example: in Book VII, at 532c, I was brought up short
by Socrates' statement that

>   the persisting inability [my emphasis] to
>   look at the animals and the plants and the
>   sun's light, ...-all this activity of the
>   arts, which we went through, has the power
>   to release and leads what is best in the
>   soul up to the contemplation of what is best
>   in the things that are,...

Contrast this precision with Francis M. Cornford's
translation (Oxford, 1945) of the passage:

>   he was still unable to look at the animals
>   and plants and the sunlight;... Now the
>   whole course of study in the arts we have re-

viewed has the corresponding effect of leading the noblest faculty of the soul toward
the contemplation of the highest of all
realities,...

I wondered: why the persisting inability (adynamia)?
How can this inability lead to understanding? Then,
what thing or power is the best in the soul, and how
does it correspond to what is best in the things which
are? Cornford's paraphrasing translation leaves no
doubt that "he" - presumably "the philosopher", but
there is no person in the passage - in due course
contemplates the highest of all realities, which the
reader already knows - or believes - is "the good".
Bloom's translation not only left doubt: it brought
me up short, and made me work and then begin to think
that there might be some relationship between what is
best in the soul and in the things which are, between
these and what follows, the practice of dialectic. From
there, I started to think other, different thoughts
about the "message" of Book VII, in relation to what
Plato says of Socrates elsewhere. And, then, to begin
to relate this discovery to others. This process of
critical, integrative reading, repeated throughout the
work, is my method.

*   *   *

This method has its limitations. It is almost
completely "internal". The role of the interpreter is
roughly that of the twelfth participant in the dia-
logue-questioning, remembering, seeking connections,
speculating about patterns, discovering, questioning
again, and of course recording. Because I see myself
as an interested participant, I learn and am shaped
significantly by the dialogue; but the influence which
plays on the interpreter, and thus on the mode of interpretation, is only the dialogue. Beyond faithful
and sustained engagement, however, this method does
have the advantages of focus and clarity.

Other interpreters use other methods. One mode
is well represented by Julia Annas, An Introduction to
Plato's Republic (Oxford, 1981), and Nicholas P. White,
A Companion to Plato's Republic (Hackett, 1979). These
are works by philosophers who rest their interpreta-
tions on the premise that Plato is doing moral theory
or moral philosophy. For these scholars, justice is
unproblematically the subject of the Republic, and the
just city is Plato's unqualified political recommen-

dation. These assumptions cause them to abstract almost completely from the dialogue as an empirical, implicitly political phenomenon, and from the dramatic action. I disagree with this - my Plato is a poet and producer, in a word an _artificer_ of political _philosophizing_ but these works are helpful, especially White's painstaking, argument-by-argument analysis.

I am indebted to White most particularly for drawing my attention to the relationship between 437b-439d and 580d-581e (_Companion_, pp.125, 225-227). These passages raise the issue of whether all three divisions of the soul are desiring or erotic. Leo Strauss, in _The City and Man_ (Rand McNally, 1964) (followed by Bloom's "Interpretative Essay" in his edition of the _Republic_), contends that they are. This premise, coupled with Strauss' belief that the key to understanding the _Republic_ is grasping Plato's systematic abstraction from the body, yields the very interesting Strauss-Bloom interpretation.

The Strauss-Bloom interpretation argues that the city, and thus practical justice, is naturally and severely limited by the natural limitations of its types of representative men. Most men are limited by physical desire and its consequences, especially private families and property. The philosopher is defined by a non-sensual _eros_, as is the political man. The philosopher desires truth, the politician honor. Although different, these desires serve to lift them above the mass of men. The task of the philosopher is to convince the potential politician, first, that honor is not a great good because it is bestowed by the fickle _demos_ and, second, that truth is the greatest good. The desire of the political type for honor is then diminished. Thus the theme of the Strauss-Bloom _Republic_ is "the education of Glaucon".

In this view, the philosopher will always be a philosopher, will always desire truth, and thus will always shun politics. What of the politician? Will he always desire honor, no matter what mode of persuasion is employed by the philosopher? If the philosopher is to succeed, the answer must be "no". The art of the philosopher - perhaps assisted by the art of the well-inclined rhetorician - must be such that it can deflect the politician's desire. It is probably important here that the philosopher is considerably older than the would-be politician.

Does this action of the philosopher improve the city, assuming that it succeeds? It is hard to see how it can. The philosopher desires truth, which requires solitude and removal from politics. He acts even quasi-politically only in his own permanent interest as a philosopher. If it succeeds, this action overcomes the desire for honor and takes from the city one of its best young politicians. At least, he becomes less emphatic in his desire to serve the city and thus win honor. At most, he abandons public life altogether.

This broad argument rests on four assumptions. First, like the "moral theory" interpretation, it assumes that Plato is a philosopher, or has primarily the interests of philosophy at heart. Second, it assumes that there is some entity "the body" which may exist apart from "the soul", and thus can be pointedly ignored or "abstracted from". Third, it assumes that there are distinct, permanent human types which remain more or less constant whatever physical, moral, or intellectual influences play upon them. The argument here seems to be that these types, but especially the philosopher, are both ideal and empirical, while the just city - however defined or understood - is ideal only. Fourth, it assumes that there is an order of reality which runs, in ascending order, physical pleasure: honor: truth. If the philosopher is to prevail, it must be because the object of his eros, truth, is more real than that of the politician and, it goes without saying, that of the lover of sensual pleasure.

All of these assumptions are, I believe, questionable in terms of the text of the Republic. I speak to them especially in my interpretation of Book VII, and of the three arguments for the superiority of the philosophical life in Book IX, but generally throughout The Politics of Moderation.

PREFACE

INTRODUCTION: THE MUTED THEMES OF THE REPUBLIC

Both on the face of things, and in the long tradition of interpretation, the subject of Plato's Republic is justice. The book's subtitle, apparently given it not by Plato but by early editors, is "On the Just". It is appropriate, and surprisingly revealing of the truer, more profound content and meaning of the Republic, to begin by considering why the first and most obvious concern is justice.

The Republic is a work of political philosophy. In this context, I mean that the Republic is philosophizing in the classical polis. Socrates and his companions are, for the most part, Athenian. They "do philosophy" in Athens, that most famous if least typical of the ancient Greek cities.

As the Republic opens, and gets under way, neither the participants in the dialogue - Socrates excepted - nor the reader know what is happening. Socrates makes the introduction of justice as the topic of discussion appear to be accidental. As the discussion continues, it seems that justice is being discussed in its own right, not as a prelude to something else. This is natural and inevitable, given life in the polis. Justice is the fundamental issue of political life and the obvious political good. The participants in the discussion are spirited men who have firm ideas or deep-seated convictions about what justice is, and about whether and why it is useful in living successfully.

Socrates knows this, and uses his knowledge to give impetus and form to a dialogue which will range far beyond its initial question of whether it is better to live justly or unjustly. He is dealing with spirited men, and spirited men wish to live political lives and to know about political matters. They want success, justly if possible, less than justly or unjustly if necessary. First of all, they want success within the context of the polis, in political life. This being so, the only question of general philosophical import which Socrates could possibly interest them in is justice. Even here, he must limit himself. They are not truly interested in justice in itself, justice in abstraction, but instead in the pragmatic question of whether justice is good <u>for</u> <u>them</u> and conducive to satisfying their ambitions.

This begins to engage the major theme: but it is worth pausing for just a moment to reflect on the attractions of justice as a topic of conversation. The real or assumed attitude of the participants toward justice is instrumental, but perhaps not wholly so. There is a certain rudimentary sense in which justice in itself <u>is</u> attractive. Justice is attractive because it is very likely that we have felt or know about injustice. Whether or not it is noble, the hatred for injustice is natural, and thus the love or desire for justice is inevitable. That this is so is the chief advantage which political life has in commending itself as <u>the</u> way of life.

But this is somewhat a digression: I return to the main theme. The concern of the participants is whether justice is good for them. Socrates must convince them that it is, and moreover that justice is good in itself, whatever its reputation or apparent consequence might be.

However, "justice is good in itself" is an ambiguous phrase. It may mean that justice is desirable for its own sake, not merely because it brings success. This is how the participants understand the phrase when the problem of justice is posed systematically at the outset of Book II. Socrates does not enlighten them further at that point, and allows justice in political arrangements to dominate the discussion during the first four books.

The second possible meaning of the phrase is that justice is <u>the</u> good: justice is the highest or greatest good. This view is implicit in any completed political science. The city - or state, or commonwealth, or political community - is the final form of organization, and the just city is the best among cities. Thus the just political organization is the highest thing and the greatest good. This view is not anthropocentric or humanistic - of course the individual human being is defined by and subordinate to the city -, but rather "polito-centric".

In the text, these undercurrents run through Book IV. By that point, it is apparent that Socrates has played a huge trick on his friends by searching for a justice which is "good in itself". The city and its arrangements are not "justice"; they are merely an example of justice. Justice itself is something else, some sort of transcendent entity, applied to and informing specific things like cities. In a word, justice is an idea. Worse than this: justice is only one of a number of ideas, and it is not obvious that it is the greatest idea. There may be a greater idea, which lies "beyond" justice and somehow "causes" justice and the other, lesser ideas to exist. This greatest idea is the good, the absolute good, which is known by that name and no other. Slowly, it begins to dawn on the dazed and then dazzled audience that it is this absolute good, and not merely justice, which they have been searching for.

The search for the absolute good is not the business of political science. Political science and political life are limited by justice. Their knowledge is of the good for the city. Not entirely in passing, it is worth noting how Socrates' concentration on the city elevates or at least changes the perspective of the participants. They began self-preoccupied: justice was worth having only if it proved to be good for them. But the focus on the city has taught them this basic and rather hard lesson: justice is what is good for the city. The standard of justice is the well-being of the city as a whole. Whether justice is also good for each and every individual is questionable, and largely a matter of indifference to political science as such.

There is an activity whose nature it is to seek to know the absolute good, and an individual who embodies that nature. They are, of course, philosophy and the philosopher. In any given progression, logical or historical, the philosopher emerges once the limits of the city, and thus of political science become known. In other words, justice is only one of the ideas, and a lesser one at that. Since it is the business of the philosopher to get involved with and know all ideas, he cannot stop with justice. Inquiry into the city as a whole implies inquiry into wholes which are not merely political or human. It implies inquiry into the whole as a whole, especially that inquiry when it seeks to know the cause of the whole. The simplest empirical observation, which in principle is absolutely forbidden to a mature political science, tells us that the city is only part of the whole, and a small part at that; and certainly that the city does not cause the larger natural whole. Whether or not it is caused by that natural whole is another question, but again a question beyond the limits of political science.

In very broad outline, these are the concerns of the first part of the Republic, which extends through the end of Book VII. On reflection, it turns out that the search which their inability to define justice satisfactorily sends them off on is a search for the absolute good. To put it another, more personal way, the cause of the search is the desire of the participants to live successfully. Either way, the logical goal of the search is knowledge of the absolutely existent or the absolutely real. Whether or not justice is the good, the participants begin to believe that they must know the good, and become involved with the good, if their lives are to have an absolutely firm foundation.

Two things should be noted now. First, their search takes them very far from ordinary political life, defined by some imperfect notion of justice. A gradual loosening of political ties occurs. Seeking to know justice itself - that is, to define it - requires that they first become fully aware of the idea of justice implicit in their own native political arrangements, and then that they subject that idea to logical criticism. This leads Socrates and his friends toward justice itself, and thus toward the best political arrangements in which true justice is made manifest. By the standard of logos - of ordered speech, of reason, of the defining activity - ordinary political life is seen as inferior to truly just political life.

Second, the best political life, once discovered, must itself be subjected to logical criticism. In other words, having arrived at what justice is, logos must then wonder whether justice is the good. Here, logos and common sense appear to agree that this is very doubtful. To common sense, justice appears to be merely hard and necessary, not desirable in itself. Logically, justice does not seem to be flatly equivalent to the good. Socrates defines justice as each thing being itself, and not some other thing. This is pure justice, but logic questions whether severely individuated things can possibly constitute a coherent world; and, if not, how a justice which destroys the cohesion of the world can be believed to be any good at all, let alone the absolute good.

xviii

With this, the main theme in all its fullness begins to emerge. In methodological terms, philosophy is the defining activity. It moves the dialogue along from the opening question, "What must one know, do, or be in order to live successfully?", first to the question, "What is justice?", and then to the question, "Is justice the greatest good?". Since the answer to the last question is "no", the participants are carried successively beyond themselves; their own city; the most just city; and finally all human limits. In this way, the enormous power of critical philosophy is revealed to them dramatically, or should I say dialogically?

*   *   *

Although it is not usual to view them as such, the first seven books of the Republic constitute a very long introduction or, probably better said, a sustained approach to the basic question posed by the work. One would think, since the answer to the question of whether justice is the greatest good is in the negative, that the basic question would then be, "Well, if justice is not the greatest good, what is?". In one sense, this is the basic question; in another, it is not; and in any case, this is not the form which it takes. This will become clearer if the second broad section of the Republic is considered.

In fact, the second part of the Republic begins at the outset of Book VIII, which makes the work - or at least my analysis of it - appear unbalanced. But this is an accident, although a revealing one. Book VIII begins the treatment of the inferior regimes, from the second best, timocracy, to the worst, tyranny. But this treatment was "scheduled" to begin at the end of Book IV, with the conclusion of the discussion of justice in city and in soul. At that point, a dramatic outburst forced Socrates to make explicit things which he had chosen to leave concealed. The most attractive of these things is the sexual arrangements of the Guardians, but by far the most basic of them is the power of philosophy as an agent critical of political life.

Critical philosophy does two things. First, it undercuts the traditional basis of the city. That basis is opinion: philosophy, which seeks absolute knowledge, is impatient with opinion. It is disinclined to examine carefully the complex relationships among opinion, political life, and the nature of the human soul. To a philosophical logos soaring toward perfect clarity, opinion looks gray and confused, if not pitch black.

Second, philosophy refounds the best city. Having discredited opinion as a basis, philosophy has a political obligation to provide a new, more solid basis. The new basis should be knowledge, discovered by philosophical method. However, there are problems here. One is that philosophy is critical not only of opinion, but also of any "knowledge" which rests on an unexamined first principle, or hypothesis. By the highest standards of philosophy, a science resting on hypotheses is only a more sophisticated form of opinion. The other problem is that, in principle, philosophy is committed to an endless search. This requires that all apparently secure knowledge must be subjected to the restless, ruthless dialectic.

Given this, very great, literally infinite improvement is possible, but not absolute knowledge. The city founded on philosophy must be a progressive city. Since its basis - tentative or hypothetical knowledge - keeps changing, so must the superstructure or form of the city change to keep pace with its foundation. In Book VII, Socrates emphasizes the tendency of the philosopher to escape the city altogether. The explicit reason given is the desire to see the absolute good; but a philosopher with any minimum political awareness must be troubled by the insecurity of a city which is in a nearly continuous condition of flux.

Based on imperfect science, a failure of science brings the progressive city down. The failure is in the science of breeding, upon which the character of the rulers depends. This failure opens Part Two, which is the tale of the fall from the city of progressive science, through various inferior cities, to the horrors of an erotically-based tyranny.

To this point in the text, the broad argument of the Republic is this: aiming at the absolute good does not secure that good, but instead results in a wholly questionably, fundamentally non-political science; in the pursuit, in turn both the traditional justice of a particular city and the ideal justice of the best city are left behind as inferior goods; finally, the science depended upon quickly proves unreliable and leads to the fall of that city in which philosophy attempts to reach beyond justice to the absolute good.

I will comment on the implications of this broad argument in a moment; but first a remark or two on the progress or, rather, the decline of Part Two is necessary. There, the inferior regimes - timocracy or the rule of honorable men, oligarchy, democracy, and tyranny - are derived from one another, and discussed. The fall from the best to the worst is very rapid, at least measured in textual terms. Whereas the establishment of first the just and then the progressive city takes seven books, the fall to tyranny takes less than two books.

The reasons for the slow ascent but relatively rapid decline are never made explicit, but they are implicit in the relationship between the just city and the progressive city. The just city takes a long time to establish because it is based on the combination of good character and right opinion. This is developed slowly, through education in music and gymnastic. The ascent from the just city to the progressive one is faster, but still relatively slow. In the progressive city, philosophy and knowledge are substituted for right opinion and character. This takes time, since the man of character, formed slowly, is conservative. But, through a combination of critical arguments and dazzling promises - to say nothing of the "exile" of all those over ten years old - , philosophy succeeds in overcoming tradition and establishes the progressive city. This city, resting on hypothetical knowledge, reaches lofty heights despite, or perhaps just because of its unstable base.

By the standards of philosophy, right opinion is not absolutely certain. Good character is also questionable, especially insofar as it rests on right opinion. But these are far more stable than progressive hypothetical knowledge. In the progressive city, character - or some likeness of character - rests on science: the wholesome individual is a result of sound scientific breeding and advanced intellectual education. Any more traditional supports of good character and political stability have been stripped away, as unscientific obstacles to progress. Thus, when science fails, the fall to and through inferior regimes is quite rapid.

xxi

THE POLITICS OF MODERATION

Very nearly the last thing which occurs to the philosopher in the brilliant, unstable City of Progress is the sight of the absolute good. The route to that sight, the sight itself, and the consequences of the seeing all combine to induce in him profoundly disquieting second thoughts. After all, in the dramatic narrative the sight of the good comes much too late, even for the perfectly selfish philosopher. The price paid for the lofty perch required to view the good is not only the loss of the progressive city, but also the sickening plunge into tyranny.

The good is seen, or perhaps only glimpsed, in the last leaping flames of the dying city of progress. Given the demise of that city, and its political consequences, second thoughts occur. Among the second thoughts are these. First, it occurs to those who think that the search for the absolute good - broadly speaking, the philosophical activity - was not a very good idea. The city limited by ideal justice - by an implicit acceptance of justice as the good - was orderly and stable. Everyone had a function and a place, except of course the philosopher, and look at the difficulties which letting loose philosophy have gotten everyone into! Why, then, not return to the just city? Why not agree to hold that justice is the good, and prohibit anyone from questioning that convention?

Are there problems with the thought of returning to the just city? Perhaps there are. For one thing, it is hard to see a city which denies free speech and free inquiry as just. More fundamentally, the just city does not exist, except as an idea. It is based on the idea that justice is each thing being perfectly itself and no other thing - an idea full of logical and political difficulties; on a rigid convention mandating belief that this idea is the good; and on a prohibition of critical discussion of that idea or, at best, a tacit agreement to remain critically silent. Thus, the just city is not only fictional, but also has not abolished philosophy. It has merely arrested philosophy in mid-career, allowing it to reach to the idea of justice, but not beyond. This may be practically possible, but it is evidently unjust to the frustrated philosopher, and thus involves the just city in a hopeless if unspoken contradiction.

This second thought having proven fruitless, or productive of too-bitter fruit, a related one should be discussed briefly. This is another return, not to

the supposedly perfect justice of the just city, but
to the particular justice of some particular past historical city. This too is unsatisfactory. First, the
historical city does not claim to be fully just, but
merely acceptably so. Second, this claim is almost
certainly fraudulant, since an acceptable justice would
have been defended and perpetuated. Third, this city
too now exists only as an idea, in need of historically
inclined philosophers to reconstruct it in thought. In
short, this project suffers from all the difficulties
of a return to the just city, without the attraction
of that other project, the allure of a perfect or near
perfect justice.

*   *   *

At this point - it is the transition from the
second to the third and final part of the Republic - a
frustration and near despair must set in. Discipline
after discipline has been introduced, allowed free
play, and found wanting. Rough and ready practical
political science has been unable to create a just or
stable regime. "Normative" political science, cogni-
zant of ideas or forms, has articulated the just city,
but has been unable to justly limit philosophy. Philosophy has reformed the just city into a progressive
one, in order to use the city as a springboard to the
sight of the good. But it is doubtful that philosophy
can really know the good - how can it be sure that that
fleeting glimpse was the good?; and the hypothetical
sciences which philosophy leaves in its wake prove to
be unstable bases for political life. In the eighth
and ninth books, an observational political science of
psychopathology is presented, but all that this science
can do is stand by ineffectually as bearable regimes
degenerate, and political life darkens into tyranny.

All of this has occurred only in thought and
speech, among the participant in the dialogue. In
fact, only a few hours have passed: they are still
sitting in Cephalus' house. Around them, Athens still
stands, unmoved - at least as yet - by their thought
and its vast implications. Cities, regimes, sciences,
and whole ways of thinking have not risen and fallen.
Thought has leaped ahead and beyond. This is the way
of thought, to project beyond what now is, to what may
be or even must be. Everything is as it was, and yet

different, for thought sees all things, and is critical of them, and somehow changes everything which it touches.

Further second thoughts ensue. Critical thinking is untrue to itself if it is not critical of itself. The difficulties with a return to the just city induce this thought: perhaps justice is not the good. But this is a previous thought, which when fully developed led to the search for the absolute good. The consequences of that search are now known, at least in thought. A more comprehensive and thorough kind of second thinking emerges. This critical, reflective thinking is the foundation of the final part of the Republic.

The premises on which the argument has proceeded thus far are these: there is an absolute good, and that absolute good is an idea. Within that frame of thought, the philosophical question can be sharply focused: is justice the greatest good and, if it is not, what other idea is? In Part Three, the shortest and, indicatively, least argumentatively clear and direct portion of the work, these premises are questioned. But very little of the questioning is explicit, which makes the final portion difficult both to characterize and to get a good grasp on.

The third part begins, literally, in political wreckage. The fall of the highest, most progressive city, and the inability of either philosophy or science to arrest that fall have resulted in tyranny. The original choice, between the life of the just man and the life of the tyrant, is posed again. Tyranny has been shown to be the worst of political circumstances, and the participants have no inclination to choose the tyrant's life. Well and good; but, in rejecting the tyrant's life, are they thereby choosing the life of the just man? And, if so, what exactly are they doing in choosing the just life? Are they thereby choosing justice, in spite of both the intrinsic and the consequential difficulties with the idea of justice? Further, if they choose justice, does this imply a return to the just city, with all the doubts and difficulties of that project?

It is apparent that the first two parts of the Republic have not really resolved anything. Socrates and his friends began with the question of how one should live one's life; whether one should be just or unjust; broadly, with the question of what life to choose. Very near the end, and again at the very end of the discussion, they return to the same question. They may have been dissuaded from tyranny, or argued out of it, but that does not make the positive choice of a life much easier or clearer.

But this does not mean that nothing has been accomplished. Ideas have been examined. More to the point, lives - and cities - based on ideas have been identified and discussed. The critical question implied is this: are ideas firm and sound bases for a life? An adequate response requires a comprehensive study of the nature of ideas. The Republic is not that study. Exactly what an idea is remains a mystery. Two ideas - justice and the absolute good - are considered, and the generally unhappy consequences of founding upon them are shown.

Yet, the practical problem remains: a life must be chosen. If, as is implied, ideas are a questionable foundation, how then should the choice be made? The final part establishes a context within which choice is possible. One way to characterize that context is to say that it is both post-political and post-philosophical. I do not mean that politics and philosophy are absent or irrelevant. They are not. Once thought begins, justice and an absolute good are unavoidable ideas. But the first blush of youth is off both politics and philosophy. Both their excesses and their limitations are known, in the Republic in thought, perhaps elsewhere through experience. No longer can either of them solve the problem easily or unquestionably. Instead, each of them becomes part of the problem, an element to be weighed, balanced, accommodated, and adjusted. Human life and human choice acquire depth and dimensions absent when single, simple imperatives govern; which is to say, human life and human choice become fully human. "Fully human" does not mean "unsupported"; but it does mean incompletely or at least unsimply supported. In other words, it means that choice becomes truly choosing.

Once this is understood, elements in the Republic previously sublimated or overlooked begin to become evident. By far the most profound and significant of these elements is moderation. It now becomes apparent that, all along, at every turn of the text, moderation has been a contender. It has been an alternative, competing good, but it has not been very prominent or

attractive. This is due in part to the clarity of
justice and the powerful appeal of the absolute good,
and in part to moderation itself. What is obvious
about moderation is that it is quiet and unobtrusive,
qualities which make it unappealing and nearly contradictory to the sharply logical mind. What is not
obvious about moderation is what kind of thing it is.
Is it a thing unto itself or a component of other
things, distinct in themselves? If it is good - and
perhaps even that is questionable - is it a great good?
Or, as its name seems to suggest, is it only a middling
good, not very much pursued or valued?

There is a certain irony about moderation in the
Republic. It is long eclipsed as one or another good
or discipline makes its claim and is carried to excess.
Then, upon reflection, moderation appears. But even
then moderation has no definite place and no thematic
treatment, but is now seen to be ubiquitous; and even
then its value is questionable. It appears to be of
worth only relative to the excesses of the more obvious
goods; but, in each particular instance, those more obvious and attractive goods outshine moderation, and
cause it to be rejected or discarded. This naturally
leads to excess and disaster, but it does not establish
the absolute worth of moderation. Is it greater than
these other goods even though it appears to be less, or
just because it is non-excessive while they are or tend
to be? After all, can it sensibly be claimed that moderation is the greatest good? And, if it could, would
it?

Then, there is the problem of whether moderation
is a purely human good, rather than an absolute one.
Part Three establishes an understanding of humanness
as the context within which choice occurs. Within this
context, the "pure" lives based upon single ideas are
seen to be partial, and thus misleading. The question
then becomes, is there a life based on moderation? and,
if there is, what kind of life on what kind of basis?

The temptation is to seek a philosophical answer
to these questions. One would write a New Republic,
this time with the subtitle "On the Moderate". One
would attempt, through inquiry, to "know" moderation,
as one attempts to define and thus know justice or the
absolute good. But the movement of the Republic, which
is a movement from justice to moderation, is a movement
away from seeking intellectual answers to practical
questions. This serves to identify the category which

moderation should be placed. It is neither absolute
nor "objective", nor purely human, which suggests
"relative" or "subjective". Instead, moderation is a
practical good. This implies not only that moderation
exists and thus is known "practically", perhaps through
some faculty or combination of faculties which may be
called "practical"; but also that moderation has an
integrity which defies or overcomes intellectually conceived dualisms like "objective-subjective" and "ideal-
real".

The terms of Part Three confirm this argument.
It begins and ends with composite images, of the well-
ordered soul and of the cosmic whole. Each of these is
a complex whole of parts. Each may be analyzed, and in
fact the parts are more or less explicitly known. But
analysis is perverse or, as more contemporary language
has it, analysis is a category mistake. A whole existing living thing - I am casting about for a vocabulary
- is "known" through participation in it, not through
detached dissection of it. In the Republic, however,
terms and concepts are not imposed artificially, or
should I say inappropriately? In Part Three, Socrates
the philosopher turns poet, and tells stories. Given
this, it is perhaps of some use to entitle this part
of the work "Tales of Wholeness".

Emphatically, this does not mean that the Republic
trails off into mysticism. Socrates the poet - or
poet-legislator - is as lucid as Socrates the philosopher. What Part Three does is to make more explicit
the other great contender which has remained relatively
implicit throughout the Republic. That contender is
music. What music is for Socrates is not a simple
thing. It is about time to begin the music of the Republic - insofar as I have been able to interpret and
record it - , and so it is enough to say this: the
moderate soul - or city, or cosmos - is musical. More
to the point: the moderate life and moderate human
being are musical. There is a basis here, for moderation and choice.

THE POLITICS OF MODERATION

CHAPTER ONE
BOOK ONE

First, the place and time of the Republic should be mentioned. The place is Athens, but not the city proper. Athens had, and has, a port called Piraeus, located five or six miles to the southwest. In Socrates' time, Piraeus was known as a center of radical democratic sentiment and activity, especially during the reign of the Thirty.(1) The conversation about justice occurs in Piraeus at the home of a wealthy resident alien named Cephalus. Cephalus was originally from Syracuse, and apparently was in the business of manufacturing shields.

The dramatic date of the Republic cannot be fixed precisely. No particular political or military events are mentioned. The city appears to be relatively peaceful and relaxed, and neither defeated nor demoralized. Socrates seems to be between 50 and 55 years old, which would make the date 417 or 416. Probably the conversation occurs somewhat before the first great Athenian expedition sailed for Syracuse in 415. At any rate, those at Cephalus' house have both the time and the inclination for leisured discussion.(2)

*   *   *

Socrates narrates the dialogue. Book One opens, not at Cephalus' house, but on the road leading from Piraeus to Athens. Socrates and Glaucon, one of Plato's older brothers, are walking back to Athens after having observed a religious festival and having offered prayers to the goddess being honored. They are overtaken and ordered to wait by the slave boy of Polemarchus, Cephalus' oldest son.

Polemarchus arrives with Adeimantus, Plato's other brother, Niceratus the son of the general Nicias, and some others. Polemarchus is interested in philosophy, and wants Socrates to stay in Piraeus with him. However, he scarcely knows how to go about it. He threatens Socrates with the superior numbers and strength of his group. Socrates hesitates, preferring to leave with Glaucon or at least to be persuaded to stay. Finally, Adeimantus intercedes, mentioning that the religious ceremony will continue with a novel torch

1

race on horseback at sunset. Socrates and Glaucon agree to stay, and go home with Polemarchus. The group arrives at Cephalus' house. There they find a number of others: the father Cephalus; Polemarchus' brothers Lysias, the orator, and Euthydemus(3); the sophist Thrasymachus, a teacher of rhetoric from Chalcedon on the Bosphorus; and two Athenians, Charmantides and Cleitophon. Of this rather large group, Glaucon, Adeimantus, Thrasymachus, and of course Socrates will take the leading parts in the long discussion which now begins.

*   *   *

They do not simply sit down and begin to discuss justice. Socrates is there because others enjoy his philosophical conversation, but after all he is a guest, not a conductor of classes on set subjects. Some preliminaries are required. Cephalus greets Socrates warmly and mentions that, as he grows old, he becomes less concerned with the pleasures of the body and more interested in the pleasures associated with speeches. In a polite way, Cephalus is letting Socrates know that he may have some use for him, now that his active life has ended.

Socrates' reply is in kind. Cephalus does not believe that what Socrates does is of any value to a real man: Socrates believes that the only subject which Cephalus could possibly enlighten him on is old age. Equally politely, he asks Cephalus what things look like from that vantage point.

When Socrates came in, Cephalus had just finished performing a sacrifice to the gods. As he and Socrates talk, it becomes apparent that old age has an effect other than weakening sexual desire. The shocking realization that he is about to die forces a man to wonder whether there is an afterlife and, if so, what judgment awaits him. Cephalus is a man who has been devoted to money and to pleasure, in roughly equal parts. He must now, quite suddenly, become philosophical, or at least pay some attention to the questions which philosophy asks. He must review his life, and consider whether he has gotten more than his share of money and pleasure, and whether he has gotten them justly or unjustly.

2

Faced with death, he must finally give some thought to the fundamental questions of this life, and the next.

Nothing in his life has prepared Cephalus for this moment. Where shall he turn? Who knows about these things, so remote from the daily pursuits of an active man? Does Socrates? Certainly he is concerned, even preoccupied, with these things, but does he have any answers, or only questions? Cephalus, however, does not even think to ask Socrates, since he has another source of knowledge about justice, the gods, and the afterlife. He has the poets, and especially Homer. It is the poets who have taught the Greeks about these things.

It is important to understand Cephalus' attitude toward the poets, since it is this that sets him apart from the younger generation. The poets are Cephalus' teachers, but in a special way. The poets do not so much give Cephalus things to think about as things to do. They give him precise practical instructions on how to live his life successfully, and Cephalus follows these instructions without puzzling over their truth. For example: Cephalus is now about to die. It is very possible, to put it mildly, that he has committed some unjust acts, although they have gone undetected or unpunished. What to do? It is the case, according to the poets, that the gods punish unjust acts. But it is also the case that the gods are propitiated - not to say bribed - by sacrifices, and especially generous sacrifices. The poets even tell how to perform these sacrifices. Cephalus is a wealthy man. He can afford generous sacrifices. He also believes that he may need them. He does not pause to wonder how a just god can justly permit injustice to go unpunished: he leaves such questions to dreamers like Socrates. Cephalus' logical soul is not sufficiently developed to squirm before such questions. But he is wise enough not to stay around and hear them. To continue to believe what the poets say, he must close his ears. Close them, and believe the poets, he does, in the most practical way. He goes off to perform further generous sacrifices.

Before he leaves, Cephalus is made by Socrates to give a definition of justice. Actually, nothing could be further from Cephalus' mind than defining justice, or anything else. He has no idea what this novelty of "defining" things is all about. Cephalus' concern is to do what is necessary to save his skin. But this last statement is not quite true, and its untruth is

3

what gives Socrates his power and his authority. Cephalus wants to save, not his skin - which is dry and
wrinkled, anyway -, but his soul. He thinks he knows
how to do it, but he is not quite sure. He also thinks
being just has something to do with saving his soul,
but he is not sure of that either, and he is very far
from having thought through what justice is. The best
guide he has is the tradition developed by the poets,
but he is not sure enough of its truth to enjoy, or
even listen to, questions about it. The younger men, a
generation or two of logical argument and political
turmoil removed from Cephalus, are much more open to
questions. They too want to save their souls, among
other things, and they know they need a new teacher.

For his part, Socrates takes full advantage of
the ambiguity of the situation. In the Republic, he
will appear to be the devoted enemy of the poets. They
are bad teachers, and their teaching must be replaced.
But the poets have done Socrates a great favor, which
he seizes upon and uses without acknowledging his debt.
Through long usage, they have convinced the Greeks that
there are gods, that men have souls, and that there is
an afterlife. Socrates will take these basic beliefs
as unquestioned premises. Thus, his reform of the
poets' teaching will be one of details, albeit large
details, rather than fundamentals. While subjecting
the tradition to severe criticism, Socrates nevertheless accepts its basics, and carries it forward. This
pattern of resting arguments on unquestioned hypotheses
is crucial to understanding the Republic.

Socrates' closing exchange with Cephalus shows
that it is not clear or obvious what justice is. Cephalus has an opinion, and that opinion is not free
from contradiction. Thus the rules of the game - a
game that Cephalus will not play, for better or for
worse - are established. They will search for a definition of justice which does not contain or imply
contradictions. Everyone will play by these rules:
all definitions will be subjected to logical analysis
and criticism. Socrates' practice - the practice of
precise logical discussion, or dialectic - will rule
the gathering. Long before philosophers become kings
in the just city, Socrates and his art become, by tacit
agreement, temporary king in Cephalus' house.

*   *   *

4

The royal, even god-like game begins. It occupies the remainder of Book One. Not everyone chooses to play, since the game, so apparently playful, is nevertheless felt to be dangerous. Cephalus, of course, leaves, although with a laugh. Most of the rest sit silently. To play the game, one must be willing to expose one's opinions, and risk the possibility - and, given Socrates' presence, the probability - that one's opinions will be shown to be wrong, or at least very imperfect. For most, this hurts considerably. Silent attention is the prudent policy.

Only two choose to play. One is Polemarchus, a special case. He may not know what justice is, or care very much, but his father's opinion has been impeached, and as a dutiful eldest son and a brave man, Polemarchus moves to defend it. But he does not defend it as his father's, or his own. Sensing the prevailing tradition with the sureness of a sleepwalker, Polemarchus defends his inherited opinion as that of the poet Simonides. The opinion - that it is just to give to each what is owed - proves to be a general statement of Polemarchus' own real and characteristic opinion, that it is just to help friends and harm enemies. After some argument, Socrates succeeds in persuading Polemarchus that it is never just to harm anyone. They agree, as friends, to fight always against the opposite opinion. Polemarchus is content.

The other player is Thrasymachus, the teacher of rhetoric. He too is a special case, but of a different kind. Thrasymachus is on the prowl for students, and has scented the promise of Cephalus' wealthy and somewhat uncultivated household. It is not duty, but a combination of professional pride and personal gain that cause Thrasymachus to fling himself into the argument, and at Socrates.

Thrasymachus is a clever and experienced man, familiar with the way of politics. He knows that Socrates is the master of the game at hand, and that his own art of speech-making is at a distinct disadvantage. Thrasymachus is good with words, but only when addressing an audience, not when responding to critical questions. Having been compelled by circumstances to play, he silently resolves on a tactic. He will terrify Socrates, accuse him of being an intellectual coward, and thus intimidate him into silence. This done, the way will be clear for the demonstration of his own

5

art. Thrasymachus' ferocious entry into the game is not so impassioned as it may appear.

Thrasymachus' behavior indicates that Socrates' rule is not settled or secure. Thrasymachus wants to replace Socrates and his art, dialectic, with himself and his art, rhetoric. He would rule, not by searching for the essence of things through defining them, but by making persuasive speeches that favorably impress his listeners and win him adherents.

This episode points to the crucial problem that confronts Socrates, and will later form the core of the Republic. His art is not well adapted to ruling. More, it has almost nothing to do with ruling. Only under the most favorable circumstances, and with men of the very best natures, can Socrates' art rule even a small gathering for a short time. Put it this way: one Thrasymachus can be controlled and tamed, although with difficulty; two would destroy the discussion.

Thrasymachus' art, on the other hand, is much more at home with the normal practice of politics. It is not politics, inasmuch as it uses only persuasion, but it is a part of politics. Thrasymachus is not as disadvantaged as the Republic makes him appear. He has something useful to sell to the politically ambitious. Although it is not always evident, Socrates is the disadvantaged one. He must induce young men, and politically inclined young men at that, to believe that their highest concern should be the well-being and eventual salvation of their immortal souls. To do this, he must turn them completely around, away from the spurious allures of political life.

But this is to look ahead, to the heart of the Republic: back to Thrasymachus and his art. His definition of justice mirrors his preoccupation with practical politics. He says that the just is the advantage of the stronger, and proceeds to elaborate what this means. In every city, one group or one man is stronger than everyone else. This group rules, and makes laws which are to their own advantage. The laws say what is just and what is unjust, and must be obeyed by everyone, or punishment follows. In this view, the just is the legal, and the legal is what advantages the ruling group. This is the reasoning which underlies Thrasymachus' definition.

This is a powerfully persuasive definition, which seems indeed to capture the very essence of actual political life. It implies, not only that justice is self-serving, but that what is just varies from place to place, and from time to time. If accepted, it must defeat forever the search for a justice which is constant always and everywhere. If his art is to survive, let alone rule, Socrates must attack this position with all his strength.

Socrates does have one advantage. Almost unwittingly, Thrasymachus has continued to play the game. He has defined justice, and this act of defining contains the seeds of his undoing. Although Thrasymachus does not believe that justice is constant, he nevertheless has given a single definition of justice. This ambiguity corresponds to the ambiguity in his definition. He says that justice is a product of the rulers, a convention which varies from city to city. But his definition is that the just is the advantage of the stronger. The definition is more general than the examples from which Thrasymachus draws it, and it carries justice beyond politics. Although he does not understand the significance, Thrasymachus has defined justice not essentially as political or conventional, but as natural. If he were to make justice truly conventional, Thrasymachus would have said that justice is what the rulers say it is, and nothing more. Instead, his definition implies that justice exists in nature, as a persistent thing, independent of the action of this or that ruling group.

Socrates' questions take full advantage of this deep ambiguity in Thrasymachus' opinion. What, he asks, if the rulers make a mistake? Then, is their justice imposed on others, to their advantage? Bit by bit, Thrasymachus is drawn around to this position: the rulers are truly rulers - rulers strictly speaking only when they are ruling perfectly, without mistakes. More generally, an artisan, or artist, is truly an artisan only when he is performing his art perfectly and flawlessly. For the first time, a pure idea - not of perfect justice, but of the perfect artisan - emerges from the discussion. Given his enormous pride in his own art, it is an idea peculiarly acceptable to Thrasymachus.

Socrates now has a pure idea - indeed, one of the basic ideas of the <u>Republic</u> - to work with. He and Thrasymachus agree that there is such a thing as the perfect artisan, perfectly practicing his art. Now, all the special arts - medicine, navigation, and so on-and all existing artisans must be seen in this new light, and a strange and powerful light it is. Never mind what the actual people whom you and I know do, how careless they are in their profession, how much they neglect their patients or take advantage of their clients. Instead, think always of the perfect doctor, healing perfectly, of the perfect builder, building flawlessly. Think of what one is when one is only one's art in its pure and perfect form.

All is not roses from here on out, but Thrasymachus is essentially tamed. He must concede that true arts and true artisans act for the benefit of those over whom they rule. He does not pause to consider what this principle implies for his own art. Instead, he gathers himself for a last rally. With the dying gasp of the cynicism born of his experience, Thrasymachus adduces the example of the shepherd. The shepherd obviously does not rule in the lasting interests of his sheep. But the wedge of the pure idea has been driven forever. Do you mean, Socrates asks, when he is being a shepherd, or when he is being a diner, or a money-maker?

The game is over. Thrasymachus must concede, yes, there is art of the money-maker; and no, it is not the same as the art of the doctor strictly speaking or the shepherd strictly speaking. Each artist except the money-maker rules - that is, practices his art - for the advantage of those over whom his art rules. Thrasymachus falls silent, and a crucial political lesson is implied, one which will determine the structure of the just city. If there is to be proper rule, for the benefit of the ruled, the art of ruling must be separated from the art of money-making. The rulers must be rulers only, money-makers never. They must not be serving their own selfish interests as they rule.

With this, more than controlling and taming Thrasymachus is accomplished. The audience now has some first notion of what an idea is. It is pure; it is unmixed; it is one thing and only one thing. Soon, this idea of an idea will be linked with the idea of justice. Justice will be understood as the purity and perfection of a thing as itself and nothing else. In other words, justice will be unbreachable integrity: it will be oneness, and not manyness or otherness. But this idea contradicts very much of our experience

8

of ourselves and of the world. Much of Thrasymachus'
virtue is that he thinks his experience to be the real
truth about things, and says so. In time, his worldly
experience will be raised to philosophical understanding, and have its effect on justice understood as integrity and perfection.

NOTES TO CHAPTER ONE (BOOK ONE)

1. Following the disastrous defeat at Syracuse in
413 B.C. - a defeat accomplished with Spartan aid - ,
Athens was thrown into prolonged civil struggle. Inevitably, the democracy was blamed for the debacle at
Syracuse, and the hand of those who opposed democracy
was greatly strengthened. A series of revolutions in
the form of the Athenian government followed. Demo-
cracies, oligarchies, and more moderate regimes followed one another in rapid succession. They were given
names like 5000, the 400, and so on, indicating the
number of effective political participants.

Military defeat and political upheaval came together following the final Spartan victory in 404. In
combination with the occupying Spartans, a group of
extreme oligarchs established a regime known as the
Thirty. The leading figure of this group was Critias,
a relative of Plato and companion of Socrates. The
policy of Critias and his associates was simple. They
intended to purge democratic Athens of democrats.
Under the guise of legality, they proceeded to plunder
and murder the leading democrats. The democrats
inside the city, and those who had been driven into
exile, organized against the oligarchs. Under attack,
the Thirty appealed for help to the Spartans, who then
occupied the Athenian acropolis. Full-scale civil war
followed, during which Critias was killed. Finally, a
reconciliation was brought about, the Thirty were
turned out, and a democratic government reestablished.

2. A. E. Taylor, Plato (London: Methuen, 1960), pp.
263-264, places the dramatic date a few years earlier.

3. Polemarchus and Lysias were among those involved
in the struggle against the Thirty. Polemarchus was
executed by them.

THE POLITICS OF MODERATION

CHAPTER TWO
BOOK TWO

At the end of Book One, Thrasymachus restates his basic thesis to say that injustice is more profitable than justice, and thus that the unjust man is better off than the just one. Socrates defeats this opinion by further developing the idea of a pure art, along these lines. Thrasymachus is willing to concede that injustice, although supposedly profitable, nevertheless produces discord. Despite his cynicism, his experience will not permit him to say that injustice, when in control, produces order or harmony or good results. As the argument proceeds, Thrasymachus also agrees to these points: that each thing has its distinctive work; that it can do this work only if it is in good condition or, in other words, possesses its distinctive virtue; that the work of a soul is to rule or manage; and that the virtue of a human soul is justice. All this having been granted, it follows that only justice can rule well and produce good results. Thus, it is the just rather than unjust man who, through good rule, produces benefits for himself and for others.

As Book Two opens, Plato's brothers Glaucon and Adeimantus react strongly against this argument. Part of their objection is that Thrasymachus has given up too easily. They set about remaking his argument, drawing upon the opinion of the masses and the poets. The masses say that justice, although a necessary agreement among men, is hard and unpleasant. The poets say that it is the reputation for being just, and the practical benefits which that reputation brings, that really are good. Neither the masses nor the poets value justice as good in itself. More than this: both doubt that justice really exists, independent of the agreement or opinions of men.

This is the real basis of the brother's reaction. The argument has gotten off the track. Its purpose had been to discover what justice is, but somehow the question became, is justice advantageous or not? Socrates has succeeded in persuading Thrasymachus that it is, or at least in beating down the opposite opinion. But this has taken them not closer to, but further from, the just itself. The brothers insist that Socrates return to the search for justice. They present opinions which they themselves do not believe, opinions which imply that there is no such thing as true or natural justice, to force him to discover justice itself.

There is a beautiful clarity and simplicity about this request. Tell us only what justice is, in itself, purely. Show us the idea of justice. Don't tell us where it came from or what its effects are or what people think about it or why they desire it. And, show us injustice also, in itself, as it really is, not as popular opinion understands it. Show us true justice and true injustice at work in the souls of the just and unjust man. Show us those souls, in all their beauty or ugliness. Show us what is, not what is believed to be.

But, can Socrates' task be so simple? Will anyone want justice, or desire to be just, unless being just also has good consequences and makes one happy and prosperous? Who will be just, if justice is only hard and painful, and even then brings disaster upon one? The brothers may be lovers of truth, or of ideas, but they are also young men, influenced by what they hear, in need of deciding what kinds of lives to lead.

The ambiguity of these considerations governs Socrates' response. He will seek to discover the idea of justice, but not using the pure logical dialectic. Socrates makes two crucial decisions, which determine the shape of the rest of the Republic. First, he will look for the "larger" rather than the "smaller" justice. The smaller justice is that of a single man, the larger that of an entire city. Second, he will not take the city as already established, but will cause it to come into being. He will, so to speak, build a city in speech. In this way, they will be able to watch its justice come into being as well.

The plan, then, is to create a city in speech. To what extent this is Socrates' genuine intention is unclear, but it is certainly not what happens. Not a single city, but very many, are created: this creation takes almost the whole remainder of the Republic. One city flows, as it were, into another. The cities are different, not physically of course, but in their principles. The principle of the first is necessity, the second luxury, the third courage, and so on. As well, each succeeding principle, and thus each succeeding city, follows more or less inevitably from the one before. Thus, each city has some of the features of the others, as well as certain differences.

Why mention this now, before even the first city is built? For this reason: the purpose is to find justice in the city and, using this device, to discover justice pure and simple. This suggests that there is a just city, that is, a city whose principle is justice. The just city is the equivalent, somehow, of the just man, only "larger". Its discovery is the political goal - or, more properly, the political-philosophical goal - of Socrates, Glaucon, and Adeimantus.

There is a problem here, however. Each city will follow from the previous city, and bear a certain resemblance to it. Assuming that there is a just city, at least in speech, what does this imply about the other cities? That they are unjust - or only that they are less than perfectly just, but have some justice in them? Apparently, the latter. But, if every city, no matter what its principle, has some justice in it, what exactly is different about the just city? Is it full of justice, to the exclusion of all else? But, if it excludes all else, is it still desirable? Livable? Possible? Can there be too much justice? These questions, in one form or another, occur repeatedly in the Republic. They suggest that the perfectly just city is going to be very difficult to discover, let alone to create in practice.

*   *   *

The first city is hardly built before it falls prey to this kind of question. Socrates calls it "the city of utmost necessity", and seems very pleased and satisfied with it. It is based on two principles of human nature, one obvious, the other controversial.

The first principle is that human beings are not self-sufficient, but need the aid and assistance of one another to survive. The second is that we are naturally different from one another. Thus, not only is life made pleasant, nay possible, if one of us builds and another farms and a third weaves clothing, but by divine dispensation one of us is by nature a builder, another a weaver, and so forth. There is a perfect natural division of labor and thus a perfect natural harmony, with each of us serving the needs of

13

others by acting upon our unique, and uniquely useful, natures. Everyone has his place in the overall scheme, and that place is perfect for him or her. The human beginning is marked not by cruel chaos, as Glaucon's speech has implied, but by association.

Adeimantus, at least, is so bemused by this vision of rustic harmony that he forgets all about justice. Who needs justice, in any ordinary sense, when order is natural and perfect? But his, and Socrates' contemplation of the perpetual abundance of the City of Necessity, the Greek Garden of Eden, is shattered by Glaucon. Where, Glaucon wants to know, are the fancy desserts, and all the other things civilized men live for? Perfect natural justice cannot survive Glaucon's overdeveloped desires. With a mental sigh, Socrates turns his back on the City of Necessity.

Is the City of Necessity just? The question is left unanswered. In it, each man practices a single art, apparently to perfection. What a paradox! The completely artless city is the city of perfect art. But where is justice, if justice is the virtue of the soul which permits it to rule or manage well? The City of Necessity has no need for rule: there is no managing to be done. Nature is both perfectly expressed and perfectly restrained. Because nature has made each man a perfect artist, there is no need for justice, if justice is the art or the virtue of ruling well. Paradox upon paradox! Justice perhaps is one man, one art, and the one art that is not needed in the perfectly just City of Necessity is the art of justice. Should we not give thanks for Glaucon, whose simple-minded desire for luxury saves us from these logical whirlpools?

Still, the City of Necessity is permanently alluring. What if? What if we could be stripped of all artificiality, especially all artificial desires? What if we were free, simply free, to express our own unique natures? Then, wouldn't we find what was right for us, simply right, fully realizing our unique selves? Wouldn't all of us, simply and perfectly, serve one another by acting completely on our own unique individual impulses? Wouldn't there be the simple peace and harmony and joy and fulfillment that Socrates describes? The City of Necessity, and its principles, are the essence of the anarchist or primitive communis-

14

tic vision. Just because it has no need for political
philosophy, it becomes a permanent part of the tradition of political philosophy.

*   *   *

Nowhere is Glaucon's humanity more evident than
in this. His desires, which destroy the City of Necessity, are thoroughly artificial. What he wants is
nothing necessary, but what advanced civilization and
his over-refined tastes have taught him to want. The
simple city, glowing with ruddy health, is now swollen
with luxuries, and with those whose business it is to
provide them. The anarchist vision abruptly dims:
what is the City of Luxury after all, if not a place
where, unchecked by natural necessity, everyone acts
upon their own unique impulses? Political philosophy
begins to look more necessary.

There is doubt about the justice of the City of
Necessity. There is none about the injustice of the
City of Luxury. Two things are noteworthy here.
First, of course, is the injustice. The city wants
more of everything, and can get it only by taking it
away from others. The City of Luxury too is paradoxical or, more accurately, dialectical: so soft, so lost
in its own pleasures, it is compelled to become aggressive and, in time, even hard.

Second, surprisingly, the City of Luxury is more
truly a city. The City of Necessity is only questionably a city: it is more an unorganized gathering of
amicable rustics. The City of Luxury cannot afford
this disorganization. Although sunk in luxury, it must
act as one to take what it wants away from others, and
then to defend its plunder from its enemies. Political
philosophy becomes not only necessary, but with the
emergence of a real if unjust city, possible as well.

With this surprise comes another. Luxury brings
into being war, and war in turn begets justice. Somehow, the principle one man, one art holds even in the
City of Luxury. Since there must be war, and defense,
there must also be a corresponding art, and a group of
men who practice it. These men are called the Guardians. In Book One, the discussion with Polemarchus show-

15

Guardian

ed that justice is useful for guarding things. Now, a group which is dedicated to justice as guardianship emerges.

The guardian class, then, embodies the opinions of the loyal and brave Polemarchus. It is the political representation of those opinions. Since much of the next three books will be taken up with the Guardians and their way of life, it is worthwhile to reconsider Polemarchus' opinions at this point. This will help in understanding the place, and the problems, of justice in the city.

Socrates' discussion with Polemarchus showed two crucial things about justice. First, it established that those who are best at guarding are also those who are best at stealing. This implies that the Guardians' relationships with the rest of the city - at this point, a city dedicated only to its own selfish luxury - will be a very uneasy one. The city will depend upon the Guardians to protect and defend it; but it must also fear that the strong, lean, united Guardians will turn on it and take for themselves the goods they are supposed to defend.

Second, Polemarchus' own definition of justice is helping friends and hurting enemies. This is exactly what the Guardians must do, in protecting and defending the City of Luxury. Polemarchus' opinion is an excellent one for a Guardian to hold, especially if no one looks critically into that opinion. If one were to look critically, one might ask, for example, how exactly are the decent and brave Guardians friends of the unjust money-makers? But looking critically is exactly what Socrates the philosopher does. Examining Polemarchus' opinion, he discovered that it is never just to harm anyone. This implies that the Guardians' notion of justice is imperfect, and thus that the city will never be perfectly just as long as the Guardians are the ruling class. The non-Guardians' fear of the Guardians is more justified than it appeared at the first glance.

*   *   *

The emergence of the Guardians modifies thoroughly the entire nature of the city. Their art is war. This conforms to the principle one man, one art, but in a

16

much different fashion than in the City of Necessity. There, everyone was naturally adapted for their particular art. Now the question arises, is there anyone whose art naturally is war? Either answer is suspect. If there is, it is impossible that the city can survive internally. But if there is not, it is equally impossible that the city can survive externally. The dilemma appears severe indeed.

It is not, however, unsolvable. To resolve it, the second foundation principle of the City of Necessity must be modified. Now, one no longer has one's art naturally. One may be naturally inclined in a certain direction, here toward guardianship, but one acquires one's art through education. Leisure acquires a new meaning. It is no longer merely a respite from practicing one's art, but the very means whereby the art is acquired. Thus, if it is to be even minimally just, the city cannot function without leisure. The place and function of the money-making or producing classes also becomes more apparent. They are to provide the material prerequisites for leisure to the more "political" classes. FORM " - UNIVERSAL

As the city begins to become just, it acquires an outline or form. In general terms, it consists of functionally differentiated classes, each of which has several needs and each of which provides for one of the several needs. However, although each class has several needs, each class does not have each need equally. This elemental fact makes cooperation and justice possible. To illustrate: the Guardians need defense and material goods. They provide all the defense, for themselves and for the producers. The producers need defense at least as much as the Guardians, but they also need material goods much more than the Guardians. In fact, the producers need more of everything than the Guardians, except leisure. The Guardians' art is such that they need much more leisure than the producers. Thus, justice between classes begins to exist, as each needs more or less, and different, and each provides what it is naturally inclined, and then trained, to provide.

This is the foundation of the true city, which is neither the City of Necessity nor the City of Luxury. In the true city, things are not so necessary, and leisure is crucial. Both of these facts point the way toward freedom, or at least choice. Because arts are not simply determined naturally, each individual begins

17

to have some choice in the way of life - that is, the art - he will develop. Because leisure is crucial in providing for the development of the various arts, non-productive free time must be available. There is a certain kinship - they are distant cousins - between leisure and luxury. This is why the true city grows out of the City of Luxury, however estranged it may finally be from it.

None of the arts in the true city are simply natural: all require more or less development. This being the case, we might expect that Socrates would now begin a discussion of iron-working or wheat-farming or money-management, until all the arts needed by the city had been considered. But Socrates the erstwhile stonecutter, supposed to be so fond of visiting crafts-men and tradesmen, says not a word about these things. However vital, these people are left to acquire know-ledge of their arts by themselves, through practice.

Instead, Socrates directs the discussion toward the education of the Guardians. They will have the physical resources to dominate the city. They will have the leisure which, if improperly used, can sink the city back into dissolute luxury. Their natural spiritedness is required to defend the city, but that spiritedness must be elevated, rather than be allowed through neglect to descend to brutality or sensuality. They are the crucial middle class, and their education has priority.

It is worth mentioning another reason for this emphasis. It is evident that the true city is not simply natural. It has a natural base, and individuals are naturally somewhat inclined toward their respective arts, but the easy natural harmony and differentiation of the City of Necessity are gone. Now, human beings are and are not naturally different. Because justice in the city demands differentiated classes, some natur-al differences must be heightened. This is done most effectively through education.

With the problem of the Guardians' education, a basic change occurs. Up to this point, things were determined by necessity - by the necessary logic of events. For better or for worse, they were beyond human control. Now, a new element enters in, beyond desire, beyond the spiritedness of the Guardians. It is rationality, or prudence, or calculation. It is the exercise of human deliberation and foresight to

18

shape men and events. Now, Socrates and the brothers become something more than observers and chroniclers of the passing historical scene: they become legislators.

*   *   *

The city which they design is not Sparta, although it certainly has "spartan" features. Socrates begins where they all are, and they are in Athens. Despite all its faults, Athens, not Sparta, is the point of departure for the ascent to the true city. Athens alone provides the freedom and leisure to speculate, and the flexibility of mind to take speculation seriously. Socrates ironically compares the Guardians to that philosophical beast the dog. But the germ of philosophy is in the Guardians who emerge from the swollen city. Whatever has placed it there, the very looseness of an Athens has allowed it to live: the tightness of a Sparta would not. With philosophy alive, all other changes are possible: without it, the city and the soul in their completeness are impossible.

Given this understanding, the education of the Guardians becomes a much more difficult and subtle matter. But the first problem - a problem which nearly wrecks the entire project at the outset - is discovering whether there are any persons naturally fitted to be Guardians. The bodies of those who would be Guardians must promise speed and strength; their souls, philosophical gentleness and great spiritedness. This potential for the rarest integration of apparently opposed qualities must exist in the young Guardians. If such human beings are not to be found, the true city is impossible.

Do such wonderful natures exist? Can they be found? Ah, but the questions are too solemn, and miss the tone here. At least, they miss Socrates' tone, and even Glaucon's. Their playful labor is the creation of a tale, a tale of the true city, a city which may or may not exist anywhere except in speech, but in any event rests upon a wholly hypothetical natural or material foundation. The education of these wonderful natures is a tale within a tale. Only Adeimantus is solemn. Yes, he believes implicitly, such natures may exist: let's get on with their education, and thus keep on the trail of justice.

And yet, who's to say that Adeimantus' solemnity, his inclination to true belief, is simply naive? Who knows the power of a true education? Who can be certain that nature has failed to provide a sufficient number of satisfactory human beings, capable of being shaped and molded by that education? We are moving out of the realm of mere natural necessity. Outside it, the power of thought to move and shape must be allowed to be substantial. Nature need only do its part: it need not provide, ready-made, perfect Guardians. In fact, they need not spring from the earth - but more of such things soon enough. In truth, perhaps Adeimantus' solemnity is genuine seriousness: at any rate, it keeps us, still hopeful, on the trail.

The trail is that of justice. Socrates and Adeimantus agree: consideration of the Guardians' education will aid in understanding how justice - and injustice - come into being in a city. At this point, the meaning of this is quite mysterious. All we can do is note this supposed relationship between education and justice. Evidently, the city is to become just through the Guardians' education.

Now, at the outset of the education, Socrates conducts a little exercise in the logic of division. Is not the proper education divided into gymnastic, for bodies, and music, for souls? Yes Is not music divided into non-speeches and speeches? Yes. Are not speeches divided into the true and the false? Again Adeimantus replies, yes. All right, then, says Socrates, we will begin their education - and the beginning is the most important part of every work, especially here - with false speeches.

Our natural reaction to this remark is astonishment. Why begin, of all things, with false or mostly false speeches? Are not any of the other alternatives more sensible, more useful, as starting points for producing warriors? How possibly can justice be served by falsity? These and other questions crowd in upon one another. What is this paradoxical, dialectical Socrates up to now?

Paradox is exactly what Socrates is up to. Taken as a whole, this final portion of Book Two reveals that Socrates is much more afraid of the true lie than of the false truth. The true lie is an untruth told in, and told by, and told to the highest and truest part of the soul about the things which are the highest and

20

truest things. This condition is the most terrible and hateful thing. It has as its reflection or imitation the true lie told in speech.

By comparison, the false truth is mild and harmless, nay even salutary. The false truth is a tale told to the uninformed soul concerning the things which we do not and cannot know, the ancient things. Far from harming the young soul, this largely false tale strengthens it by approximating a truth which is beyond knowing, and thus beyond telling. It stamps upon the young soul the outlines of a model of the truth, and thus prepares it to receive, God willing, the truth pure and simple.

Socrates' choice of a starting point, then, is not quite so astonishing. Soul itself, he appears to believe, is the source of all else, good and evil, just and unjust. Thus, the young soul must be properly molded, and it cannot be molded by pure truth. Why is not obvious, but perhaps for this among other reasons. It is questionable whether pure truth can be put in words, and of course the young soul must first listen to tales. All this being so, it must first listen to tales mostly false but nevertheless pointing toward the truth.

*   *   *

The remainder of Book Two and much of Book Three are taken up with tales about three kinds of ancient things: first gods, then heroic ancestors, and finally the origins of the city. Concerning the gods, this statement poses two problems: first, it is proper to speak of the gods as ancient?; second, can tales which are false in any sense properly be told about the gods?

Adeimantus too is bothered by these questions, especially since Socrates begins by saying what the poets Homer and Hesiod should not have said about the gods. Yes, that's right, he says, they should not have said these things: but, what should they have said? What are the models for speech about the gods?

In response, Socrates proposes two models. He says first that they are acting as founders now, not as poets. The models certainly reveal this, and other things as well. Banished from the city are the charm-

21

ing - and thought-provoking - if not always edifying
tales of the Homeric gods. In their place are put
these models: first, gods - or, the god - cause only
good; second, a god is only its simple, unchangeable
idea or form.

Socratic music is intended to mold the young, very
impressionable soul. It does this, first with gods and
later with heroes, by forming simple models. The gods
are eternal, good, beneficient, unchanging, and truth-
ful. Stories about them, devised by the city's poets,
supervised by its legislators and, it eventuates, preserved by its Guardians, impress these divine qualities
upon the receptive young soul. Socrates does not con-
struct any sample stories - this is not the work of
the legislator - , but no doubt they are as simple and
unambiguous as the models which they are intended to
convey.

The intention and content of this music raises
two interesting questions. First, by the standards of
Homer, Hesiod, and Aeschylus it is very simple and
unsophisticated. Is it too simple? Does it betray the
poet's art, and the truths about the nature of things,
especially first things, which that art conveys? Evidently Socrates does not think so, partly because he
believes that the traditional poets' tales are both
ignoble and false, partly because the audience is the
very young. Young souls are being formed: they are
unable to judge the truth or falsity of what they hear:
they are able only to receive it. The nature of the
gods may or may not be knowable. The Republic will
have much more to say on this, and what it says will
not be simple. But here, Socrates' purpose is not to
tell the truth about the gods. He is not doing theo-
logy or even philosophical religion. His concern is
very elementary religious poetry, which presumably will
form young souls in ways conducive to the guardianship
of the city.

This raises the second question, the implications
of which will take time to unfold. Although not in
just so many words, the tales about the gods contain a
teaching about divine justice. Divine justice is doing
only good. Gods do not hurt enemies, dominate the
weak, tell lies, or refuse to return things borrowed
because they suspect the folly of the owner. Their
justice is not any kind of human or political justice.
Certainly it is not the justice of helping friends and
hurting enemies. Yet the Guardians' souls are to be

formed along the lines of divine justice. The question
is, is this justice sound for Guardians? Will it form
their soul for the preservation of the city? Or, will
it make them so simple and gentle that they will be
unable to believe that they have enemies, or that they
must sometimes withhold the truth? Beyond this, will
it make them unable to exercise any rule? From the
very partisan, very human point of view, the old Homeric tales don't look so bad. Yet they are full of
ambiguities and scandals which are unhealthy for the
young soul. The question becomes: how far can high-
minded philosophy proceed in its reform of traditional
poetry? Or, to ask it otherwise, how far may divine
justice be known, let alone realized in human affairs?

THE POLITICS OF MODERATION

CHAPTER THREE

BOOK THREE

Socrates' thoughts have not quite carried him to a complete reformation of poetry. He is still concerned with the ancient things, and with providing models of them for the poets to follow in making tales. The basic model is of gods as ideas. The philosopher-legislator fashions this model for the poets to follow. Heroes are to be the semi-divine embodiment of two ideas, courage and moderation. The Homeric heroes, Achilles above all, are to be trimmed of undesirable characteristics until they are simply courageous and moderate and thus good models for the young Guardians to follow. Thus, the Guardians are molded by a model created by the poets which is itself modeled after the philosophical original. They are, so to speak, the sons of sons of the reformed gods.

Are these sufficient, as models and tales? Socrates says no, in addition there must be tales about human beings. However, no existing tales about human beings are corrigible, since all writers, whether in poetry or in prose, show human beings as lovers of injustice. Tales about human beings must wait until justice is discovered. Thus it is suggested that whereas courage and moderation have hitherto been discovered and discussed adequately and thus may be assigned to heroes as characteristics, justice has not. Justice will be the characteristic of such men, and tales will be told of the best of them, for example Socrates. More than this: the discovery of justice awaits the introduction of a new mode of discourse, which is neither pure prose nor pure poetry. Having hinted at the limits of pure philosophy, The Republic quietly points toward the province and the power of political philosophy.

It is appropriate, then, that the question of ways or styles of speaking be introduced next. Adeimantus, apparently such a lover of pure form, has given these forms no thought at all, and finds the going very hard here. This is because, while the place of substantive models and tales in the young Guardians' education is obvious, the place of ways of telling is far from obvious.

25

This should be noted, concerning the basic question of education and justice. Socrates becomes concerned with the form of tales after he has discussed the heroes as models of courage and moderation. With these virtues, what matters is telling the proper tales, without much attention to their form. Only when the question of justice arises does the form of speaking become crucial.

Now, the poets do not simply tell tales, good or otherwise. They are more than simple narrators: they are also imitators. By speaking as if he was them, Homer in a sense becomes the priest of Apollo, and then Agamemnon. He must somehow contain these opposed characters, and many others, within himself. But the poet is even more than narrator and imitator, although Socrates does not speak of this. His great poem is produced by bringing out each of these characters; placing them in the proper dramatic relationship to one another; and then placing each of these dramatic combinations within his overarching narrative. The poet, then, is the taleteller: but this means to be the creator, orderer, and imitator of many others.

Why does Socrates conceal the true nature of the poet? Many interesting answers are possible, but this is most obvious. If Socrates acknowledges the poet to be a creator, the question must arise: how can one be the imitator of that which one has created? Socrates wants Adeimantus to understand the poet simply as the combination of narrator and imitator. He thus conceals the extent of the poet's power, and the analogy between the poet's art and his own.

Thus, complex questions are resolved into one simple question one perfectly adapted to Adeimantus' soul: namely, should the Guardians be allowed to be imitators? The answer as well is simple. The Guardians are to be one thing and one thing only. Almost all imitation will compel them to be many rather than one. The only imitation permissible is that of good, upright men when they are in the best condition. Virtue alone may be imitated. A consequence of this is that narration will be much more prevalent than imitation.

But what sort of education is this? Has the reform of traditional education, however flawed it might have been, left anything capable of educating? Can these few, simple tales, simply told, mold souls? Poetry, with its power and its charm, seems all but

26

banished in both form and substance. Has it been sent
away too soon, before its necessary work is done? In
short, has justice been so demanding that the indispensible means of education have been abandoned? Can all
impure things - mixed things, as Socrates calls them -
be eliminated from human affairs?

*   *   *

Certainly Glaucon would not have put the question
in this way, but, unlike his brother, he is naturally
disinclined to be sure that the answer is "yes". Socrates has said that human nature is minted in very
small coins: Glaucon is an embarrassment of riches.
When Socrates now says that everyone can infer what
their reforms imply for modes of rhythm and harmony,
Glaucon for the second time threatens to undo simplicity. He laughs aloud, remarking that he may not be
included in this agreeable "everyone".

Glaucon's nature is deeper and richer than Adeimantus': this is manifested in his interest and talent
in all kinds of music. He does not share his brother's
rationalistic desire to purge the existing world into
simplicity. But now his failure of critical reason
leads him to betray his own interests by participating
in Socrates reform of the musical modes. The sensual
and sentimental modes are eliminated; there will be no
love songs - not even Platonic ones - in the just city.
Only two modes - a violent one for courage, and a
voluntary one for moderation - are allowed to remain.
As a consequence, only musical instruments which are
simple and which produce these simple, acceptable modes
are retained. Thus does the many-sided Glaucon begin
to grow more simple, at least in speech, and more acceptable for admission into the city which his brother
and Socrates are building.

Make no mistake about it: at this point, the city
belongs to Socrates and Adeimantus, not Glaucon. But
Socrates understands what Adeimantus does not, that
there is more to education than the imitation of pure
ideas. There are Glaucons in the world, and the city
needs them very much. Glaucon's soul is open to the
non-rational - or at least the non-logical - ,to the
purely musical. Just because Socrates understands the
power of music to insinuate itself into the innermost
part of the soul, he must insure that the Glaucons of

the just city are formed by the proper music, which is in large part good, not bad words. The proper music need not be discovered. It exists, but so does the improper, and thus so do many-sided men, and bad, as well as the simply graceful. It is within the power of music to produce grace, and prepare the way for reason, and it is this that Socrates, so unmusical, must aim for.

More than music is in question here, if the Guardians are to be made graceful. The poets are further simplified, and made to appear as merely one of the kinds of craftsmen who serve the city. If the city is more than the Guardians, it is above all the Guardians - especially, the Guardians' souls - who are the city, and who must be served. The young Guardians must have good images impressed on them by all of the arts. Their senses must be developed in the right environment: the city in all its parts and works must be supervised by the legislators to insure that their products help impress the right disposition, or _ethos_, on the Guardians.

Socrates' intention here is remarkable. He means to make the whole of the city - streets, buildings, sounds, sights, songs, stories, everything - a reflection of the ideas. Having appeared for Adeimantus' sake to constrict education to purely rational models, he now opens it so that the entire physical and ethical city is a school in which the ideas are represented everywhere, in many forms, and are taken into the souls of the Guardians by every available means in order to mold those souls. Only such a comprehensive education can satisfy the unconscious longing in the soul of a Glaucon.

These remarks shed light on the nature, education, and place of the craftsmen and producers, about which almost nothing is said directly. They reveal that the non-Guardians are no lumpenproletariat crushed beneath the heel of super-educated rulers. On the contrary: they are practioners of arts which produce things of beauty. True, they set the stage and provide the material for the Guardians; but the stage they set is a magnificent one, and besides they themselves are on it. Can it be doubted that the craftsman and farmers are thoroughly absorbed in mastering arts which produce such beauty and goodness, or that the practice of these arts is anything but completely satisfying to them? They are an indispensible part of the _idea_ of the city:

28

they produce and are surrounded by beauty. What more could they want? The apparently austere Adeimantus, grasping the richness of the producers' existence, will soon complain that it is the Guardians who are disadvantaged, and who should be dissatisfied by Socrates' scheme. The more knowing Socrates will not be so sure.

* * *

Now it is Glaucon, and not Adeimantus, who is caught up in the reform. Glaucon thinks himself musical, and allows Socrates to flatter him on this score. But it turns out that Socrates knows the true music, since to be truly musical now means to have the ideas in one's soul, at least some of the ideas. Glaucon does not have these ideas: he does not even know what form an idea takes. But he does know that ideas are beautiful in some sense, and, above all, he wants to continue to believe that he is musical, truly a person of grace and rhythm and harmony. If he must get involved with ideas to hold to this belief, well then, by Zeus, he will.

The true music exacts its toll in abandoned pleasures. Glaucon the passionate lover of boys becomes a gentle parent to them: Glaucon the lover of desserts gives up his Attic cakes. Here, the soul merges quietly into the body, and music into gymnastic. In both, the keynote now is simplicity, and the result a moderate soul and a healthy body. This sort of person has little if any need of lawyers and physicians. Thus are the three traditional professions - ideas need only philosophers to interpret them - banished or at least sharply demoted in the just city.

The banishing of the professions has a number of dimensions. The Guardians must care only for their city: the practice of their "profession" is indistinguishable from the well-being of their city - but no usual profession can accept this standard, or meet this test. Also, the usual professions care for the law, the body, and the soul, and are justified on this basis. But in the just city, everything cares for the soul. Moreover, everything springs from the soul: orderliness does not originate in the law, nor health in medicine.

29

Is it surprising, then, that Socrates now argues that gymnastic does not exist chiefly for the body, but for the soul? At first glance, it is not. Don't the Guardians need both hardness and softness, and doesn't gymnastic supply the one, and music the other? Glaucon agrees with this, but in so doing again reveals his lapses in memory and self-understanding. They have already agreed that there is to be a harsh and a gentle mode, for courage and moderation. Music would seem to be sufficient in itself, without gymnastic. Then too, Glaucon himself evidently has not neglected gymnastic, yet is not closed to music nor overly hard.

What relation, then, has gymnastic to the soul? This question implies a far greater one, which soon will form the basis of Book Four: namely, what is the nature of the soul? Thus far, they have spoken of it quite simply, and have been concerned only with the virtues of courage and moderation. These have been treated as if they were sufficient, the most desirable condition of soul being a balance or mean between them. This would leave the soul a battleground, and would not go beyond Polemarchus' theory of justice. But the discussion has shown that the true music is somehow related to the forms of virtue. Now, Socrates begins to reveal that the soul is complex, and that music properly understood does not inform the spirited portion, but rather the philosophic. Gymnastic exists for the proper condition of the spirited portion.

The way is thus open for a division of the Guardians. The division is fundamental, between those who will rule, and those who will not. But the philosophical basis of rule is not completely laid. The tales and speeches told of the gods and heroes are not simply true: the musical modes heard through the ears are only representations of the ideas, and can only prepare the soul for true understanding, not provide it. Philosophy is impossible without music, but musical education alone is not sufficient for the full development of the philosophical portion of the soul.

The Guardians, then, are divided. Those who believe themselves to be one with the city - to act for it, when they act - and who hold firm to this belief, they rule. The rest do not. Less firm in their attachment, they assume lesser tasks.

Are the Guardians just? Every effort seems to have been bent to make them one thing and one thing

only. It seems that they should be just. But their
justice is questionable, because their wholeness, their
simplicity is questionable. They are divided among
themselves, into rulers and non-rulers. The rulers see
themselves as indistinguishable from the city, but the
city is not one. They are devoted to a particular physical and ethical thing, the city, which is not a
single idea and may not even be the representation of a
single idea. They have been raised to be courageous
and moderate, but their musical education falls short
of philosophy. They are supposed to be devoted to a
single art, guardianship. But Socrates has long since
shown Polemarchus that guardianship is useless when inactive; useful only when analyzed into several distinct
arts; and, when active, most likely productive of injustice. The Guardians can claim to be just only if
justice is possible without wisdom. Nevertheless,
their education is the necessary prerequisite for
justice.

At the heart of the problem of the Guardians is
the question of what wholeness or simplicity or unity
is. At this point, the Guardians reflect Adeimantus'
understanding of these things. Wholeness is purity,
achieved by the banishment of complexity. One is whole
when one is pure, and one is pure when one is untouched
and unbroken. Polemarchus' inactive guardianship and
Adeimantus' purified Guardians are cut from the same
cloth: that cloth is pure white. The world of Polemarchus and Adeimantus remains a world of friends and
enemies, of pure and impure, of either-or. This is
what the irrepressible Glaucon finds so boring and,
finally, so false about it.

And yet, there is nobility about this city. The
Guardians are tested and retested, to see if they have
true belief and can endure in it, through the five
great enemies of belief: time, force, deceit, pleasure, and pain. In this sense, they are and remain one
and the same. They must endure, without anything very
sweet to sustain them, or fall by the wayside. Their
virtue above all is courage, not the courage founded in
wisdom, but the harder courage of endurance in difficult circumstances.

The famous ending of Book Three - the noble lie -
sums up the nature of this city. It is not perfectly
true, and apparently for this reason not perfectly
just. Nevertheless, it is noble. Its nobility is
steadfast endurance in the face of terrors and tempta-

tions. The best of the Guardians are, so to speak, passed through the fire to determine if their gold is genuine. If it is, they rule: if not, they are relegated to subordinate roles.

The noble lie is the end of music education. It is the fundamental tale told to all, to explain how the city came into being, why it is as it is, and why each has the place in it which they do. It is the basis of education in political virtue, since it makes what is in large part artificial - the place and function of each person in the city - seem completely natural. In the end, the great genius of music education is not its truth, but its power to conceal the truth, especially the truth about itself. It is largely responsible for the order of the city, by raising up the Guardians to a kind of courage. But its final act is to create a tale concealing its own power of education, a tale which represents the order of the city as a product not largely of music, but entirely of nature. In so doing, it more than reconciles each to his place in the city. Much more, it joins all together in belief. It gives everyone a shared fundamental outlook on the world. That outlook is not true in any scientific sense: the wholeness of music is not a philosophical wholeness. Nevertheless, it has truth - political truth - in it, since it simultaneously joins all together, and differentiates each from the other. It makes both common life and rule possible and acceptable. As such, it is the musical basis of a city not only decent but even noble.

*   *   *

As Book Three ends, Socrates is describing the way of life of the Guardians. It is a simple, regimented existence which permits then to be devoted to their art without distraction. Their lives are to be austere, noble, and more or less just. But what, wonders Adeimantus, is noble about this mean, propertyless existence? And what sort of justice is this, which leads to apparent unhappiness? It now appears to Adeimantus that popular opinion is right. Justice is not soaring purity, but drudgery. Worse than this, it doesn't even lead to prosperity. The Guardians seem to have the worst possible lives, hard in themselves, and without any payoff for their justice. Adeimantus calls upon Socrates to give an apology for what he has done to the Guardians.

THE POLITICS OF MODERATION

CHAPTER FOUR

BOOK FOUR

Although not immediately evident, Book Four opens a
whole new phase of the Republic. Books Two and Three
have been taken up with the basic formation of the
Guardians: Books Four through Seven will treat the
greater questions raised by the Guardians' existence.
As before, Adeimantus is naive, supposing that justice
leads in some easy, painless way to happiness. But he
is also partly right. He senses that something is
wrong with the Guardians' lives. They lack something,
and that something can justly be called happiness.

Socrates' apology will require that he raise and
answer these sorts of questions. Is the best life one
totally devoted to the city? Even more basically:
what is the best life, and why is it best or happiest?
Further: is the best life a just one, or do the demands
of justice somehow interfere with the best and happiest
existence? Having approached the best, the measure
begins to become the good.

*   *   *

Socrates does not begin with these general questions. Instead, he makes a long speech which is a more
philosophical version of the noble lie. The noble lie
is for the many: Adeimantus is more refined than that.
This portion of Socrates' "apology" is designed to call
Adeimantus back to his great love of purity and unity,
which more or less coincides with the basic principle
of the city. Adeimantus, one must not forget, is a
reformer, deeply interested in a certain kind of politics.

Each person in the city, Socrates says, must perform his own function. A potter is not really a potter
if he spends his days in revelry instead of making
pots. Much less is a Guardian a Guardian, when he is
doing something other than guarding. Each must be what
he is supposed to be, rather than merely seem it, if
the city is to be happy, and it is the well-being or
happiness of the city which takes precedence over the
happiness of any individual within it.

This austere and selfless doctrine immediately silences Adeimantus' doubts about the happiness of the Guardians. He then raises another, related doubt: how can this poor city defend itself against a wealthy one? In effect, Adeimantus is asking this: isn't money a part of any political situation, and an absolute necessity for political survival?

Again Adeimantus has not quite grasped what is implied by this city he has helped create. It will not need money, to pay soldiers or buy their supplies. The Guardians do nothing but guard: they are always soldiers, always ready for war. They are always supplied with what they need to live and fight, and they need very little. They have been bred and raised to be courageous and moderate, and they prove themselves to be. So far from wanting money and property, they will actively reject it, if it falls their way in war. They will give away wealth, to those foolish cities which desire it. Placing no value on money, they will not see money given to others as a bribe, or shameful. They will conquer, always, but they will reject all the fruits of conquest, empire included, so that the city will not lose its unity through growth, and the unnecessary desires and practices which growth brings with it. The city will remain one, itself, unchanging. It will be ever ready for war, always successful in war, and never corrupted by war. All the institutions of the city will cooperate in producing this steadfast character. Adeimantus, that deeply conservative radical reformer, is delighted by all this constancy, to Socrates' quiet amusement.

This completes the founding of the city, or at least seems to. The legislators agree that all things depend upon good character, that combination of good natures and good education. Their legislative efforts have been directed to this, and above all to music education. They are willing to leave other sorts of laws, concerning marriage, contracts, and so on, aside, relying on good character to choose wisely, and believing that these other laws are of little effect without good character. Aside from music education, only the laws of religion are considered fundamental - indeed, greatest, fairest, and first -, but of these, narrowly defined, they profess to know nothing. They are content to leave them to the oracle of Apollo at Delphi.

*   *   *

Adeimantus is easily satisfied. He probably would
be willing to let things rest, but Socrates reminds him
that they built the city to discover justice, and its
relation to individual happiness. Evidently, Socrates'
apology for the Guardians' happiness satisfied Adeimantus more than Socrates. Socrates suggests to Adeimantus
that they call in Glaucon and the others to search for
justice. Is Socrates dissociating himself from this
city, which perhaps more suits Adeimantus' tastes than
his? In any case, again Glaucon does not permit him to
escape. He reminds Socrates that it is his holy duty
to support justice however he can.

Socrates agrees, it is true. He has said this: it
is his duty. Searching for justice takes precedence,
apparently over all else. But he is full of doubts
about this city they have created. He has already
questioned the goodness of the Guardian's education.
Now, he implies that it is questionable whether the
city has been founded correctly. Socrates the philosopher is far from at ease with the work accomplished
by Socrates the legislator and his young colleague.

With this separation between legislation and philosophy, the classical questions and problems raised by
political philosophy begin finally to emerge. If the
city has been correctly founded - and Socrates the
legislator thinks that it has - then it is perfectly
good; and, if it is perfectly good, then it is wise,
courageous, moderate, and just. These qualities -
wisdom, courage, moderation, and justice - taken
together constitute goodness, or make something good.
If three of the qualities can be found in a given thing
- here, in the city - then that which remains must be
the fourth quality, namely justice. Thus, the search
for justice - the philosophical quest - will presuppose
that the other three qualities exist in the city, and
can be known and identified.

This procedure is strange, and very interesting,
and most instructive. First, it presupposes something
wholly questionable, that the city is good. Second, it
presupposes that the meaning of "good" is known. Third,
it presupposes that almost all of what makes up goodness is known. Fourth, it presupposes that the qualities making up goodness are present in a city. Fifth,
it presupposes that whatever remains once certain
qualities have been identified is a single quality.

THE POLITICS OF MODERATION

Sixth, it presupposes that the single remaining quality
is justice. In short, it makes massive presuppositions
about methods and qualities which philosophers find
wholly questionable. It makes the resolution of a
vital philosophical - and practical - problem rest on
these presuppositions. In so doing, it implies that
there is something essentially hypothetical in the
nature of political knowledge or political science.
And, perhaps most intriguing of all, this procedure is
initiated by an avowed philosopher for whom the search
for justice is a holy quest. Long before the parable
of the cave, at the very outset of this central phase
of the Republic, Socrates hints at the very great pleasures which the philosopher must give up in order to
serve the city. He must act as if he knows, when he
does not, and when his greatest pleasure is questioning
and investigating. He must participate in a search
which he himself has turned into a pseudo-search. Only
later, once the search has found what Socrates has
buried, can he even suggest how incomplete and unsatis-
fying it has been for him.

Thus, for the moment, Socrates' eros for goodness
must give way to Glaucon's eros for justice. He begins
with a statement which only Glaucon, blinded by a peculiar combination of conventional politeness and his
own nature, could fail to question. Wisdom, says Socrates, is plainly that which comes to light first in
the city.

At first glance, it appears that no effort whatever
has been made to place wisdom in the city; and thus
that nothing could be more preposterous than Socrates'
claim that the city is wise. At least, it is a fact
that the Guardians' education has been in courage and
moderation, not in wisdom. Why then does Socrates say
that, in his opinion, the city is really wise?

Socrates reasons from an obvious fact, that there
is knowledge in the city. The carpenters have knowledge, the smiths have knowledge, the farmers have
knowledge. However, each of these kinds of knowledge is
partial or specialized, and thus should not be called
wisdom. There is another kind of knowledge, that of
the city as a whole. More exactly, this knowledge is
of how the city can best deal with itself and with
other cities. Possessed only by the Guardians, it is
called good counsel. This knowledge alone deserves
the name of wisdom.

38

Socrates does not discuss good counsel in detail, saying only that it is possessed by the smallest group and ruling part of the city; and that it is because of this knowledge that the city is called wise. But he does leave Glaucon with the opinion that wisdom is political science. In other words: Socrates implies that from the point of view of justice, or of the desire for justice, to be wise means to have practical knowledge of what is good for the city as a whole; and, of course, how to keep and maintain those good things. Justice demands political science, and is satisfied with it, precisely because political science implicitly is limited by the good of the city. Thus the best of the Guardians, devoted completely to the well-being of the city, can be called wise as long as they act to secure that well-being. Because they rule, their wisdom becomes that of the city as a whole.

What is remarkable about this discussion is how ordinary and commonsensical it makes wisdom appear. A city is wise if it conducts its affairs well: by analogy, a man would be wise if he did the same. Wisdom seems to be prudence, and the sign of its presence to be success or, at most, well-being. Glaucon, eager to find justice, is satisfied that wisdom has been discovered. But it is worth noting that Socrates makes wisdom the first virtue, and that it rules.

Courage is next, and it too is found to be political, rather than natural or philosophical. Courage belongs to a part of the city; conversely, what a part of the city possesses is political courage. Socrates uses a powerful analogy here. The Guardians are "dyed-in-the-wool" believers that what is terrible is what harms the city: simply, they are "dyed-in-the-wool" citizens. Courage is that virtue of endurance and persistence which preserves this belief. Above all, their education aims at making them courageous, at "dyeing" right opinion deep in their souls. Metaphorically, the cloth will wear out - or tear - before it loses its color. Apparently, courage is the most colorful virtue. But, for the Guardians, it resides in their souls, rather than in flags and banners and robes, as we will see later on.

*   *   *

39

THE POLITICS OF MODERATION

As we know, Glaucon has put Socrates to test after test, refusing to allow him rest. Now, Socrates begins to repay Glaucon, by putting him to a little test. There are, he says, two virtues remaining, moderation and, of course, justice. What if we were able to find justice directly, without bothering about moderation? Glaucon passes the test with flying colors. Whatever the strength of his _eros_ for justice, he replies that he does not want to find it unless they also discover moderation. This apparently moderate reply links moderation and justice, and wins Socrates' approval. Socrates says that it would be unjust not to search out moderation before justice. Is he implying that justice must be discovered in its proper place? Or, that there is no justice without moderation? In any case, Glaucon's desires and the demands of justice coincide. Moderation must be found next.

Wisdom and courage have been found easily, or so it appears. Wisdom is found in the rulers. Courage seems to be found in all the Guardians, both those who rule and those who do not. But there are some problems here. First, it is not evident how the rulers became wise. Second, moderation seems to have been placed in all the Guardians, by the use of gentle music. In general, the virtues as they are discovered in the city do not coincide with the Guardians' education.

These are mysteries enough, but moderation presents a greater one. It is the great way or passage that must be traversed to reach justice. If the city is to be a city, united and complete, it must be moderate. But what is moderation, and where is it found, and how does it develop? Socrates speaks of moderation leaving tracks, as if only its effects could be seen. Moderation is a mastery by better of worse, say by rulers of non-rulers, or necessary pleasures of unnecessary; yet moderation must be found in that which is ruled as well as in that which rules. It is both order and harmony; yet it is also that which makes order and harmony possible. Moderation is of the city as a whole; yet it is also present in every part. It tempers each part so that each can associate properly with the other, and thus form an orderly and organized whole. Moderation does just what its name implies, it moderates or softens some person or part so that it is not too harsh or alone or resistant, and yet does not cease to be its individuated self. Altogether moderation is a wonderful mystery. Nowhere is the need and power of the proper music more evident than here.

Moderation, then, belongs to the city as a whole, but also pervades every part of it. It prepares the way for justice, and perhaps makes justice practical. The long search is almost over: Socrates and Glaucon have justice in sight. Caught up in the excitement and near conclusion of the chase, each vows to do what he is best able - Socrates to lead, Glaucon to follow - and so finally discover justice.

Long, long ago, when Glaucon set the search in motion, it was for justice itself. Discovering justice has always been their purpose, and ultimate goal. But they decided to seek justice in the larger thing, the city, because it would be more evident there. This caused them to create city after city, no one of which was perfect. Now, as they are about to discover justice, the wisdom, courage, and moderation of their search is evident. They have not merely discovered justice: they have discovered it in a certain way, a way which has deepened their understanding.

Their search has been prudent, since it first sought not justice itself, but practical manifestations and examples of it. It has been courageous, since it was long, and would have been easy to abandon when it did not reach its goal immediately. It has been moderate, since it refused to give up the rest of virtue in a head-long rush toward a part of it. Even now, as justice begins to come into view, they will first stop to examine political justice. This reminds them again that they are men, very dim of sight and much in need of aid from one another, in both the theory and practice of justice.

Justice, then, is not to be looked at directly, at least not yet. But even in its political manifestations, justice is a magnificent thing. Justice, or the search for justice, causes all the other virtues to come into being. In the simple City of Necessity, there was a kind of natural justice: each was inclined naturally toward some one necessary art. The rustic prosperity of this city gave rise to the desire for luxury, and thus to the injustice which that desire engenders. Wanting more, the city was forced to war and defense: for this reason, it was compelled to depend upon spirited men. But it could not simply trust these men: their raw spirited courage was a threat to internal security. Their spiritedness needed moderating and refining, and so the music education was devised. That education resulted in the virtues of moderation

41

and political courage. But wisdom of a kind was needed to develop the music education, and then to preserve it.

Justice is the fourth, final virtue which completes the goodness of the city. But it is evidently not equal to one of the other virtues, or merely one-fourth of the whole good. Socrates and Glaucon agree that justice is the <u>rival</u> of the other virtues. This implies, first, that it may well be equal in weight to all three taken together and, second, that in some sense justice may be at odds with them. More than this: it seems that justice causes the other virtues, preserves them by making each part exercise its distinctive virtue - and yet is merely what is left over after the others are found. Then, is justice the greatest virtue, to be valued above all, or is it some remnant so inactive as to be nearly useless? Again, Socrates' wisdom in compelling Glaucon to consider moderation before going on to justice is evident.

*   *   *

All this suggests that justice will not be simple or easy or unproblematic. Yet Socrates' definition of justice seems to be simplicity itself. After their long search, he and Glaucon find justice rolling around at their feet: justice appears to have been close at hand - or foot - from the very beginning. Justice is everyone performing his own function, or doing what he is naturally most fitted for: in a word, justice is everyone minding their own business.

This is political justice. It defines the role of each person in the city. Each must have his own work and do it well, without neglecting it and without meddling in the business of others. This is especially true of the Guardians, who are responsible for the well-being of the city as a whole. If they were to neglect their work, or allow non-Guardians to interfere with it, the city would perish.

Only this definition of justice, tempered with moderation, can produce a well-ordered city. Justice cannot be pressed too far, either in the direction of too much control by the rulers, or too much independence by the non-rulers. Either extreme destroys the possibility of everyone having their own business, and thus being just and practicing justice. But heeding the gentling voice of moderation dissolves apparent dilemmas and makes possible a just, harmonious city.

In many respects, the Republic could end here. Political justice has been discovered, or brought into being. The just city has been shown to be a possibility, and at least its outlines have been sketched. The basis practical education which produces justice has been discussed in some detail. Moderation has been revealed as the indispensible agent which tempers justice and binds the city together; and something of its nature and effect have been suggested. True, justice as such has not been found, or proved to be good; but sound common sense says that an attractive, practical political science has been set forth.

But Socrates is not seen merely as the spokesman for sound common sense. Glaucon is not one who can be deflected so easily from his erotic pursuits. Adeimantus has not gotten over his preoccupation with pure forms. More generally, philosophy does not relinquish so readily its searching questions, or its strict logical standards. And in the background, silent now but watchful, Thrasymachus and his associates have not forgotten their doubts and cynicism about human nature. In short, moderation does not conquer so easily in the practical world.

The basic question is this: Can human beings be just? Can they mind their own business? Logic asks: if everyone is to mind their own business, how can it be the Guardians' business to mind others' business, or everyone's business? And, how can non-Guardians have a business of their own, if the Guardians regulate their activities? Philosophy asks: are human beings so complete and self-sufficient that they can be content with one and only one business? If so, what do they need with a city, and rule? Eros asks: can creatures attracted sexually to one another possibly avoid all sorts of entangling affairs? Cynicism asks: can nosy, aggressive, restless, jealous, power-loving men ever cease meddling with one another's affairs, and causing each other trouble? The extremes of human activity, good and bad, conspire to raise doubts about the likelihood of human beings minding their own business. The question will not go away: can human beings be just?

THE POLITICS OF MODERATION

The justice of the individual human being, then, must be examined. This will complete the long search for justice itself, and return from the larger thing, the city, to the smaller, the individual. But a decisive change in the original plan now occurs. It is not man, body and soul, who is to be searched for justice, but soul alone. Socrates chooses to treat the individual as equivalent to the soul, and to ignore the body. Of all the voices just now raised, that of eros of body for body is least heeded.

This method - the analysis of soul abstracted from body - raises doubts about the comparison between city and individual. This is another form of the basic question of the Republic. Little by little, its dimensions will become evident. Here, this can be said. To a great extent, the city is its rulers, the Guardians, and the Guardians are their qualities of soul: wisdom, justice, and, above all, courage and moderation. The good city is one in which the rulers have virtuous souls, and in which their virtue rules, guides, and influences the ruled. Body does not enter in, at least not in any erotic sense. The city is not sexually attracted to other cities. Functioning properly, the rulers are only their qualities of soul. That they happen to have bodies is irrelevant to the Guardians as Guardians. Consequently, it seems much more permissible to abstract from body in the case of the city.

Socrates assumes, however, that city and individual differ only in size, but are otherwise identical. In other words: the form of the just city is identical to the form of the just man. The just city has three classes of natures: those of the rulers, or full Guardians; those of the auxiliaries, or lesser Guardians; and those of the various producers. It is just when each of these classes minds its own business; and moderate, courageous, and wise due to other virtues possessed by one or more of the various classes.

It remains then to ask, does the individual have these same three forms in his soul, namely, a ruling form, a supporting form, and a producing form? Glaucon is eager to inquire, Socrates not so eager. Again he expresses his doubts, this time about their method. That method is a comparison based on the assumption of identity. Behind this method lies a political science based on hypotheses. Socrates does not explain his doubts, saying merely that there is another longer method that would be more satisfactory. But it may well be that methods appropriate, even necessary, in political science are not philosophically acceptable when seeking justice itself. They agree to continue using the existing method, but Socrates clearly has his reservations.

*   *   *

As they proceed, however, the argument changes subtly. It becomes both more formal and precise, and more dialectical. Formality is needed, since justice itself is being sought; a dialectical approach, since justice is being sought through the comparison, and interplay, of city and individual.

First, the effect of material factors is assessed. Certain geographies and climates produce certain human types: the north, spirited men; the center, lovers of learning; the south, money-seekers and pleasure-lovers. These types influence or determine completely the character of cities in their respective regions. Thus, purely material factors are an element, but cities generated solely by these factors are partial or incomplete. Materialism alone, Socrates implies, cannot produce justice or virtue, in cities or in men. But these factors may well place definite limits on the development of virtue. The good city must be geographically fortunate, and of moderate climate.

Next, the individual removed from particular circumstances is considered. Socrates poses a great question: what is the cause of human action? Assuming that actions are divided into the spirited, the learning and knowing, and the desiring, is each of these kinds of actions caused by a distinct portion of the soul, or by the whole soul?

To determine the nature of the soul and the cause of human action, Socrates proposes a test, or trial. The trial will be conducted according to this law: the _same_ _thing_ will not do or suffer opposites in the same respect in relation to the same _thing_ at the same time. In other words, the law is this: a thing is itself, and not something else. As itself, it can only be itself, and behave as itself. If there are apparent differences in behavior in relation to the same thing, respect, and time, then more than a single thing is present and behaving. This is the law of identity, or

45

non-contradiction. Applied to persons, it means that
if a person is inconsistent - if he shows signs of a
struggle with himself - concerning a given issue or
object at a given time, then more than a single element
in his soul is involved. The circumstances of the
trial are that everything "external" is held constant
and so, according to the law, there must be more than
a single "internal" thing involved to cause the inconsistency.

The meaning and cogency of Socrates' remark about
method now become more apparent. Justice itself, so
far as it can be known, is not far off. But, even now,
justice cannot be apprehended directly, with no assumptions or hypotheses. The law of identity is not established. It is a law, without which the logical trial
cannot proceed. Obviously, it is the philosophical
equivalent of the political law. It must be taken as
given, if the trial is to proceed. Without it, with
it in doubt or questioned, there is no trial. Thus,
even here, in a realm free from almost all particular
considerations and limiting circumstances, there is no
trial - and, by implication, no justice - unless the
prior existence and governing power of the law is
granted. Political philosophy, especially when it is
closest to philosophy, must respect the law.

Thus Socrates and Glaucon, with the fundamental
law and various clarifications of it established, conduct the trial of the soul. They first consider desire, agreeing that each desire is a desire for the
thing which is like itself or which fulfills it. For
example, thirst is the desire for that which satisfies
thirst (drink), and hunger for that which satisfies
hunger (food).

Glaucon finds this simple enough, but now Socrates
introduces a distinction. Not all desires are desires
for a specific thing, related to the desire, which fulfills the desire. There is another class of desires,
not so clear and obvious. The second class seems to
be not for specific, correlated things, but for a
general thing or for itself. One might say, there is a
desire for that which satisfies desire. But Socrates
does not satisfy anyone's desire here, saying only
that, for example, there is knowledge of that to which
knowledge is related, and then there are particular
kinds of knowledge like house-building and medicine.

46

This interesting distinction - one great general desire, and particular desires - is now put aside. Instead, Socrates considers particular bodily desires and asks, don't we often desire something and yet not act on the desire? Certainly, Glaucon replies. And, isn't that which forbids us to act calculation, or reason? Apparently, says Glaucon. Then, aren't there two distinct parts in the soul, the rational calculating part, and the irrational, desiring part? Glaucon believes so.

Then, is there also a third part, the spirited?; or, is spirit the same as one of the other two? The eager, erotic Glaucon thinks that it may be the same as desire. His answer is not unusual: it's easy to believe that anger, and spiritedness generally, appear when a person wants something and doesn't get it; and that anger then becomes the ally of desire in trying to get what it wants. Then, anger is either a part of desire, or something very closely allied to it.

Socrates' response to Glaucon's unremarkable opinion is remarkable. It is most spirited, and is intended to move powerful impulses within Glaucon; in turn, disgust, shame, pride, and finally, the love of justice. Socrates wants to persuade Glaucon that spiritedness never allies itself with desire against calculating, reasoning speech. But experience and observation alone do not yield that conclusion. Glaucon is compelled - not physically, but by appeals to shame, disgust, and so on - to agree with Socrates.

It is evident, then, that spiritedness is the crucial middle portion of the soul. It is perhaps naturally associated with desire, but that alliance is a dangerous one. Together, desire and spiritedness can run roughshod over reason. Spiritedness must be detached from desire, and made obedient to reason. But reason alone cannot do this. Calculation must produce speech which moves spiritedness through appeals to emotions like shame and pride. These emotions first move spiritedness into alliance with reason, and thereafter bind it in place. Spiritedness is made to believe that the noble man does not use anger to satisfy unreasonable desires. It appears, then, that spiritedness is capable both of a certain kind of understanding, and of right desires: it has ideas of nobility - and baseness - and is capable of desiring the one and loathing the other. This accords well with its intermediate position between reason and desire.

This establishes, to Glaucon's satisfaction at least, that there are three elements in the soul, corresponding to the three classes in the city. But it leaves crucial questions unanswered. If calculation and spiritedness are allies, are they opposed to desire? If they are, is the soul then factionated, and a battleground? If it is, then how can the individual act as one, or coherently? The effect of conducting the trial under the law of non-contradiction is evident: there must be signs of inconsistencies to establish the existence of distinct elements in the soul. This is fine, and scientific. But the demands of scientific method are not so fine in practice. There, the evidence of distinct elements in the soul is struggle and inconsistency, finally preventing coherent, integrated action. On the other hand, it is difficult to discover distinct elements in the integrated individual. They cannot be seen, as the distinct classes in the city can. These considerations suggest two basic difficulties: first, the comparison of city and soul is doubtful; second, the nature of the soul is much more open to question than that of the city.

These philosophical problems are ignored. Instead, Socrates leads Glaucon to agree that the private man is wise, courageous, and just in the same way and because of the same things as the city. This done, they can attend to the practical problem of forming the parts and the whole properly. Calculation must rule with spirit as its obedient ally, each of them having first learned their business and been tempered by the proper mixture of music and gymnastic. These must be set over desire, to insure that desire minds its own business rather than trying to rule the entire soul.

The soul is just, then, when each of the three parts minds its own business. But the discussion suggests that none of the three parts naturally minds its own business in the way demanded by an integrated, harmonious soul. There is nothing to suggest that wisdom naturally rules. Naturally, spiritedness seems likely to ally itself with desire. The natural tendency of desire is to grow so big as to fill the whole soul, and bend it to desire's wishes.

Then, is justice unnatural? This is not the likely conclusion. It may be quite natural for each portion of the soul to mind its own business. But, this tendency does not lead to an integrated soul, but instead

48

one going off in all different directions, or one in which constant quarrels occur about which portion should direct the soul. The trial of the soul, under the law of non-contradiction, reveals this: evidently, what is not simply natural is the integrated, harmonious, orderly soul.

*   *   *

Long and winding paths of speculation and reflection branch off from this point. Socrates and Glaucon do not wander off on these paths, but instead remain practical. It seems that souls do not naturally assume an orderly pattern. Therefore, each of the parts must be educated to understand its own special business, and its place in the scheme of the soul. The soul is just when the business of each part is not merely its own, but also is defined in relation to each other part and to the activity of the entire soul. Justice is thus shaped by moderation, which Socrates identifies with the friendship and accord of each of the parts about which should rule and which should be ruled. Moderation tempers each of the parts, relates it to the others, and binds the entire soul together. Without it, the soul is rough, jagged, and irregular: with it, smooth and orderly.

Finally, the just soul looks like this. Each part has the educated, moderated, developed inclination to attend properly to its own business. The desiring part desires the particular objects of particular desires: the spirited part becomes aroused and takes action to guard the whole soul: the calculating part makes judgments which govern both the parts and the whole. When the soul acts, it acts as one, because there is an overall coordination based upon and following from specialized function. In a word, the soul is a whole of parts founded on justice and integrated by moderation.

The trial of the soul can now be seen more clearly. Justice is the power which produces parts naturally differentiated from one another. It is not clear whether these parts are also naturally related or associated or interdependent. What Socrates argues is this: moderation is what holds things together, in this case the soul. Evidently, the soul passes the test - that is, it acts well - when moderation creates unity from natural diversity, binding the parts of the soul together harmoniously. A man works on his soul to produce this condition. He seeks those actions which develop and strengthen this condition, and calls them just and fine. He calls wisdom the knowledge which supervises these actions, and names unjust those actions which undo this condition. In all of this, the soul, the man, are being tried. The work of a man is to make his soul good. The trial is to determine whether he has done his work properly, in other words, whether he is just.

This has almost the formal elegance and beauty of a proof: justice is minding one's own business, and the business of a man is the well-being of his soul. Therefore, the man who attends satisfactorily to his soul's well-being is just. He seeks everything which furthers this business, and avoids everything which destroys it. Socrates and Glaucon rest, if only for a moment. They believe that they have found the just man and city, and what justice really is in them.

*   *   *

While they rest, we too may pause, and review what has been accomplished. The just city has been established, but only as a means to discover justice in the soul. Justice is the power which makes each thing what it is, and thus provides the basis for an orderly, integrated world. This integration is accomplished through the gentling and binding action of moderation.

These discoveries mark out the pattern and purpose of a man's life. His business is to put his soul in order. It appears that the city exists for the sake of the individual; the individual, for the sake of his soul; the soul, for the sake of its harmony, its order, its perfection. There is no conflict or compromise here, only a clear order and an ultimate peace. This knowledge casts a whole new light on human affairs. All else fades into insignificance in the face of the brilliant glow cast by the perfected soul. Now, if a man is to do his appointed, appropriate work - if he is to be just - he must labor unceasingly for the perfection of his soul.

This is Socrates' message, a message evidently founded on solid reasoning. But this message, this

light, so clear and brilliant, casts all else into
shadows and doubt. What is to become of the city?
What justice can there be in the lives of most men,
limited by nature or education or both to the performance of merely necessary tasks? How can these individuals be concerned with the perfection of their souls?
What of the best, naturally strongest, fully educated
men? Are they to withdraw from the cares of everyday
life, and from the guiding of those less blessed, to
preoccupy themselves with the beauty of their own
souls? How much do they need the city and - more to
the point - how much does the city need them?

These questions point to one great question: Is
it possible to have both a just city, and just men?
At first, the question is startling, since it seems
obvious that there cannot be a just city unless it is
composed of just men. But the long search for justice
reveals that the proper work of a man is painstaking
attention to the condition of his own soul. Now, it
is the case that the just city depends upon each class
minding its own business and performing its proper
function. No class is given the function of attending
unceasingly to the beauty and harmony of their individual souls. Such a concern is an intense preoccupation
with soul, if not with self, and evidently distracts a
man from both the care of the city and the performance
of his particular function. In a world illuminated by
the beauty of souls, the city goes begging. On the
other hand, if a man devotes himself body and soul to
the city, and to his task within it, his proper function as a man - his true business - is neglected.
Then, in the ultimate sense he is unjust, even while
contributing fruitfully to the justice of the city.
It appears that one is either for oneself - that is,
for one's soul - or for one's city. If one fails in
the first, the man is unjust; in the second, the city
is unjust.

Thus, the great and central question of political
philosophy comes to light: is it possible to do justice both to oneself and to one's city? If we serve
the one - whichever one - can we help but cheat the
other? For a man who would be just, who would do his
duty, who would mind his own business in the deepest
and truest sense, no question can be more pressing, no
dilemma more apparent. At last, Socrates and Adeimantus and Glaucon have discovered the just city and the
just man and justice itself. But, far from having
resolved all difficulties, they instead have brought

to light the greatest of all difficulties: if justice is minding one's own business, then what is one's own business? Is it the well-being of one's city, or of one's soul?; or, can these two cares, evidently so opposed, somehow be brought together?

*   *   *

So, as justice is discovered, and its depths probed, it is apparent that the problem of justice is not solved. Finally, the problem of justice is the problem of how to live one's life, of what to make one's business. By now, as the fourth Book ends, Glaucon is convinced that it is more profitable to be just than unjust. He sees no problem with being just. The just man has a fine and healthy soul in which each part minds its own business and welcomes rule by the part naturally fitted to rule. To this end, the soul seeks those good actions which strengthen it in its justice. Glaucon willingly accepts all this: what can be a greater good, or more profitable, than the health and well-being - the justice - of the soul, and who can desire any action except that which produces and preserves it? To inquire further into injustice, and its possible profit, seems a waste of time.

Nevertheless, Socrates persists, appealing naturally to Glaucon's courage. He knows that they must consider injustice, because he knows that the problem of injustice is most pressing for the man who is most preoccupied with the soul. It is the philosopher above all who believes that the ruling portion of the soul is able to direct it, and to seek healthy, soul-strengthening activities; and, above all, it is the philosopher who will be accused of injustice for neglecting his duty to the city. Socrates alone understands that it is the life of philosophy - the life devoted to the health of the soul - which raises the question of justice in its most acute form: can the best, most complete man be just and, if so, under what circumstances?

However, Socrates is moderate here, indeed more than moderate. He does not point to the problem of the philosopher. On the contrary: he is the very model of the good citizen, at least when he himself has designed the city. Perhaps in this city there are no questions about the justice of the philosopher. Socrates takes virtue as known, and associated with the regime which

52

they have designed. Injustice and vice, and their regimes, four in number, remain to be considered.

THE POLITICS OF MODERATION

CHAPTER FIVE

BOOK FIVE

Socrates' discrete silence is noticed, if not very well understood. Polemarchus believes that important parts of the argument have been omitted, and he wants to hear them. He and the others, particularly Thrasymachus, are interested by Socrates' statement that women and children will be held in common. Socrates' preoccupations are mirrored, but in a negative sense, in Polemarchus and Thrasymachus. Socrates is concerned with the soul, with the business of the best man, and with the dilemma of justice posed by the tension between philosophy and politics. His listeners, long silent, are now aroused. They are concerned with the body, with the pursuits of "a real man", and with the perhaps unjust but certainly delectable prospect of a city where one gets more than one's share of sexual intercourse.

Here, the division of city and soul into three parts is made manifest by immediate human reality. Socrates' aroused listeners correspond to the desiring portion of the soul, and the producing class in the city. Their concern is with the body, with the apparently delightful, and with sex. Socrates, of course, is the human equivalent of the calculating part, and the ruling Guardians. The brothers correspond to the crucial middle elements, spiritedness and the auxiliary Guardians. Adeimantus puts Polemarchus' desire into words; for the moment, spiritedness is allied with desire. Socrates must proceed to severe this alliance. But he is limited by the strength of desire and, moreover, by the hypocritical rhetoric - "what do we desire, but arguments?" - advanced by Thrasymachus. Not merely the majority, but also Adeimantus and Glaucon, vote to compel Socrates to discuss this intriguing domestic arrangement. Socrates is frightened by this demand, especially by the damage that it may do to his friends, but he finds himself compelled to agree to it. The female drama, as Socrates calls it, will be taken up.

*   *   *

The female drama is part of the greater drama of the Guardians. The great drama is this: will the spiritedness of the Guardians be allied with desire or with calculation? The female portion opens with a demand by desire. Desire senses that the Guardians are most vulnerable to the needs and pleasures of the body, especially sex. The question shapes up this way: how will the Guardians satisfy the demands of desire and the body? Will they go outside their own class for sex - and consequently for children - to the lower, producing class? Or, will females be included in the Guardian class? Whatever the answer, it will bear directly on the form of the city.

Socrates - or, to be precise, justice - has already decided this point. There must be a class of women associated with the male Guardians, and these women must be held in common. The demands of the body and the necessity of procreation demand intercourse with women. The provision of the best natures for training as Guardians demands that these children be born of the best possible women. The sole function of the Guardians - the preservation of the city-- demands that they avoid the distractions of private families. The conclusion is evident: the Guardians, and consequently the city, cannot be just unless there are female Guardians, held not privately but in common.

Thus, justice demands what is repulsive to common sense and normal practice, namely, that women cease being women and begin doing exactly what men do and, further, that families of the usual kind cease to be formed. These are the first two of the three "waves" of Book Five. But these radical changes rest on a premise that is wholly questionable, if not yet explicitly questioned: that the Guardians are completely devoted to the well-being of the city and serve only that purpose. Now, the true business of a man - single-minded and whole-hearted concern with the beauty of his soul - is forgotten. It is political justice that demands the radical change.

Yet, as Socrates and Glaucon open the female drama, the tone is hardly even political. From the heights of the perfect soul, they descend to discuss the merely animate body. The Guardians again are considered noble dogs, who shepherd their flock. Yet another division into three appears: the herdsman, who breeds and trains the dogs; the Guardian dogs; and the flock which they guard. Among noble dogs, distinctions

56

are not made in the use of males and females. The best
of each sex are used for guarding, although in general
the males are stronger. Thus the question becomes: are
the distinctions in use among humans wrong-headed and
unnatural? Should the best women be used in approxi-
mately the same way as the best men?

Notice that these questions are different than the
initial ones. They were, how can the justice of the
male Guardians be assured? How can they be kept from
having more than a single business? Socrates had
responded simply, by having women and children in
common (and thus preventing private pursuits and pleasures), and left it at that. But the curiosity prompt-
ed by Socrates' response has opened new questions.
Now, the whole issue of the status of women must be
explored. No longer can women be left in the background, essentially serving the needs of men who are
to become just. The demands of justice spread, and
threaten to upset all conventional human relationships.
Socrates sought to make light - or, perhaps, dark - of
the female drama, but now it too is placed on center
stage. No wonder Socrates feels that he has been
thrown into the sea and faced with great waves.

So, what began as a joke - old women stripping to
do calisthenics - is made to become a serious question:
do men and women differ in nature? If they do not,
how is it possible to assign them anything but the same
education and the same business? Now, the definition
of justice must be applied to practical situations.
But now justice is not first tempered by moderation,
nor are its implications left discretely unmentioned.
In the little community of the dialogue, democratic
desire has ruled, and demanded that all aspects of justice be brought into the open.

*   *   *

The discussion of women is very interesting, not
only for what is said, but also for what lies behind
it. Socrates must discuss the status of women, but he
must also keep in mind the original questions: how can
the justice of the Guardians be strengthened? What
arrangements will move the Guardians away from an alliance with desire, and into one with prudent calculation? In other words: the status of women cannot be

57

considered apart from its effect on the best man. These unspoken consideration shape Socrates' discussion.

Socrates begins with a classic - and crucial - question: is there woman's work? But he does not ask it that way. Instead, he asks, is there any human activity in which men, as a class, do not excel women? No, Glaucon replies; while individuals vary, men are generally better than women at all pursuits. This striking answer leaves women in a curious position. They are not assigned a particular kind of activity which nature has made their own - strictly biological considerations are left aside -, but are associated with men in all human activities. But that association is not one of equals. Across the board, women are inferior to men. Thus, while females are first and foremost human beings, and only secondarily if at all "women", they are decidedly inferior human beings when evaluated according to their ability to engage in characteristic human activities. Or, so Glaucon at least believes.

However, the situation is not such as to leave all women in a permanent - and losing - struggle with all men. Indeed, the classes "men" and "women" melt away as practically meaningless. Instead, human beings are differentiated by their natural inclinations to various pursuits. This is virtually a return to the first, simple city Socrates loves so, but without the tacit assumption that it is an all-male city except for necessary procreation. Now, in the just city, women will participate in all practices as their distinctive individual natures demand. There will be women Guardians and, presumably, women shoemakers and women farmers as well.

Slowly but surely, Socrates is dragging the city away from the threat posed by desire, and returning it to its proper concerns. The practical disregard of male and female rests on the premise that persons are essentially their souls, not their bodies, and that souls differ in inclination. Those women with souls of potential Guardians will be educated in music and gymnastic, and will be elevated by their original nature and their education above other women. They will be the best women because they will have the best souls. But the best souls are those which keep desire in its proper place, and understand the relative place of soul and body. Although they don't know it, Polemarchus and Thrasymachus will find themselves ruled over by women, if they are sincere in their desire to learn about the just city. The city will be well-ordered not because women are admitted to Guardian status, but because naturally higher, properly educated souls are associated in ruling. When Socrates says that women Guardians will be assigned lighter tasks, he rests his conclusion on a relative weakness of body, not of soul. Finally, bodily weakness is not decisive, given the supposed similarity of souls.

In this way, the first wave is escaped. Women Guardians are found to be both possible and beneficial. But the city is subtly changed. No longer can we speak of the justice of the male Guardians, and how to strengthen it. Now, Guardians are male and female, associated by the similar configuration or form of their souls, and having all things in common. If only because the lower, producing class looks upon the Guardian class in amazement - and, very possibly, in envy - the city is not the same. Something of its moderation, resulting in a consensus about ruling, is gone. It is not easy to see souls when bodies, especially young, unclothed bodies are so evident.

*   *   *

No sooner is the first wave escaped--if it is escaped - than the next, even larger, looms up. Unmoderated justice demands not only that women be Guardians. It also requires that the women belong in common to the men; that the children which result also be in common; and that neither natural parent nor natural child know one another's identity. Glaucon, who at points had difficulty with women Guardians, has far more difficulty with this new law.

Hearing Glaucon's doubts, Socrates reminds him again of the dogs and birds he keeps. These are spirited animals trained for guarding and, especially, hunting. Earlier, inclusion of females among these packs was the basis for including women among the Guardians. Now, Glaucon is asked about breeding practices for hunting dogs and noble cocks. Isn't it true, Socrates asks, that not all are bred? Instead, aren't the best bred with the best, in their prime? And, wouldn't any other practice result in lowering the quality of the pack? Glaucon agrees that these things are so.

There is, then, both a purpose and a pattern in this breeding. The dogs and birds are being bred to be the best at hunting, and must be of a certain initial nature and temper established by careful, selective breeding. They will then undergo extensive, very pointed training. Of course, it is strange to speak of these animals "practicing communism" of females and offspring; but Glaucon's mind, at first closed, is being opened to consider seriously the desirability of communism among the human Guardians. Inevitably, given their close association and common exercises, they will have sexual intercourse with one another. The question is, how should the rulers order and arrange this inter-course?

Socrates is circumspect here, since he knows that Glaucon is not convinced that what is practiced when breeding thoroughbred dogs and horses is therefore appropriate for human Guardians. Socrates does not permit him time to reflect on this, but instead subtly flatters Glaucon the handler of dogs by remarking how necessary eminent rulers are. This remark implies that the standard for the Guardians has never been nature, at least not in any simple sense. The master selects and breeds the dogs: his judgment about the best, rather than spontaneous intercourse, determines the quality of the pack. The rulers must do likewise.

This helps to define the communism of the Guard-ians. That communism is not natural, if natural im-plies spontaneous or anarchic. Sexual intercourse among the Guardians is a natural necessity, but there is no indication that it would result in communism of women and children if permitted to take its natural - that is, unguided - course. The actual communism is carefully arranged for the sake of justice. The Guard-ians must be both naturally fit for their task, and free of any concerns which would interrupt it. Their breeding, training, and way of life are determined by their function, and directed by the rulers. Their communism makes sense and is justified - is just - only within this context. It is the communism of a class dedicated completely to the well-being of the city.

If the communism is not natural, then is it volun-tary? Is it enforced? Evidently, it is neither. The Guardians do not form themselves into a communist society. Neither do the rulers simply command then to do so. Instead, the rulers arrange "marriages" among the Guardians on the principle that the best should

60

breed with the best. This happens only when marriages are carefully, subtly guided, using a mixture of incentives and deceptions. These devises make the arrangements for procreation appear more or less natural. Equal attention is given to post-natal care, to insure that mothers do not become attached to their own children.

In this way, good Guardians are born, develop, and practice their art. Every phase of their lives is regulated to insure that the best use is made of the best material, and that the strongest possible bonds develop. These bonds are not natural in any ordinary sense, since some Guardians procreate no children, and those who do don't know who they are. The natural human bonds of parent and child are distracting and disruptive for Guardians. In their place are put complex artificial - more precisely, quasi-natural - bonds, which thoroughly disguise any natural connections. As a result, every Guardian has many fathers and mothers, brothers and sisters, sons and daughters, to say nothing of less direct relations. In name at least, and presumably in the minds of the Guardians, the ruling part of the city is one enormous extended family.

Is this good? Is it good that the city be a family sharing everything? That depends, Socrates says, on a further question: what is the greatest good for a city? Is it not that which binds the city together and makes it one? And, is it not the community of pleasure and pain which does this? Glaucon agrees. He believes that when the city feels pleasure and pain, joy and sorrow, as one - as an individual human being feels these things - then it is united.

Poor, mislead, forgetful Glaucon! He is being overwhelmed by the second wave which, like the first, drowns moderation. Long arguments have shown that it is moderation, not the common sensation of pleasure and pain, which binds the city together. The city is not united on a physical level, because it feels as one; instead it is joined in opinion, with each differentiated part agreeing who should rule and accommodating itself to the rest. CRITIQUE.

Communism does not seem to be doing its job. The spirited Guardians must be moved away from desire and allied with calculation. But common possession of women and children, resulting in this political

61

"family", appears to be obliterating moderation and
compelling a preoccupation with physical pleasure and
pain. More and more, the Guardians' existence is on
the bodily level. So far from beginning to think, they
hardly even believe any longer; instead, they merely
feel. Given this, how can they help but understand
right and wrong as pleasure and pain? Evidently, the
waves - are they not waves of desire? - are washing
away all of that long education in courage and moderation. It does not appear that these communistic Guardians are truly dyed-in-the-wool.

The practice of the communist "family" reveals
itself as an elaborate play, if not an outright sham.
Its member will say the words of kinship and concern,
but will they mean them? Will they do the deeds, as
well as say the words? After all, what are their ties?
They are not the ties of blood. Since these specialized "parents" do not raise children, neither are they
the ties of longstanding concern, common practices,
and shared experiences. The Guardians may share
experiences, but not as a family - an integrated unit
founded on natural differentiation - does. Moreover,
it is never made clear exactly how these Guardians feel
one another's pains, and for good reason. Common sense
says that there is no such thing as common sensation.
The family,let alone the city, is not equivalent to the
individual body, which itself is different from an
individual human being. Forms of address and code
words of commonality may cover up these differences,
and may even be heartfelt, but this is the most which
they can do. The differences remain. One may want to
feel another's pain, or pleasure, but one can do so
only vicariously, at one remove from natural reality.

However, natural reality no longer governs the
minds of the Guardians. The parallel between city and
soul is all but lost. In the well-ordered soul, wisdom or good counsel governs. Justice is only one of
the virtues, and it does not rule. Socrates' implicit
teaching is that justice alone is not, and cannot be
the greatest good. Now, among the communistic Guardians, the desire for justice rules. All of the other
virtues are forgotten, or sacrificed to this desire.
Glaucon becomes the advocate of this movement and thus,
in effect, the spirited ally of desire.

The desire for justice is perplexing. Justice is
that power which makes each thing itself, and not something else. Justice is the end of the institutions and

practices of the Guardians. They are to be freed from all other concerns, so that they may do nothing but guard. But something goes wrong. The desire for justice becomes the desire for unity. Why? The desire for justice is the desire that each thing - or person - be perfectly itself. The desire for unity is the desire that each thing cease to be itself, and become perfectly one with all other things. These desires, seemingly almost identical, produce exactly opposite results. In other words: the desire for justice, when pushed to extremes and permitted to displace all the other virtues, results in the complete destruction of justice.

Having succumbed to desire, Glaucon follows helplessly as Socrates leads him down its paths. Having been stripped first of their clothes and then of their property, the Guardians are reduced in fact to little more than animals in a herd. All the characteristic political institutions are abolished as unnecessary. For example, the Guardians are free of lawsuits, because they settle their differences by fighting. The distinctively human virtues have been drowned by the desire for justice. Now, only fear and shame remain to restrain them from the ultimate expression of their equality and unity, direct assaults by the young upon their elders.

Is this life happy and desirable? Glaucon, headlong in his pursuit of communal justice, believes that it is far happier than the life of an Olympic victor, to say nothing of a farmer or shoemaker. Are there any grounds for his opinion? Perhaps there are. These Guardians are free of all the everyday cares of men and women with families and possessions. They are not separated from one another by any differences other than those which result from immediate physical desire, and these are quickly, if violently, resolved. They have all their physical wants satisfied. They are relieved of the necessity of reflecting upon, and facing up to, the consequences of their behavior, especially their sexual behavior. They are given prizes by the city, and buried by it. In short, they experience physical satisfaction and apparent utility, free from care and anxiety. Evidently, the communism of the Guardians results in a life of organized, satisfied bodily desire. This life appeals not only to Glaucon but to the rest of the company as well, if their silence is to be taken as agreement. They, Adeimantus included, are willing enough to give up the

hard, austere life of the Guardians - to say nothing
of the search for practical injustice -, in exchange
for this much softer existence.

*   *   *

For the eager Glaucon, all that remains is to discover how to realize this way of life. But Socrates
is carried forward by his thoughts. His thoughts are
of war. The very austerity of the "old", moderate
Guardians made war both unlikely and unnecessary. The
way of life of the "new", openly communistic Guardians
seems to make war inevitable, or at least so Socrates'
preoccupation implies. The softness of the end is con-
tradicted by the hardness of the means.

Is this a return to the swollen city of excessive
desire? Probably not, although it shares with that
city the tendency to fight wars. Those in the swollen
city wanted luxury, and had to behave unjustly to get
it. The situation now is much more complex. This city
is ruled by desire, but not for the normal objects of
desire, like money or sensual pleasure. Instead, its
desire is hardly appropriate to the desiring portion of
the soul. Evidently, in this city, the functions of
the desiring and the calculating portions have gotten
mixed up. Rather than calculate, the calculating portion desires, but its desire - perfect justice - has an
abstract, intellectual quality foreign to natural or
normal human desire.

This city is very dangerous, due to the nature of
its injustice. It is not unjust because it wants too
much pleasure, and uses violent means to get it. This
is a relatively simple form of injustice. In this city,
the parts are perverted. They do not do their own
work. The ruling class desires. The spirited class -
the communistic Guardians - are also at least tinged
with desire. It is anyone's guess what becomes of the
producing class: they begin as normal, but it is
doubtful that they can stay that way. Here, injustice
has the form - a grotesque form - produced when natural
functions are confused, and thus debased. In these
circumstances, desire is limitless, because it is unrelated to the natural objects of desire and thus incapable of fulfillment.

This is a city very different from the city of
excessive natural desire. It presupposes the emergence
of mind and thought; a high degree of organization;
and an approach to the problem of the proper function
of human beings. It is nearly philosophical; but, just
at the point where a philosophical understanding of
function is about to be realized, the rulers of this
city are perverted by desire. This perversion takes
the form of a desire for perfect justice, untempered by
moderation, and subserved rather than ruled by calculation. Its politics - the politics of its rulers - are
the politics of the most unholy war.

It becomes evident that this city - the city of
perverted desire - is, for all its perfectionism, far
from good. In immediate human terms, it is the perversion of the potential Guardians Adeimantus and Glaucon:
it combines Adeimantus' attachment to abstract purity
with Glaucon's undiscriminating eros. Its rulers,
lacking knowledge of the proper objects of desire for
each portion of the soul, become fanatics. In the
process, they pervert the lesser Guardians, who are
transformed into conquerors. Education in music and
gymnastic is forgotten. In its place is put the practice of war. From their earliest days, the "Guardians"
become creatures of experience: they are exposed to
war, employed in war, judged by war, and rewarded for
war.

In this city, both true differentiation and true
unity are destroyed. Its typical experience, war, best
illustrates this. As the conquering warriors see
things, the wars they fight are fundamentally national
and racial. They are Greeks, and barbarians are their
enemies by nature. They have lost all ability to see
true differences, which are differences in soul unrelated, they once believed, to differences in sex, let
alone differences in dress and custom. The justice
implied here is at best that of Polemarchus, with its
division into friends and enemies. But this perception
of war divides the warriors from the rulers. There
are perhaps some shreds of moderation - or at least
humanity - left in dividing the world into friends and
enemies, and believing that one must help one's friends
and injure one's enemies. This is not the view of the
rulers, who are far more perverted than the warriors.
At the last, the warriors do have their raw experience
as a basis for judgment. The rulers are further yet
from reality. Their unspoken justification for war is
their desire to achieve perfect justice. Finally, even

their desires separate them from the warriors, who are now only instruments of their fanatic purpose.

Glaucon, however, thinks none of these harsh and disquieting thoughts. He is a spirited man, and is more than convinced that this regime is simply good for a city. For Glaucon, it is the best regime, since it satisfies his most basic desire. It beings unity of spirit and purpose to the warriors, and this unity brings with it victory and honor. These will, in turn, produce and then gratify his other desires. In a flash, Glaucon sees all this: at last, he has found his spiritual homeland. This vision of perfected desire exhausts his patience. He demands, nay virtually commands that all else by dismissed, and the means of realizing this blessed regime be discovered.

Thus, a strange alliance is nearly consummated. It is the alliance of various kinds of desire - for victory, for dominance, for pleasure - with spiritedness, and with an abstract and rigid understanding of justice. In human terms, were Socrates to join, it would include all members of the company. If formed, it would provide something like unity, but not the unity of Book IV. That unity was a whole of differentiated parts joined by moderation under the rule of wisdom. This spurious unity is based on the equality of each of the parts. Underlying this equality is the reduction of each part to desire, although different, selfish desires. This coincidence of interests makes the alliance possible. Indicatively, it is Glaucon, the active man of many, varied desires, who most approves of this regime.

*　　*　　*

For some time now, Socrates has gratified desire. For his trouble, he has been swamped by two great waves. He is at the point of ceasing to be master of the ship, and being forced to play the role of a helmsman commanded by the desires of others. Now, Socrates knows that there is a third, even greater wave coming. That wave will enable him to re-establish command.

This great figure, of the three waves, points up the perilous, paradoxical position of the philosopher. The waves are waves of desire, of each portion of the soul in turn. They are part of sailing the human seas.

They cannot be ignored, or simply opposed. They are
great waves, on a broad sea, and the ship is small.
As they come, the waves must be ridden out or, better
still, used to moved the ship - is it not the soul? -
closer to port. Great knowledge and skill are needed
to know and do these things. But the philosopher is
never completely free from doubt - it confines his wars
to speech -, and besides is never called upon except
in extremis.

Now, Socrates resumes command, but in a way that
seems again merely to serve Glaucon's desire. But
first he reminds the impatient Glaucon that they have
been seeking knowledge, not action. Glaucon concedes
this, and also that action is necessarily less perfect
than speech. He agrees to be content with some approximation of the justice they have produced in speech.

This exchange, coming where it does, requires some
discussion. Glaucon's desire has overwhelmed him; he
longs now to put into practice what has been spoken
of. He must be recalled to philosophy, or at least
forewarned by it. Philosophy and the philosopher will
now become the subject of the Republic, and grave
doubts will be raised or implied about the justice of
the philosopher. The true work of the philosopher is
to discover a pattern or design unseen and untranslated
into practical reality. He must be judged by the goodness of this pattern, not its realization. Both the
pattern and the philosopher are compromised when they
are forced into practical action.

So, just as at the outset when Polemarchus compelled Socrates to accompany him, so at the exact mid-
point of the Republic is Socrates again forced to act
against his will. He has been compelled to show justice in the flesh. Now he is compelled by spiritedness
to put justice into practice. Desire and spiritedness
have forgotten that in the first place they merely
sought justice in itself. But they should not be
blamed: each has acted according to its nature. Perhaps wisdom should be blamed, for not taking sufficient
account of those natures. At any rate, against its
will and against its nature, compelled by its continuing association with spiritedness and desire, wisdom
must now take command. To be sure, wisdom counsels
moderation in practical expectations. It remains to
be seen whether counsel is sufficiently restraining.

One further thought, before the third wave des-
cends. This is the dramatic and decisive moment of the
Republic. Socrates is called upon to be not wisdom
embodied, but a complete human being, the manifest
integration of all the virtues, and qualities of soul.
He must do more than know: he must show justice in
action. His business becomes the human business: the
care of his soul cannot remain private, but must be
displayed through the most heroic action, the bringing
into being of the just city. Nothing less will do for
the fulfillment of the eros of each portion of the
soul, spiritedness and desire as well as wisdom, and
thus for the fulfillment of the entire soul. The chal-
lenge to Socrates is, become complete! Act! Realize!
Again we must see how this squares with moderation.
But it is now evident that the eros of the soul is not
only for self-perfection, but also for philosophical
action.

*   *   *

Unless the philosophers rule as kings or
those now called kings and chiefs genuinely
and adequately philosophize, and political
power and philosophy coincide in the same
place, while the many natures now making
their way to either apart from the other
are by necessity excluded, there is no rest
fron ills for the cities, my dear Glaucon,
nor I think for human kind, nor will the
regime we have now described in speech ever
come forth from nature, insofar as possible,
and see the light of the sun.

The third wave is the alliance of wisdom and
spiritedness. It seems to cancel, and more than cancel,
the first two waves. But its placement immediately
following the discussion of war understood as the quest
for justice raises a shadow of doubt about this. In
any event, after an initial outburst Glaucon appropriately offers himself to Socrates as an ally. There is
a hint here of the decisive part moderation must play.
It will require the greatest moderation for this alliance to exist as an alliance. Wisdom and spiritedness
are not natural allies, as the first two waves have
abundantly shown. Moderation must first bring them
together and then, once they are allied, must act both

to keep them together and to prevent them from losing their distinctive identities. It must work in wisdom to bring it to action, and especially in spiritedness to allow it to accept the direction of wisdom.

Of course, these qualities - wisdom, spiritedness, and moderation - cannot be seen, and are known only by their activities. Their alliance is not like that of Socrates and Glaucon. That is an accidental, wholly temporary alliance of partial or incomplete human beings. As such, it may be the best possible, but it is far from the best thinkable. The true and lasting alliance is "in the same place", that is, in the soul of an individual human being. This is the moderate man, a lover of wisdom who, through the circumstances of possessing political power, is in a position to act comprehensively.

Together, Glaucon and Socrates will withstand the attack. Apparently, the attack is from those who disbelieve in the union of philosophy and politics, not from that great wave itself. First Socrates says, they must distinguish who these men are, and show that it is natural that they philosophize and rule. Their character, he implies, will be the basic defense.

They agree that each kind of man - the erotic, the honor-loving, and so forth - has his characteristic desire, and that desire is for all of the kind of thing desired. According to this, the philosopher is one who loves and desires all kinds of learning. Glaucon suggests that this definition would include some strange types, of men and learning. Socrates agrees: these are not true philosophers. He amends his definition: the true philosopher is the lover of the sight of the truth.

To his credit, Glaucon wonders what this means. But his ignorance is not complete. He already knows, or has heard, that there are ideas or forms - for example, the fair and the ugly, the just and the unjust -, and that each idea is one. But ideas are seen in and through actions and things, and thus appear as not one but many. Those who see, and love, the things and actions are not philosophers. Philosophers love the idea itself, apart from its manifestations, because the ideas cause beauty or justice in things and actions, and thus alone are real and true. The amazingly uncritical Glaucon, who believes in the goodness of justice because it brings manifest pleasure and honor, agrees

to all this. He takes offense only when Socrates calls
him an erotic man. Socrates, it appears, has wooed
Glaucon away from desire - with the implicit promise of
the sight of the truth - and made him an ally.

Thus is Glaucon awakened to true reality, the
reality of the philosopher. The philosopher knows,
what is. At the other extreme are those who know not
what is not. In between are those caught in the dreamworld of opinion. Each of these - what is, what is
not, what is and is not - generates a different power,
in turn, knowledge, ignorance, and opinion. The world
of the senses, made up of many things, lies in the area
of opinion. It is ambiguous, partaking of what is and
what is not, and thus a place of inconstant judgment.
In opinion, the same thing appears at one time to be
fair and another time ugly, at one time just and another unjust. This is because that thing partakes of both
what is - the fair, the just - and what is not - the
ugly, the unjust. Those who love the sensible, visible
things are in the power of opinion. They are distinguished from the philosopher, who loves what is, which
is constant.

CHAPTER SIX

BOOK SIX

Thus ends Book V. Socrates would prefer to leave it at this. His brilliant argument has established him as a philosopher, a lover of the things which are. Whether he has escaped the power of opinion, and seen truly, is another question. The immediate problem, however, is to apply this understanding of the philosopher to the ruling of the city. Is there any reason to believe that philosophy and political power can be brought together?

The first question is, who should rule? This question has been asked and answered long ago, in Book III. Then, it was decided that those Guardians who held firmly to received opinion should rule. But now philosophy has appeared, and shown that opinion is only a dream rolling around between what is and what is not. By the standards of philosophy, men held in the power of opinion are not fit to rule. The virtues of the previously ruling Guardians - courage and moderation - are thus downgraded, or at least cast into some doubt.

The function of the rulers is redefined accordingly. No longer do they merely guard the inherited laws. Such men, the men of opinion, are scarcely different than the blind, or so Glaucon comes to believe. Now the Guardians know what is, timelessly and truly. Undetermined by opinion, they see these things, and use them as a pattern by which to order the city. Only those laws which conform to the pattern of what is, are retained. The rest are discarded, and new, philosophically determined laws put in their place. In a word, the Guardians are hardly Guardians any longer. Instead, they are radical reformers. Not only courage and moderation, but justice itself, are cast into doubt by philosophy which responds to desire and attempts to realize the idea of justice.

In the light of the apparent effect of philosophy on courage, moderation, and justice, the second question is crucial: do these philosophical candidates for ruling have the other virtues, and experience? Socrates speaks of these latter qualities - those of the "old" Guardians - as entirely apart from theoreti-

cal knowledge. To answer the question, the nature of
the philosopher must be understood thoroughly.

*   *   *

Socrates proceeds to draw out eleven characteristics of the philosopher. The first is a love of learning the nature of that which is, the last his own
measured and musical nature. At the center of these
characteristics is the philosopher's indifference to
death. The overall image is of a gentle soul removed
from the normal concerns and immune to the temptations
of the world. By any ordinary standards, no less likely candidate for political power could by found, or
imagined.

This is not the brothers' reaction. When Socrates
asks whether the city should be turned over to such
men, once they are perfected by education and age,
Adeimantus breaks in. He does not deny that such men
should rule, but disbelieves that Socrates has depicted
philosophers accurately. Instead, he has misled them
bit by bit with his series of questions, until this
philosopher presented in speech is quite different from
those who actually exist. The latter are at worst
queer or even vicious, and at best useless to the
cities.

Adeimantus' indictment has three counts: philosophers use speech unfairly; they are odd or vicious;
they are useless politically. How does the philosopher
Socrates respond? He agrees, but very judiciously. He
ignores the first two charges, and proposes to answer
the third through an image. The image is in keeping
with that of the three waves. Imagine now a ship, out
of command. The shipowner is powerful, but not very
bright. The sailors are fighting over who should
steer, and will use any means available to seize the
helm. They know nothing of the true principles of sea-
manship, and deny the claim of anyone who says they do.
There is much more, as Socrates develops the image in
loving detail.

Thus the philosopher, indicted as useless, brings
the counter-indictment. Practical politics is a mad-
house or, more exactly, a ship of fools. The uselessness of the philosopher is not his fault. He should
not have to beg to rule; instead, those in need of his

art should seek him out. In short, the non-participa-
tion of the philosopher in politics is to be blamed on
politics.

Having said this, Socrates begins to answer the
charge that philosophers are vicious. But before hearing this portion of the counter-indictment, a comment
or two is necessary. Socrates has cast some doubt on
his, and philosophy's, judiciousness. Supposedly, he
is seeking to show how and why philosophy and political
power are to be joined. Actually, he levels a blast at
politics, accusing it of failing to do what is natural,
namely, seek out rule when it needs it. How, one wonders, can cooperation or conjunction result from this
lack of moderation? But more than this, Socrates seems
to be misrepresenting the philosopher's art. That art,
as defined so far, is to search for the truth. Nowhere
has it been established that philosophy is the art of
ruling.

What then of the first, unanswered charge, that
philosophy uses speech to gain an unfair advantage?
Is Socrates, through his own speech, demonstrating the
truth of this charge? Or, is he showing Adeimantus the
cut-and-slash ways of politics, where one attacks one's
opponents and defends oneself as best one can? It is
certain that the Socrates who accuses and attacks politics is not the gentle, other-worldly philosopher
depicted in the exchange with Glaucon. Now, the philosopher actually involved with politics takes it in its
own terms and, using his superior intellectual skills,
evidently conquers it. Philosophy and politics may
come together, but it will not be the gentle mating
first envisioned. This association does not appear to
be characterized by moderation, at least not at the
outset, but rather by domination. The rule of wisdom
transforms moderation from its natural gentleness into
something far more calculating. Evidently, moderation
in politics has a different form than moderation in the
soul. As before, it keeps things together, but now is
a different, more vigorous way.

Now, what of the vicious? Again, Socrates concedes Adeimantus' charge: most of those considered
philosophers are vicious. But again, philosophy is not
to blame. Socrates defines again the true philosopher's nature. It is that of the just man of Book IV,
the man whose concern is for the well-being of his
soul, who seeks the things which are with the part of
his soul fit to grasp these things, and who possesses

the other virtues as well. The true philosopher is the _idea_ of man.

Socrates' repetition makes it clear that the nature of the city's potential rulers has changed. These men are different than the spirited puppies of Book II, who at best become faithful Guardians. They were not so rare, and much less full of potential. Philosophical natures are very few, very potent, and capable of great deeds, good or evil. Unless there is divine intervention, the quality of education which they receive will determine what kind of use is made of their great potential.

*   *   *

What corrupts these men? Not, Socrates thinks, the sophists. That argument is itself sophistic. It is made by the biggest sophists, those who truly educate young men, and turn them out just the way they want them. Adeimantus is puzzled. Socrates, who has studied more than the things which _are_, enlightens him. This powerful educator is the multitude. It assembles in various public places: it raises a great uproar: it praises some things, and blames others: its deafening voice floods the hearts and minds of the best young men, drowns their private education, and causes them to say what the many say, do what they do, and be what they are.

The multitude who hold political power employ what means are necessary. If praise and blame are insufficient, they use dishonor, fines, and death. Adeimantus the would-be reformer listens solemnly, and agrees. But threats and punishment are rarely needed. Their opinions are already in the young, placed there by those private wage earners the sophists. They study the angers and desires of the many and, calling them wisdom, organize these things into an art and teach it to those who pay them.

All of this seems full of bitterness and contempt, and Adeimantus is moved accordingly. But Socrates' remarks, and particularly the powerful image he employs, are equivocal. He compares the multitude to a great, strong beast, and the sophist to the beast's trainer. The trainer observes the beast and learns its nature. To some extent, the beast can be control-

74

led, even trained, and the trainer learns how to control it. This experience, turned into a practical art, is taught to the trainer's - or sophist's - students. They will ride the beast, making what use of it they can or will.

Socrates' genuine quarrel with the sophists - and, by implication, with the many - is quite specific. Because they work for wages, they are prone to say what serves their financial interests. In the image, they tend to teach the rider to let the beast run wild. Not enough training occurs, of either rider or beast. Consequently, both are very ungentle. Were the trainer more disinterested, were the rider firmer, were the beast better trained, a more noble use would be made of all. The implicit teaching of the sophist is that the beast is all but uncontrollable. This leads to inconsistent handling, either too harsh or too relaxed. Socrates' implicit teaching is that, under the proper circumstances, moderation can make the best, noble use of the beast. But again, moderation in politics is not dreamy gentleness. It is firmness, in the education of the rider and consequently in the handling of the beast. It is doubtful that Adeimantus is capable of this, so Socrates gently but firmly moves him away from politics, and toward a distaste for the sophists.

Not only the public and the sophists act to ruin the best natures. Friends and relatives are guilty also. Now, Socrates makes the philosophical nature not only great in soul, but also gives it a beautiful body, noble birth, and wealth. The philosopher appears to be a god among men. What else would he do but rule? What else could ordinary men do but submit, gladly, to his rule? But this is not the picture which Socrates paints for Adeimantus. Instead, the philosophical nature is flattered, seduced, and, if necessary, threatened by those who wish to use him in their own interests. Everything necessary is done to keep him away from philosophy. But little persuasion is needed: this bright and shining young man is vain and full of himself. He is led to betray his great gifts, and easily put to others' purposes.

The corruption of the philosophical nature is marked by a certain irony. The bright young man betrays his great gifts, but those gifts, of body, soul, breeding, and circumstance, also betray him. Others desire them, or their effects. They use what means they can to secure them for their own purposes, and thus pervert them. Thus, Socrates argues, the consequences of great natural and political gifts in a world of unequal distribution is the betrayal and abandonment of philosophy.

Adeimantus not only accepts all this, but seems almost pleased by it. Has he forgotten that the first characteristics of the philosophical nature are its love of truth and hatred of falsehood? Can it be that the weight of the other, bodily, and political goods is such that they overcome the desire for truth and permit perversion? But a deeper, more interesting question is raised by the ironic perversion of the philosophical nature. That nature, well and fully endowed, is shining and evidently strong. Yet it is overcome - easily overcome - by the petty tricks of petty men, as well as by the pressure of the masses. Again, Socrates seems full of contempt for these little arts. But is he? And, are they so little, if they subdue and pervert the great natural gifts? In short, is there not much more to politics and its practices than the philosopher is willing to grant explicitly? The more basic irony seems to be that the evident rejection of politics contains its implicit acceptance, or at least implicit acknowledgment of its place and power. In a subtle and indirect way, grounds are being cleared for the union of philosophy and politics.

The extent of the irony is revealed in this: the consequence of the influence of the many, of professional teachers, and of friends and relatives is that the best natures enter into politics or, as Socrates and Adeimantus agree to call it, are "corrupted". Whether what they do in politics results in good or evil, and why, is another question. Austere philosophy, meanwhile, is abandoned to inferior men, unfit to associate with her. These men desire the name of philosophy, not the true intercourse which begets truth. Only a very few good natures actually associate with philosophy. This is through some accident of birth or health or circumstances which disqualifies them for political life.

The consequence of the relative attractions of politics and philosophy is the worst of all possible worlds. The potentially best natures go into politics uneducated by philosophy. Once there, they adopt the ignoble impulses of the many and, using their personal power, magnify the harm done by these impulses. Philosophy is the proper activity for these best natures, but is unable to charm them as politics does. They leave philosophy to unsuited suitors who misuse her and produce nothing but ill-formed offspring. The few good natures who do happen into philosophy look on in dismay at the horrors produced in both philosophy and politics. They are unable to do more than mind their own business and thus save themselves from injustice and unholy deeds.

The sum of Socrates' counter-indictment, then, is this: the best natures are corrupted because politics is corrupting, and politics is much more attractive to them than philosophy. The essential question implied is this: how is it the best nature - a lover of truth, and so forth - is attracted to that which is much less good than itself? The answer implied accounts for both the attraction and the effect of politics: politics attracts and corrupts the best nature because politics is powerful. Perhaps it is not more powerful than philosophy: this has not been decided. But politics is more powerful than the best nature when that nature is unstrengthened or unfortified by philosophy.

Socrates holds out this hope: the best nature can survive, uncorrupted, in the best regime. Somehow, the best nature is the middle term between philosophy and politics. In any but the best regime, it is dragged one way or the other. If it goes into philosophy it is useless to all but itself; if to politics, it becomes corrupted. Living as he does in an imperfect regime, Adeimantus has seen these two conditions. Only in the best regime, when it preserves an understanding of its principles, can the best nature be both uncorrupted and practically useful. There, that nature joins in itself philosophy and politics. Here, the best nature itself is moderation, serving as it does to link two powerful and usually opposed forms.

*   *   *

Thus the question becomes: how can a city take philosophy in hand without being destroyed? Socrates leaves little doubt here about his own opinion: philosophy is more powerful than politics. Neither does he leave much doubt about his own eagerness. For the first time, Socrates does not have to be compelled against his will to continue the discussion. Evidently, joining philosophy and politics, if only in speech, is very close to his heart's desire.

How does Socrates proceed? He does not give philosophy the kind of obvious power that politics has, in order to make philosophy more attractive. Instead of this great and dangerous revolution, he proposes a modest adjustment. Philosophy is not very attractive or appropriate for the young; yet this is just the time when present cities give it to them. Socrates reverses this: give the young the things they like naturally, train properly the minds of the mature, and free the old to pursue philosophy. Adeimantus notes that his reversal would damage Thrasymachus' interests, and so be opposed by him. Socrates, full now of moderation, responds in the most soothing and politic terms. He goes on to provide, free of charge, brief instruction in the new, philosophical rhetoric. Thrasymachus' silence is impressive.

Having made his peace with the sophists - or their representative - Socrates addresses the problem of the many. Earlier, they agreed that it was impossible for the many to be philosophical. Then, the many were portrayed explicitly as a great and powerful force opposed to philosophy and good rule: but, even then, the possibility of a gentling of the many was implicit.

Now, in a stunning political maneuver, Socrates blames the few for the ill-will of the many. The many, he argues, are not bad-natured. They dislike philosophy only because those whom they identify as philosophers are a disorderly and disputatious lot. Thus, the grounds of their dislike are also the grounds for winning their favor: the many are open-minded and changeable inasmuch as they judge by what they see. If what they see - in this case, philosophers - change, so will their opinion change.

The true philosopher has nothing in common with these pretenders. He has no time for their nasty disputes. He looks upon the regular and orderly pattern of the things which are and models himself after them. He thus becomes as beautiful as a human being can be, and is seen as such by the many. But more than this: if necessity demands it, he acts publically, and molds the dispositions of others as well. They too take on some of the order and beauty of the original pattern.

Predictably, Adeimantus is fascinated by all this pure order and beauty. For him, these kinds of objects of philosophy remain supremely attractive. Pressed by Adeimantus, Socrates explains how the philosopher will reform the city. He will act as the greatest artist, first wiping clean the tablet he will draw on. Then, using as his guide the just, the fair, and the moderate by nature, he will form the human material in their image, looking back and forth from one to the other, and correcting and revising as necessary. In this way, human beings will become as near and dear to the gods as possible.

This picture, so attractive to Adeimantus, is full of unreality. It blots out from his memory what has been said before. It changes entirely the character of political life, from lively and full-bodied to flat and two-dimensional. Moderation is now an idea, rather than a quality of speech and soul. Before, under the old, conservative Guardians, a noble lie was sufficient to order the city. Now, a philosophical reformation is to occur. It will not use the human material at hand, and make the best of it. Instead, the city must be purged - the tablet must be wiped clean - and human nature reconstructed. Adeimantus literally cannot resist the power of Socrates' presentation. He is persuaded, very quickly, that the many will become agreeable to this vast reformation, and that philosophy and political power very possibly may be joined.

If Adeimantus is convinced, what of Socrates himself? There is a new eagerness in him now. Does he believe that such a reformation is possible, or desirable? What he says is this: it may be hard, but it's not impossible, and they have already agreed that it is desirable. What he indicates, or implies, is this: the philosophical reformation of the city requires activities and institutions beyond anything which they have created in forming the city of the old Guardians. The old city was a city of right opinion: the new city is, or portrays, the truth.

Much is made here of the moderation of the many. It is taken to be an indispensible condition for the rule of philosophy. But profound change in the character of the city is implied here also. Before, the city was seen essentially from the point of view of justice. Each element in it had its distinctive function. Moderation bound together the functionally differentiated elements. Now, the city is viewed differently: the essential division is into the many and the few. The many look upon the few, and are attracted or repelled according to what they see. They have little if any distinctive character of their own. In other words, they are more moderate than just, and their moderation is not the handmaiden of justice but rather a kind of softness and pliability. Now, the city has become much less a coordinated whole of parts and much more a drama with very few actors and very many spectators. Ironically, the more that truth, pure and simple, becomes the standard for the city, the more the city is divided politically, and the more judgment is based on appearances.

*   *   *

These changes determine the remainder of Book VI and all of Book VII. By now, it is completely evident that the nature of the Guardians has changed. In this city - the City of Truth, if not the true city -, philosophers will rule. As Socrates says, philosophers must be established as the most precise Guardians. "Most precise" means "in the true sense" or "perfect in their art" or "without error". The education of these rulers cannot be limited to music and gymnastic, which are intended to produce the character that preserves right opinion. The traditional education must be revolutionized to produce philosophers who also rule.

However, this statement of things is not very precise. The old education, and the kind of character formed from it, is not discarded, at least not completely. The steadfastness it produces is needed in the Guardians. But steadfastness which is not sufficient for rulers who are also philosophers. They must be more than regular and orderly and willing to stand their ground; they must also love learning, and be good and quick at it, and remember. The natures of the spirited puppies of Book II and the loyal Guardians of Book III and the magnificent philosopher of Book VI are now to be brought together, and the education of them is to occur in turn.

Socrates realizes that all this education - physical, musical, and now intellectual - sounds very tedious. He begins to hint to Adeimantus - and the others - that there is a kind of study greater than all others, and that this study has something wonderful at its end.

Although he has heard these things before, Adeimantus is, or pretends to be puzzled and forgetful. Socrates reminds him that he has heard many times that the idea of the good is the greatest study. Nothing else, justice included, is complete or finally worthwhile without this knowledge. After all, what good is anything if we don't know what is good?

Adeimantus doesn't pause to wonder: how can anything just, as they have defined justice, be other than good? Instead, he allows Socrates to persuade him that there is much dispute about the good, and that no one adequately understands it. But there is this about the good, which sets it apart from all else: everyone truly wishes to possess it. They are not satisfied with apparent good, as they may be satisfied with apparent justice or apparent beauty. Again, Adeimantus does not question the truth of Socrates' proposition. He is persuaded that every soul finally longs for the good, whether or not it knows anything about it.

By now, it has been amply demonstrated that Adeimantus has very little memory. If he did, he would recall that, long ago, Socrates suggested that there is a desire which is not specific, a desire, as it were, for that which ends desire. This suggestion raises interesting questions about the nature of the soul, and its prior division into three elements. It also gives a glimpse of the other, longer road of inquiry which they did not take in Book IV, and which does not depend on hypotheses.

Adeimantus understands none of this. He wants Socrates' opinion about what the good is. When Socrates suggests that he doesn't know, Adeimantus says, well then, say what you suppose, as your supposition. He cannot grasp that the long road, the philosophical road, is one which questions all suppositions, and finally leaves them behind. Neither can he imagine the effect of philosophical practice upon the neat political order of the city which they have created. Gently, without saying these disquieting things, Socrates begins to persuade Adeimantus to give up his rather mild desire to know the good, or rather to hear another's opinion about it.

But Glaucon is not so easily satisfied. It appears to him that the good is something wonderful, obviously greater and better and more final than even the just. As always, in the last analysis Glaucon takes Socrates

more seriously than Adeimantus does. He wants passion-
ately to know the good or to see it, on whatever terms,
using whatever procedures. He refuses to let Socrates
withdraw from the argument now, when they are so close
to finishing. Socrates agrees to satisfy him, not by
showing him the good itself - it's out of range of
their present thrust -, but instead telling him about
what looks to be a child of the good.

*   *   *

They begin their exercise in philosophy. First,
they agree that there are many fair things and many
good things, but only one fair itself and good itself.
The many things are seen but not thought, the ideas
thought but not seen. When they reflect on the senses,
they discover this. Seeing is different than the
others. To see, we need not only something to see
with, and something to see, but a third thing, light,
which yokes them. Glaucon, whose name is related to
light and sight, is a bit blinded by all this. He
agrees that light is more honorable than the other
senses' yokes, which he has just denied to exist.

And, Glaucon, which of the gods in heaven does
light come from? The clear-eyed Glaucon replies, the
sun. We have, then, these things: sight; that which
sees - the eye; that which is seen; light; and the
source of light - the sun. The sense of sight, in
truth, is different: that which is seen is not the
source of the light by which it is seen, unless one is
looking directly at the sun, a rare and dangerous
occurance.

The sun is what Socrates calls the child of the
good, begot in a proportion with itself. The sun is
in the visible region, the good in the intelligible.
Analogous to the above, we have: knowledge; that which
knows - the soul; that which is known; truth; and the
source of truth - the idea of the good. Just as the
sun is different from and the source of light, so too
the good is different from and the source of truth.

It is far from clear how Socrates arrived at all
this, or whether it is true: but Glaucon has no interest in such questions. Here is philosophy which he is
at home with. He is dazzled, and all but beside himself. He wonders aloud whether this beautiful thing

the good can be other than pleasure. Socrates hushes
him, and shows him more wonders. If the sun is the
source of all generation, growth and nourishment, but
is itself beyond them, then the good is the source of
all existence and being, but likewise beyond them.
This comes close to finishing Glaucon. He bursts out
in amazement, and begs Socrates not to stop until all
is revealed.

Then, says Socrates, think of these two as kings -
the sun of the visible realm, the good of the realm of
thought. Next, take a line and divide it into two
unequal portions, one portion for the class of things
seen, the other for those thought; and then divide each
portion in the same proportion. Socrates does not say
which portion of the line - the visible or the intelligible - is longer. There is no easy or obvious solution
to this riddle, which Glaucon ignores. He is passive,
and wishes to be told, not to inquire actively.

First, consider the visible segment. In one portion place images - shadows, reflections in water and
mirrors, and so forth. In the other, place those visible things whose shadows or reflections appear in the
first portion. These visible things are all plants
and animals and human artifacts. These make up the
visible world, or seem to. But Socrates excludes in-
animate matter, except as fashioned into artifacts.
His visible world is a living world, literally a world
full of soul.

Before considering the intelligible, Glaucon
agrees to one more argument, and one more proportion:
the truth of the visible in relation to the reflected
is in the same proportion as that of the knowable in
relation to the opinable. If we assign values of one
(1) to the reflected and three (3) to the visible, then
the knowable and the opinable - the visible realm taken
as a whole - stand in the relationship twelve (12):
four (4). This may or may not resolve the riddle of
the length of the lines.

These calculations, and others like them, take us
above the basic division, into the realm of thought.
It is evident from the calculations that one portion of
the line of thought depends upon hypotheses or assumptions, and leads to conclusions based upon the hypotheses and no sounder than the hypotheses. This is
clear enough, once the calculations are done and

reflected upon. But Glaucon has not done them, and calls for further explanation.

Socrates enlightens Glaucon first about the area of hypotheses, from the point of view of the geometer. The geometer's concern is mathematical forms, like the square, which strictly can be seen only with the mind. To aid his reasoning, he draws a particular visible square, which is an image of the mathematical "square itself". In turn, the visible square can be reflected in a mirror, thus creating an image of an image. Throughout, the geometer assumes that the square exists, and does not attempt to prove it. His thought thus rests on a hypothesis, and cannot go beyond it. In keeping with the riddle of the line, Socrates leaves unclear the origin of the idea of the square.

This leaves the area of non-hypothetical intelligence, which is most difficult to grasp, and about which Socrates says little. Hypotheses stand on the border between the two realms. But, while they rule in the mathematical and related sciences, they are subjected to critical questioning in the area of non-hypothetical thinking. Here, logical argument rules. Slowly, through critical questioning, it leaves behind all hypotheses, and begins to travel freely toward its destination. Its destination, according to Socrates' argument, is the good. What it travels through, and how, and what part of the argument reaches the end – all of this is an inexpressible mystery. But, whatever remains of it, it does reach the end, which is the beginning. There, the argument stands, free of everything but itself. Of course, it goes without saying that the argument must be good to get there. Bad arguments, of which there are many, simply go astray. But let's be precise, here of all places. They go astray, very unsimply, following long and foggy trails ending in nothing.

From the beginning, the argument starts back, but not as it has come. It came by grasping hold of hypotheses and then leaving them behind. It returns by a way much more marvelous and inexpressible even than the journey out. Now, it is free of everything but itself, and can create its own way undependent upon hypotheses. What is this way? Perhaps, we think, very beautiful and rich and clear. Ah, but these are words and ideas of the senses, and the way back no longer needs such things. Its necessity is the necessity of thought, not of sight, nor of sight and thought mingled as they are in hypotheses. Its necessity is the necessity of pure argument, and it creates a way which moves unerringly from logically necessary form to next logically necessary form until the whole panoply of logical necessity is completed.

*   *   *

Glaucon does not fully understand, and his sense of the intellectual beauty of the activity of pure argument is not well developed. Instead, this activity appears to him as, long ago, he made justice appear to the many: long and hard and doubtful. His reaction is not without reason, even if the reasons are unknown to him. There is a remarkable resemblance, of a certain kind, between the justice of Book IV and the good of Book VI. There, justice was a paradox: it appeared to be at once the power which makes each thing what it is, and yet a residue left behind when the other virtues are discovered. Here, the good is the greatest power in the intelligible world, the cause of being and truth. Yet it too is something outside the ordinary human world of vision and speech, of seeing and knowing. It seems to be something left over after all the parts of that world are spoken of and accounted for. Perhaps it is the cause of every good thing, or of goodness in every thing. But, beyond this, what can be said of it, or known about it? Goodness seems to be as purely formal as justice, and much more an object of belief than of knowledge. The paradox of the good is that argument without belief about it shows it to be an object of belief. How real then is the apparent resemblance between justice and the good? Philosophy, or at least logical argument makes the good appear much less real than justice. But perhaps this is only fitting. The method of discovering justice was analogical: the method of speaking about the good is doubly analogical.

These thoughts are beyond Glaucon, who will not examine the ground of his belief in the good. But the discussion has produced in him the beginning of contempt for the sciences which depend on hypotheses. So, as Book VII begins, Socrates puts the mysteries of the way out and the way back into an image, far and away the most famous of the Republic, that of the cave.

However, more than Glaucon's disposition determines the image of the cave. Socrates makes a statement at the border of Books VI and VII, between his
accounts of the way of thought and the cave. Four conditions, he suggests, occur in the soul, corresponding
to the four segments of the line: understanding, thinking, believing, and imagining. Until now, they had
assumed that the soul has three parts; that two of the
parts have their own distinctive virtues; that each
part has the virtue justice; and that moderation is in
common among the parts. The treatment of the soul has
been, first, hypothetical, and second, in terms of
virtue. What, now, of this new treatment? Is it a
philosophical rejection, or correction, of past hypotheses? How do the four conditions relate to the three
parts of the soul? Or, does each condition occur in
the entire soul? Evidently, the critique of hypothetical thinking has upset the order of the soul and, by
implication, of the city. Every aspect of human
consciousness except pure thought is now suspect, as
the image of the cave will reveal.

CHAPTER SEVEN

BOOK SEVEN

The cave itself is an image, Socrates begins, of human nature in its education and lack of education. This is the image. The cave is underground - below the dividing line - with a long entrance open to the daylight. In the cave are human beings who have been there since childhood. They are chained in such a way that they cannot move and can look only straight ahead. Above and behind them is a fire, the source of their light. Between the prisoners and the fire is a road with a wall built along it on the side facing the prisoner's backs. Socrates likens the wall to the partition in a puppet show over which the puppet-handlers display the puppets. Behind the wall, human beings are walking along the road. They carry various artifacts and also statues of men and other animals, made of wood, stone, and every other kind of material. These images project above the wall. Some of the carriers utter sounds, while others are silent.

Glaucon finds the image and the prisoners strange. They are like us, Socrates replies, and gives this explanation. The prisoners see nothing of themselves and of each other but the shadows cast on the cave wall which they face. Likewise, they see only the shadows of the objects passing behind them. If they name, they name these shadows; if they hear the sound uttered by the carriers and echoed of the wall, they suppose that the shadows are speaking. Their reality is the sights and sounds presented by the wall which they face. Socrates concludes, they will hold that truth is nothing other than the shadows of artificial things. Most necessarily, Glaucon agrees.

Why does Socrates say this? Why does Glaucon agree? It is not true. The prisoner's truth is not simply the shadows of artificial things. In fact, it is mixed of their own shadows and the artificial shadows, their own sounds and the carriers' sounds. Their truth may be less than true, but it is not completely untrue. If they are prisoners, it is of opinion, not of untruth. But Glaucon behaves as Socrates has predicted, like a prisoner completely unaware of his own existence and willing to believe that truth is whatever is presented to him.

This first exchange suggests several things. First, for human beings it is practically impossible to separate images and words; next, that the truth presented in words is something less than true; finally, that it is very easy to confuse "reality" - that combination of words and images in which we live - and truth. Literally, we are in the "cave" - a confusion of sights and sounds, of the natural and the artificial. The neat divisions of the line now become blurred. Because we think and "see" in words, we find it practically impossible to stand apart from this, our reality, and to comprehend any truth other than that which is contained and expressed in our reality. We are, as it were, fish, unable to see the sea because we are part of the sea. It becomes more evident why Socrates allies seeing and knowing, the sun and the good.

This confusion is the normal or natural condition of human beings. Nevertheless, Socrates calls it bondage and folly, and says that there is by nature a way out of it. The way is painful, because we are mentally stiff from lack of intellectual exercise, and because the direct light of even the natural world dazzles us at first. But slowly we begin to see those things whose shadows we saw before, and to understand that even naturally we see forms rather than flesh and blood particulars.

The former prisoner might prefer to stay at this level, studying nature, but he gets dragged away again, this time completely out of the "cave", the natural human realm. At first the intellectual "light" is all but blinding, and he can see only the shadows and then the reflections of the things which really are. But as he grows more accustomed to the realm of thought, he is able to see the various levels of real things, and finally the intellectual "sun" itself - the good.

In the image, the realm of thought appears to be very full and rich, much more so than the visible or "cave" world. This has two consequences, aside from shedding interesting light on the riddle. First, the former prisoner concludes that the good rules in the realm of thought, and is somehow the cause of everything in the visible world as well. Second, he is delighted with the change in his condition, and pities everyone who has to remain in the world he once lived in.

*   *   *

Glaucon, apparently caught up in the hope of seeing the good, leaves certain questions unasked. If the
good is somehow the cause of everything, then aren't
the things in the cave good? If they are good, why
then Socrates' dislike for the follies of the cave?
It becomes apparent that everything is viewed from the
vantage point of the philosopher. In the cave, there
are only shadows and forms. But out of the cave, in
the world of thought, things take on life and body.
For the philosopher, normal reality and truth become
reversed. In the light of thought, ordinary human life
becomes a shadowy Hades. The noble lie, in which men
are made of earth and metals, is now seen as just that,
noble perhaps, but a lie certainly. Truth, as the philosopher sees it, is soul and form and thought.

Yet, it was the noble lie, with its basic and explicit materialism, that bound together the just city,
just as it was moderation that bound the parts of the
soul together. Now, both the story of earth-born men
and the hypotheses basic to the account of the soul
have been thrown into radical, philosophical doubt.
These things - formative political myths and ethical
understanding based on hypotheses - no longer interest
the philosopher who has travelled beyond them to the
good. He has seen the light. If he returns to the
cave, he is all but blind and unable to function. His
inability moves those in the cave to ridicule and then
to anger and violence, if the philosopher attempts to
release them from their bonds and lead them out of the
cave. Or, if the philosopher is dragged into court,
he is disinclined to argue about representations or
shadows of justice, since he has seen the just itself.

Throughout this discussion, Socrates makes those
in the cave appear pitiable. But it is the former prisoner who has become truth-seeker and truth-seer who
suffers from his escape from the cave. He can no longer survive in a normal human setting: his only salvation is somehow to remain permanently outside the cave.
Socrates excuses him, saying that souls like eyes suffer from two kinds of disturbances, moving from light
into darkness as well as from darkness into light. But
eyes respond to greater darkness by opening wider, and
to greater light by narrowing to admit less of it. Eyes
naturally act to maintain a balance, to be able to continue to guide the body as a whole, and to save sight.

89

Is the parallel between eyes and souls to be taken seriously? Must it not be, since line and cave are based on the analogy between seeing and knowing? If it is, then the soul, caring for a balance and for its overall well-being and for knowing, does not respond to more truth by opening wide to admit it. Neither does it respond to untruth by simply shutting down and closing it out. Rather - (if) souls are like eyes, an unproven hypothesis - the soul looks most closely and carefully at untruth, to see if it can find some truth somewhere among it; and, it is most shy and distrustful or pure truth, making itself quite closed and admitting only very small amounts of it at any one time.

This suggests a number of things. First, an erotic desire for pure truth or pure goodness does not rule the soul. In practice, calculation does, just as it did in the earlier discussion based on hypotheses. If that was true, then is it not also true - true in practice, true for human beings - that it is moderation that binds the parts of the soul together and enables it to conduct itself as one? Second, Glaucon - for whose immediate gratification this long anti-political discussion has been conducted - lacks that quality of soul almost equal in importance to moderation: memory. Long ago, in Book III, Glaucon said something about the proper response to imperfection which it would be useful to recall now.

Finally, in light of this, what of the philosopher? What is he to do? Is he to try to escape the cave and seek the truth? Or, is he to stay in the cave, and direct the moderate light of his own soul to illuminate the unlit and thus unknown truth present in other's souls? Socrates now speaks in almost flat contradiction to the apparent message contained in the image of the cave. The argument, he says, indicates that the power of knowing is present in each soul. But only a part of the soul - its "eye" - has this power. This part, together with the entire soul, must be turned from the things which are and are not, to look upon those which simply are.

Then, is this the job of the philosopher? Is his art the turning around of souls from the darkness to the light? Again we see things as the philosopher does, although his view confirms previous hypotheses about the soul. It does have parts, and each has its distinctive virtue. But the virtues of most of the soul are close to those of the body. They do not pre-

90

exist, but are instilled by habit and exercises. The virtue of reasoning is different. It is closer to the divine: it is not instilled, but is naturally present: it functions regardless of cultivation, although for good or for ill depending upon what it is directed at. Is concern with this virtue the business of the philosopher? Does the practice of this art give him a place in the city? In a word: is the philosopher the educator of reasoning?

If he is, what of the body, and all the rest of the soul? Is it to be left to gymnastic and music, a matter of indifference to the philosopher? Or, is the entire soul somehow to accompany the reasoning portion on its journey to the good? If it does, what of the body? Can it remain behind, and belong to the city, if the soul abandons it? It is not clear whether the philosopher has now found a place in the city, or whether he will drag all human beings or the best human beings completely or almost completely outside it.

Implicit in these questions is the greater one: is the philosopher just? The awful ambiguity of justice is seen once more, but now more clearly. Justice, it seems, is not a single, simple thing. Justice is each thing being itself or, in political terms, it is each person performing one function. The philosopher seems to have a function within the city: his job is to turn souls toward the light. But, the light is outside the cave: the souls turned toward the light care for their own well-being and not that of the city. The business of the philosopher is the soul, and it is unclear how the soul can belong to the city and yet be what it is, a thing beyond all the usual human bonds and associations. But now, in the light of the good, even the question of the justice of the philosopher begins to fade, itself a matter of merely human concern. A greater question arises, profoundly disturbing politically, merely interesting philosophically: what kind of an idea is justice? Is it an idea incapable of being free from ambiguity and unclarity, a lesser idea, an idea which in the light of the good is only a twilight idea?

*   *   *

Socrates' reply to these kinds of questions is a moderate one. Glaucon asks, how can it be just to compel the philosopher to return to the cave, rather than

91

to live the better life outside it? Socrates tells his forgetful pupil that it is the good of the whole city which concerns them as founders. This seems to deny the philosophers, but does it? They are permitted - indeed, compelled - to leave the cave. There, in the light of the good, they come to have a single goal. But they are not permitted to remain permanently outside, because those who do so are unwilling to act. Human life, Socrates implies, is some harmonious compound of thinking and doing, knowing and acting. In this light - whatever light it is, wherever it is found - are not the philosophers dealt with justly? Are they not men? More: are not they the very form of man, seen in the true light of justice? Is not the nature of human life seen most clearly in the limiting case of human nature? More still: is it not possible that the apparent problem with the idea of justice - its ambiguity, its lack of clarity - lies not with the idea itself, but with that to which the idea is applied, with man?

Has justice been done? Is the life set before the philosophical nature by the founders the right life? Socrates tells Glaucon: we will say just things to them, while compelling them to care for and guard the others. Is this speech another noble lie?; or, are there now just men to whom the truth can be told? Now, Socrates is no longer Socrates, a philosopher misused and ridiculed and finally destroyed by an unjust city. He is the voice of the law of a just city, speaking to those whose function it is to aid the law in binding the city together. This suggests that moderation has returned, in the law and in those who represent the law, those philosophers who are compelled to rule.

What does the law say? It says: you are not like other men in your own city, or philosophers in other cities. We have begotten you for yourselves and for the city. You are better and more completely educated and able to share in both ways of life. You must go down in your turn to the common home and get used to observing the obscure things there. When you do, you'll see 10,000 times better than those there; and you'll know what each of the representations is, and what it represents, because you have seen the truth about fair and just and good things.

The law goes on, teaching and gently commanding. Thus, the city will be governed by us and by you; but not in a dream as are those many cities governed by

men who struggle with one another to rule as if ruling
were some great good. The truth is this: necessarily,
the city in which the least eager men rule is best
governed and freest from faction, while those with the
opposite kind of rulers are governed in the opposite
way. So, knowing the good things, in your turn you
will rule, but as a necessary, not a good thing.

Why is it necessary that those not eager to rule
govern best? Is it because they know the truly good
things, and thus can put political life in its proper
place? Is it because their knowledge of the truly good
and of the merely apparently good makes them moderate
in dealing with the mixed things of ordinary human
life? Does this knowledge of the relative goodness of
philosophy and political life produce moderation, or
only apathy and avoidance? Is a good ruler dispassionate, lacking all enthusiasm for ruling? Can any ruler
but the law be dispassionate, and yet win respect and
affection and allegiance from human beings? Will men
willingly obey other men obviously "above it all"?
Moderation - especially politically effective moderation - does not appear to be this dispassion. Moderation - at least politically relevant moderation - does
not appear to be born of philosophical understanding.
The laws must compel the philosopher to rule, while
saying just things. No doubt, given their upbringing,
they have a debt to the city. But unless that upbringing has made them truly moderate - full human beings,
understanding their humanity more fully and deeply than
mere just words can make them - , it is doubtful that
they will be good rulers.

Then, how are these Guardians - philosophers -
kings to be formed? By the Noble Lie or the Just
Speech? Is their moderation to be the result of music
or of logic? Is the city raising them for itself or
for themselves? Is their life - a life both above and
below - just, or is it an uneasy compromise reflecting
the division of their own nature? How can they rule a
city free from faction, if they are themselves factionated? How can they become truly moderate in the original meaning of the term, men whose souls are so soundly
bound together into one that their cooperation with
the laws will bind the city together in the same way?
Is it by means of the education that Socrates will now
present to Glaucon? Is this how they will become most
wise in those things through which a city is best governed? And, what are those things?

* * *

So, again, the discussion resumes. Glaucon remains eager to know how these souls are to be turned
around from dark to light, and lead up to view the
things which are. He is not so inclined to wonder what
this kind of knowledge has to do with governing a city
well; in other words, whether the things which are are
those things one must become wise in to govern well.
Glaucon is already turned around. Eager to see the
good, he has lost interest completely in political
life, and apparently in justice as well. His erotical-
ly-powered courage carries him forward.

Two absurdly disconnected criteria emerge to
determine the necessary studies: they must lead to
knowledge of that which is, and be useful to men in
war. To his credit, Glaucon indicates doubt that such
studies exist. Well, are they gymnastic and music,
the basic education of the "old" Guardians? No, not
gymnastic: gymnastic is concerned wholly with that
which does not persist, growth and decay in the body.
Glaucon doesn't bother to add that it does meet one of
the criteria. Neither does he recall the relationship
which they have established between gymnastic and the
spirited portion of the soul.

And what of music, Socrates asks Glaucon? In
response, Glaucon gives one of his best speeches, a
model of precision. Music is the counterpart to gymnastic. It educates by habituation, imparting by harmony good harmony, and by rhythm good rhythm; and also
certain other qualities, akin to these, imparted by
speeches, whether myths or truer speeches. But it is
not a study directed toward that which you are now
seeking. Glaucon doesn't say it, but music fails to
meet either criteria - useful in war or leading to that
which is.

Socrates agrees and asks, then, what studies, if
not gymnastic and music? Certainly not the arts, which
are base and mechanical. What remains? No single
study, replies Socrates, but that which applies to all
of them. And what, Glaucon wonders, can this be? Only,
Socrates says, the lowly business of distinguishing the
one and the two and the three: in other words, number
and calculation. Must not every art and science necessarily participate in them? Most necessarily, Glaucon
replies.

Do all the arts necessarily participate in number and calculation? Perhaps they do, more or less, but one above all: the art of money-making. Numbering and calculating appear to be the very essence of this art. Earlier, money-making was seen as the great enemy of all other arts: it cause a man to consider his own interests rather than those served by his art. More, it forced a man to practice two arts, and thus fail to conform strictly to justice. Now, calculation is held to be common to all the arts, and thus somehow the desired or necessary study. How are souls to be turned around by a study which appears to be the essence of that common art which mitigates the selfless justice of all other arts?

Socrates does not answer, indeed does not raise this question. Instead, he first asks whether calculation is useful in war. Indeed, replies Glaucon, not only if a warrior wants to know the order of the army, but if he's to be a human being. Then, Socrates remarks that number and calculation lead naturally to thought; but that no one uses them rightly, as things which in all ways draw us toward being. Glaucon is puzzled, and asks Socrates to explain.

Socrates gives this account. Some objects of sensation move the intellect to activity, and others do not. Those do not which are adequately known by a given sense, and do not suggest their opposite. On the other hand, those not adequately known by sense, which do suggest an opposite, involve the intellect. To illustrate, Socrates holds up three fingers - the little finger, the index, and the middle. Each finger is seen as a finger, without suggesting any opposite. Sight is adequate here: the intellect remains uninvolved.

He does not ask next, what else does sight see? Instead, these questions: does sight see their bigness and smallness adequately, regardless of where they are? What of touch? Does it reveal thinness and thickness, or softness and hardness adequately? Rather, doesn't touch sense the same thing as both hard and soft? Glaucon agrees. Then, isn't it necessary that the soul be puzzled at what touch means by "hard", if it also calls the same thing "soft", and similarly if it calls the same thing "light" and "heavy"? Again, Glaucon agrees.

It appears, then, that the soul must investigate what "the hard" and "the soft" are. But again Socrates

turns the discussion against its natural direction. He
asks, must not the soul determine whether each thing
reported to it is one or two? Glaucon agrees, but
fails to notice the ambiguity here. Does Socrates
means, is the finger one or two?, or is the hard and
the soft one or two? Indeed, what is the finger, supposedly well-known to the sight? But, at this point,
Socrates does not want this kind of question. He wants
to stay with number and calculation.

What then, he asks, of number and the one? Are
they things adequately known to the senses, or must
the intellect investigate them? Here, perhaps Socrates
again carefully displays his three carefully selected
fingers. Do we see one, or one and the opposite of
one? Glaucon's thoughtful answer captures the complexity of what we actually see: at the same time we see
the same thing as one and as many more than one. For
example, looking around the room we see one table, one
lamp, one window, one Socrates, one Glaucon, and so
forth. Each thing is one thing, and yet there are many
"ones", and, as well, each "one" is one of a class of
many. What then is one? It is not visible: the eye
cannot see one. Is it intelligible? Can the mind
"see" one? Can it imagine one, if one is not at the
same time attached to some particular or specific object? It seems that it cannot. Then, how is it that
the mind comprehends the idea of one pure and simple?
Can it purely and truly think of one in itself?

Perhaps it can, and perhaps it cannot; but two
things are evident. First, there are difficulties with
knowing "things-in-themselves", especially when the
thing is supposed to be one or unified in nature.
Again the good appears much more problematic than the
just. Second, the consideration of numbers leads to
the consideration of the one, and consideration of the
one involves dialectics. Unless numbers are taught
rote-fashion for immediate practical purposes, it is
unlikely that the rest of the specialized subjects will
be gotten to, or attended to.

Geometry is the next eligible study. Granted that
geometry is useful in war, does it lead the soul toward
being? Well, says Socrates, those who practice it now
are as ridiculous as those who learn to calculate for
the sake of making money. They speak as if they were
men of action, forever "squaring" or "applying" or doing something of the sort. In fact, the whole subject
is solely for the sake of knowing. Glaucon agrees

wholeheartedly: geometry knows what always is. As befits well-bred gentlemen exposed to the study of geometry, they leave this interesting contention unproven. The fact that geometry was found to depend completely on unestablished hypotheses is also ignored.

Here is another of those twists and turns noticed earlier. Geometry is not a more advanced study than numbers, at least pure numbers. The idea of the circle or the square is far less pure and removed from the senses than the idea of unity. Evidently, the course of studies to be followed in the ascent toward being is not a simple or straightforward one, but instead one which repeatedly turns back on itself.

Astronomy is mentioned next. Glaucon is enthusiastic; but Socrates suggests that they are beginning to go astray. Is their concern utility or truth? Are they trying to conform to the opinions of the many or the few? Or, asks Socrates, is Glaucon engaged in the argument mostly for his own sake? Bold as ever, largely indifferent to politics, Glaucon replies, for my own sake. Well, then, says Socrates, we must retreat: we are in error. He has led Glaucon to identify his own good with the truth.

They have violated the logical sequence. After a plane surface at rest - ordinary geometry - comes a solid at rest, not a solid in motion. Glaucon protests that solid geometry has not yet been discovered: but he says nothing about the logic of the sequence. In effect, they have gone from one to two to three, and are soon to go to three in motion. Evidently, the sequence is not toward what is, but away from it. Socrates' remarks on solid geometry suggest this also. The problem with it now is that it is not politically supported. Its strength is that it is charming - not useful, not true, but charming. When it finds its advocate, when its charm is politically recognized, it will become even more powerful. No doubt, the right kind of city will sponser it.

Next, solids in motion, or astronomy. Glaucon resolves to praise astronomy so as to please Socrates, not for its utility but for its tendency to lead the soul toward being and truth. Socrates scolds him, although he himself has lead Glaucon to this kind of science. It is accidental that this science studies regular motion in the heavens. Logically, it could study any kind of motion of any solid body anywhere. In

our terms, astronomy is a special case of physics. For
Socrates too, astronomy leads the soul downward not up-
ward, using the senses more than the intellect. Thus
it must be reformed, becoming not a special science of
moving bodies but instead the study of the visible representation of something much more precise and true.

What does Socrates think these truer things are?
Abruptly, the decent halts: the soul again is thrust up
into the area of intelligible forms and forced to con-
front them. They are not clear, and the soul was beginning to become accustomed to the visible things of political life, expressed in words. But Socrates snatches
the visible things away, and forces contemplation of
the idea of motion. How can there be a form of that
which moves? This is not clear: in words, it is ter-
ribly contradictory. But this kind of motion is not
expressed in words, but numbers, and true numbers at
that.

Perhaps this leads toward what is, but is it useful in war? Not useful in the way which Glaucon has
understood it, for farmers and sailors. Puzzling over
these problems, Socrates says, changes the understanding in the soul by nature from uselessness to usefulness. But, which problems, and to which kind of usefulness? The problems involved in the idea of motion, or
the problems of a soul on this rollercoaster from the
visible and political to the purely intelligible? And,
is the understanding to be made useful for theoretical
or practical questions, or both?

*   *   *

What studies give the proper character to the intelligence in the soul? Glaucon gives a charming but
not very useful answer. Socrates suggests that motion
appears in several forms, and that two are obvious.
They're not to Glaucon, not even when Socrates tells
him that astronomy has a counterpart. Motion has ef-
fected Glaucon's soul. He is blind, or rather deaf,
to that which usually is near and dear to him.

The counterpart to astronomy is harmonics. Socrates says that as the eyes are fixed on astronomy, the
ears are fixed on harmonic movement. But the eyes don't
"see" astronomy. They act as media through which regular motion reaches the intelligence. The same is true

for the ears. But there seems to be this difference. Regular motion which is visible exists in nature: regular motion which is audible is man-made. But the effect is the same: the intelligence is informed by regular and orderly motion.

Several questions arise here. Why does Socrates allude to, and apparently defer to the Pythagoreans? Have they already made an adequate study of the subject? Then, which portion of the soul is informed by this regular motion? Is it only the intelligence? Also, what is the relation of harmonics to music? Are their sources identical? Is the true music somehow "scientific"? Glaucon criticizes students of music for relying on their ears rather than their intelligence. Socrates agrees: true students - the Pythagoreans - do not seek harmony in sound, but instead rise above sounds to the problem of which numbers are "symphonic" with one another.

All of this seems purely and perfectly intellectual. Harmonics is useful, Socrates says, in seeking the fair and the good when studied this way, but useless if done otherwise. Socrates seems to have elevated - or reduced - sight and sound to number. True harmony is to be found in the world of the mind, not the senses. But why, then, does he bother with the senses at all? Why not only pure mathematics? The facts of the education are otherwise: harmonics is closer to the true, the good, the beautiful things than arithmetic or geometry. It is the conjunction of the beautiful things of the senses with the things of the mind which is almost the final stage of the education.

*   *   *

Now Socrates says, all of this is no more than the preamble to the law or, as it were, the prelude to the song. It is a very long prelude, studying each of these subjects and then discovering how they are related. Glaucon agrees: it is a very great labor. But it is not final. One can do these things, and yet not be a dialectician. Dialecticians must give and receive the reason for things in order to know what they must know. Again Glaucon agrees.

Then, don't we expect that after all this Socrates will tell us what the reason is, or at least how to find it out? Why, after all, have we been put through this? What is the purpose of this seemingly endless education? Socrates doesn't say; he only says, or asks, isn't it dialectic that sings the song, that gives the law? Reason, music, law - what are they? Are they different, or the same, and how, and why? Socrates doesn't say. He mentions again the analogy between visible and intelligible, saying that if one tries by argument to grasp what each thing is, and doesn't stand aside until he grasps the good itself by thought itself, then he will come to the very end of thought.

This is long and hard, but not strange. What is strange is this. Socrates says that it is the incapacity to look directly at the animals and plants and the sun's light - by analogy, the various ideas and the good with its emanations of truth - which leads the soul to the contemplation of the best in the things which are. What does this riddle mean? Why is it the incapacity to look directly at the truth that leads the soul to the best? What the soul is able to look at are the representations of the things themselves. This does not mean man-made copies: the best in the soul is beyond these. Does it mean, then, the representation of the ideas in words.? This would square with the dialectic, which uses arguments to go beyond hypotheses to a kind of knowledge of the things themselves. It would also be a bridge between the ideas and the good, above, and the normal life of men in a city under law.

This does not solve the riddle, but perhaps it states it adequately: are words the best in the things which are and, if they are, why? Socrates does not discuss explicitly the place of words and names in the dialectic, and its relation to political life; but he does give Glaucon a quiet little test on the subject. There seems to be no need, Socrates says, to dispute about names when great things like knowledge itself lie before us. Glaucon agrees. A very obscure statement follows, often omitted from the text. It concerns the relationship between the clarity or truth of names, and the clarity or truth of the habits of the soul. Again, Glaucon lets the subject slip away. Perhaps just because of his frustrated desire to hear the whole song of the dialectic, and to see the good, he overlooks the details, and rests content with grand opinion.

On this note, the account of the education beyond gymnastic and music ends. It culminates in dialectic:

yet we never see the dialectic in action, but only hear opinions about it. The eagerness seems gone from Glaucon. Socrates tells him that he is unable to follow dialectic in action and, quite out of character, he accepts this judgment. Why? Does he no longer desire to see the good? Is the road through geometry and harmonics and so forth - to say nothing of dialectics itself - too long and hard? Whatever the reason, Glaucon seems burned out. His restless eagerness has carried the discussion this far, but now it is only Socrates who is eager. Socrates has proved the strongest and most enduring of all. Now, every person and every desire have been tamed. Reason alone is left: Socrates is in command. The philosopher has finally become king, but his little city appears very dispirited. Evidently, he rules alone.

But this judgment needs reflection, and questioning. Socrates and Glaucon are not potential rulers. They, reason and spirit, are lawgivers - here, in speech -, although not equal partners. Their job is to establish the outlines of the city, and somehow to translate the unchanging into the political. They need not rule themselves: politics need not be confined to the one who has travelled to the end of thought and seen and known and returned. On the other hand, how can the best politics be practiced unless on the truest and soundest foundation? The discussion does not, after all, end here. They ask, who shall receive this education?

*   *   *

The introduction of higher education changes the character of the rulers. Before, men of courage and moderation who had endured various trials were chosen. Because they are time-tested, they were old men. As well, their selection was pretty obvious: those who had held to true opinion and endured nobly became rulers. But now, additional requirements exist. The new Guardian must be lovers of learning and, because the old learn poorly, they must be young. Young men - and, presumably, young women - "straight of limb and understanding" will be chosen. They too need endurance, not in belief, but in long, hard studies. But, how can this be known in advance? Mere bright intelligence does not indicate endurance - look at Glaucon, fallen by the philosophical wayside. Evidently, the question has not been answered adequately: what knowledge and what qualities are needed to rule a city well?

*   *   *

The problem is evident. The old are trustworthy but unable to learn: the young are able to learn but of doubtful character. Assuming that knowledge of the things which are is necessary to rule, it is rational to choose the young. They can learn, and may be of good character, while sound old men are unable to learn. At least, Socrates - disagreeing with Solon - says they are unable to learn. It becomes obvious that the choice here - young over old, philosophical understanding rather than mere good character and right opinion - is based on hypotheses. In other words: the course of study intended to lead to knowledge to things which are rests on opinions about the requirements of politics and the nature of human beings. Indicatively, in this context Socrates unleashes his spiritedness against the critics and perverters of philosophy. At least, he says that he seems to himself to have done this.

This, however, does not solve the problem: instead, it hypothesizes it out of existence. Does the total education solve it? The education begins very early, with its intellectual aspects presented as play. The physical and practical parts seem to be compulsory. Music is not mentioned. Socrates' plan is that each candidate be passed through these various labors and studies and fears, and that only those who take most readily to each be continued into the next phase. Comparing this with the old education, intellectual studies are added, music apparently subtracted.

At age 20, after two or three years of compulsory gymnastic, those who have done best so far are honored above the rest. What these honors are, Socrates does not mention. Then, those honored are given another long course. This course integrates all their previous studies, showing how they are related to one another and to the nature of that which is. This course is a test as well, to determine those capable of seeing these connections, and thus presumably dialectical.

Glaucon does not question how seeing connections among apparently disconnected studies is related to dialectical ability. Socrates says that this is the

greatest test of the dialectical nature. What is being
tested for? The ability to see connections? Or the
ability to determine whether there are connections?
The course itself appears to be one in method, which
abstracts from differences and discovers or proposes
similarities, perhaps in substance but more likely in
form. There are questions here. If the forms are the
same, what becomes of the separate subjects? If not,
how do they lead to being or the good or form itself?
If related - similar but not identical in form - what
is their connection and order? Evidently, these do
not exhaust the questions, since the course takes ten
years.

Again at age 30 a separation takes place. Those
who pass the various tests in this course, and prove
steadfast in studies and war and the other duties
established by law are honored. These have two obvious
qualities: they are steadfast and persisting, and they
have dialectical ability. Compared with the courageous
and moderate original Guardians, they have a form at
least of courage - but a form related as much to intellectual as physical danger and hardship -, but instead
of being musical they are questioning and critical and
intellectually very able and agile. Deep questions
about the relationship between intellectual and moral
and physical harmony and rhythm, and their bases, suggest themselves. First among them is this: is it
possible to be moderate without music? Close on its
heels is this: is it possible for the merely musical
man to know the things which are? After these, a whole
pack follows.

*   *   *

Do these qualities go together naturally? Is it
usual to find a highly critical man who is also very
steadfast? Socrates approaches the question this way.
He tells Glaucon that much guarding is needed here.
What does this mean? Socrates observes that those involved with dialectic are filled with lawlessness, and
suggests that this is understandable. Again, Glaucon
is puzzled.

Socrates explains with this analogy. Suppose that
a child is a changling. He is reared in a large and
wealthy family, but amid many flatterers. On reaching
manhood, he discovers that his supposed parents are not

his real ones, and is unable to find his true parents. How does this discovery affect him? Socrates prophesies that he will honor and obey his supposed parents and other kin when he believes them to be real. But, unless he is very good by nature, when he learns the truth he will cease to care for his supposed kin, and begin to go the way of the flatterers.

How, Glaucon wonders, does the analogy apply? Like this, says Socrates. From childhood, we have certain convictions about the just things and the fair things, by which we are raised as parents, obeying them as rulers and honoring them. Glaucon agrees. Opposed to these convictions are certain other practices, possessing pleasures which flatter the soul and draw it to them. Glaucon agrees, but should he? Is the relationship between supposed parents and seducing flatterers equivalent to that between established convictions and attractive opposing practices? Should not conviction be opposed to conviction, and practice to practice? And, who is Socrates alluding to here, one formed by music and gymnastic like the old Guardians, or one brought up on convictions? Is this why the parents are only supposed and not real?

The analogy continues. What happens when such a man is asked, "What is the fair"? He gives the answer which he has learned from the lawgiver, and the argument refutes him many times and in many ways. Will he not reach the opinion that what the law says is no more fair than it is base, and likewise about the just and the good and the other things which he had honored most? After that, will he continue to honor these things and obey them as rulers? Necessarily he will not, Glaucon says. And, now disbelieving that these things are honorable, and not finding the true things, is it likely that he will follow any way of life but that which flatters his desires? No, Glaucon replies. And then, won't he change from being lawful to being lawless? Necessarily. Isn't all this what happens to those who take up argument in this way, and don't they deserve understanding? Yes, Glaucon replies, and pity, too.

This is what happens, it seems, but to whom exactly can it happen? Can it happen to the old Guardian, an honor-lover true, but raised more on practice - music and gymnastic - than convictions? Not likely: are not his "parents" real? Can it happen to the new Guardian, not raised on practices but a truth-lover? Again, not likely. He does not have real "parents", but when his convictions are shaken his love of the truth disinclines him to follow a false, pleasure-loving existence. Then, to whom can it happen? The argument indicates, to an honor-lover not raised on true practices in music and gymnastic - instead, on convictions - who then is exposed to critical argument which does not seek the truth. These set out on the road to lawlessness.

But what is Socrates' opinion? He asks again, mustn't the greatest precautions be taken here, and isn't one of them not to let the young taste of argument? This is not the only mention of powerful things for which a taste is acquired. If the young argue, they do so playfully, to contradict and refute. This practice leads them to disbelief, and brings disrepute to philosophy. To prevent this, the Guardians will be kept away from argument until they are 30.

Does the mere passage of time solve the problem? Can the Guardians at 30 use the dialectic without becoming lawless? They have been tested, and found to be steadfast in war and studies and gymnastic. But, are they musical? Do they have the moderation - the rhythm and harmony - implanted thusly? Evidently not: there appears to be a disagreement between a complete musical education and a life seeking the things which are. Then, are they lovers of truth, and thus saved from lawlessness? They learn well, but they learn what they are taught, and they have long been involved in other pursuits. Are they now merely dogged, able to pass tests set for them by others, but lacking that love of the truth that directs a man toward the good life?

Socrates answers this way. These men will not engage in the youthful imitation of those who contradict and refute. Instead, they will imitate the man who is willing to argue dialectically and to look for the truth. Why is this? Because they are older, and attracted to different kinds of men? Because those men who argue to refute are no longer present? Because they have been well-raised? In any case, the thirty-year-olds are not autonomous truth-seekers. They are imitators of those who seek the truth. Socrates implies that their own truth-seeking depends upon the presence of such men, and the absence or at least silence of their opponents. Thrasymachus says nothing.

105

*   *   *

Socrates gives a brief glimpse of their lives. They are now thirty, under their masters, among those as serious as themselves. For five years - double the time spent in gymnastic - they exercise their minds in argument constantly and strenuously. At the end of this time, the best of them are strong and supple in body and mind, physical and intellectual athletes. All in all, they are bright young men - young persons -, if perhaps overly serious.

Now, they must be seasoned, They are sent back into the cave. There, they hold the military and political offices appropriate to people their age. Again they are tested, to see if they bear up under the pressure and confusion of the disharmonious life of the cave. Fifteen years are given over to this so that, at age 50, they have had lives roughly divided into thirds: one-third in being young and growing in a free and playful way; one-third in systematic physical and intellectual training; and one-third in managing the affairs of practical political life. At this point, they are strong, healthy, intellectually developed, handsome, and experienced.

Are they everything they must be to rule well? Not quite. There is a final step. It is necessary that they lift up the beams of their soul, and look at that which provides light for everything - the good. Then, they will use the good as a pattern to order all things - their own souls and others' private lives and, when they are ruling, the city. For the most part, they will engage in philosophy, but each will take his turn at ruling as a necessary thing. They will pass this way of life on to those younger than themselves. At the end of their lives, they will pass on to the Isles of the Blessed. The city will honor them as demons - divine beings - if the Pythia agrees, or at least as happy and divine men.

Glaucon applauds the finish given these men: it is as if Socrates were a sculptor, and not a usually unemployed stone-cutter. But his glowing last words are not free from difficulties. First, it appears that the order of entering and leaving the cave is both inconsistent with the earlier account, and improbable. Now, there is no gradual ascent, but instead an abrupt transition from the darkness of holding office to the

106

sight of the good. Why this change? Is it so that the Guardians have the promise of the good before them when they are sent into their fifteen-year exile? Perhaps, but fifteen years is a long time. They will have become very used to the cave. Will the promise of the good suffice to get them out again? And, if it does, will they be in any condition to do other than painfully begin again the long trek to the good?

There is another consideration. Socrates speaks as if the cave is permanent. Why? If the Guardians know the good, and use the good as a pattern to order all things, the city included, shouldn't the cave be enlightened, and abolished? Shouldn't politics cease to be a dark and shadowy realm far removed from the good? Evidently not: the cave stays the cave, politics politics. But, if this is so, how can the Guardians, with their wonderful education, with the promise of seeing the good, possibly be induced to labor in the cave when they know that their labors leave things unenlightened and unreformed? Is the just speech - the speech that teaches that they know whatever they know thanks to the city - sufficient? Or, is there some light in the cave, a light not inconsiderable? The basic question reappears: what must they be wise in to rule well? Is much of that knowledge found in the cave? Is that knowledge, that wisdom, of the darkness of human nature, no matter how well-trained, no matter how honored, no matter how hopeful of knowing the good? The light flickers, back and forth, but the darkness remains. The conclusion is hard to escape: what is needed to rule well is knowledge of our own ignorance, and the humility - what form of moderation is this? - the sorrowful, compassionate humility which that knowledge brings.

In this light, there is a tincture of irony about the final statements of Book VII. Is this city possible? Yes, replies Socrates; it is hard, but not impossible. When true philosophers come to power in a city, they will despise the things now honored, and instead take what is just as the greatest and most necessary thing. Serving what is just, they will set in order their own city.

This gives a slight hint about the great omission of Book VII, music. Probably perfect music makes perfect harmony in the individual soul. Perfect harmony is perfect moderation, and the perfectly moderate city is perfectly happy, to say nothing of perfectly just.

But is not the human condition philosophy, and not perfect music? Ths philosophical Guardians are not taught music because the only music worthy of their souls is the music which they, as one and as many, are searching for. The persistent search for the truth, encoded over time into law and thus into practice, is the music of this city. It may not be the true music, but neither is it a noble lie.

If this is the music, what a discordant note is the proposal to clear the city of everyone over ten years old! Is this to be taken seriously? Could disciplined men and women, dedicated to justice and the difficult search for the good, possibly even contemplate, let alone complete, such an immoderate, uncompassionate, short-sighted act? The answer to that is simple enough: Socrates contemplates it, and thus compels his listeners to contemplate it.

Glaucon agrees readily. This is the quickest and easiest way, he says, to establish a city. They leave it at this, quickest and easiest. But, is it the just way? Is it the courageous way? Is it the way a wise and moderate man would choose? Or, it is merely Socratic irony, playing on Glaucon's impulsive desire? The implicit argument of Book VII - that what is needed to govern a city well is knowledge of one's own ignorance and the consequent inclination to obey the established law and to change it only in established ways - seems to dismiss this radical proposal as ironic. But, before it is dismissed, this question remains to be answered: does an education restricted to the physical, the intellectual, and the practical ever result in genuine moderation? And, without that, is it ever certain what those possessed of great power will do? It is not without reason that Socrates and Glaucon finally avoid giving a name to the man of Book VII.

CHAPTER EIGHT

BOOK EIGHT

As Book VII opens, Socrates and Glaucon have reached the heights. The argument is over. The city of the three waves - women Guardians, women and children in common, philosophers who rule - is complete. Immediately - literally in the next breath - the descent begins. Socrates describes a life for the Guardians identical to that practiced before the waves, when they were educated only in music and gymnastic, and when a discrete silence prevailed about their domestic and sexual relations, and about the function of women.

Bold as ever, Glaucon says what is obvious: there are two different cities and two different men here. One is the just city, guarded by the spirited man of true opinion. The other is the city of truth, ruled by the philosopher who knows the things which are. The virtues of the first are courage, moderation, and justice; of the second, courage and philosophical wisdom. It is hard to see how the first possesses wisdom, at least in the philosophical sense: on the other hand, both the moderation and the justice of the second are questionable.

Now, they are to discuss the four inferior regimes - and inferior men -, lesser or greater deviations from the best, aristocracy. But, which of the two "best" regimes is best, the just city or the city of truth? Which is the best man, the spirited, faithful Guardian or the philosopher who also rules? Earlier, before the three waves, there was no dilemma. To be more precise, if there was a dilemma - a choice between the good of the city and the good of the individual -, it was not made explicit. Now, Socrates again acts as if there is no problem. He lets Glaucon's remark pass, and speaks as if there is a single best city and man.

However, his immediate silence does not obliterate what has already been said. There are now terms available to talk about the problem, and perhaps resolve it. This complex relationship can be given: there is some proportion between the value of the city in relation to the individual, on the one hand, and, on the other, the value of the things which are in relation to true opinion. In each, assume the best condition:

the <u>best</u> city, the <u>best</u> individual, <u>true</u> opinion, <u>dis-</u>
<u>covery</u> of the things which are. Does this solve the
problem? It is hard to say that the best man is a man
of opinion, or to believe that the best city can be
based on opinion. Then, <u>if</u> those who know the things
which <u>are</u> can be made to rule, and rule effectively,
the problem is solved. For those who would raise again
the question of justice, the laws are standing by with
their speech.

*   *   *

Thus, Socrates' city, the city of philosophy so
dear to his heart - if not to his earlier opinion -
seems to stand. How long does it stand? In time, an
unknown duration: in words, hardly a moment. What
happens? It is destroyed internally. How? Bad, un-
timely births occur. Why? The Guardians miscalculate.
A closer look is needed, especially since something so
great is being lost.

*   *   *

This is the essential case of the City of Truth in
operation. Part of the rulers' work is to decide when
children should be conceived. In principle, they do
this using calculation aided by sensation. They calculate what Socrates calls the whole geometric number.
He apparently knows this number, or at least how it is
arrived at. To say the least, the number is not obvious. In any case, the rulers either fail to discover
the number - which is unlikely since, once discovered,
it can merely be passed along - or fail to apply it
correctly to the practical problem of conception. The
result is future Guardians who neglect education in
music and gymnastic, and who produce children who, in
turn, are unmusical.

This the the answer that the Muses give to the
question, how does faction first occur? It gives some
insight into the city. Assume that the Guardians are
able to calculate the nuptial number. Where they fail
is in practical application, or sound practical perception. But this failure is decisive only because the
musical - and gymnastic - education is not fixed and
traditional. It is determined by each generation of

rulers. Socrates does not emphasize this, pointing instead to the qualities and calculation of the nuptial number. But the true cause of the decline - as of the rise - of the city is the fact that the rulers - theoretical not practical men - are allowed to vary the basic education in music and gymnastic.

Here, music and philosophy appear far apart. But this is unlikely. Book VII suggests that the music of the City of Truth is the truth gradually discovered and encoded into law. Does this mean that the law fails, or that the Guardians are above the law? After all, what do they guard, if not the law? But there is a difficulty here. The Guardians are also philosophers. The law is discovered only progressively. Philosophy, which discovers the truth which becomes law, is given the power to determine the law for this city. But, of necessity, philosophy may err: its essence is that it remains partially ignorant. Where it rules, its errors are publically significant, and are multiplied many times. As authoritative, it determines the music as well as the law. Now, errors in music are inseparable from errors in philosophy. Unless philosophy is perfect - which is impossible - its city must likewise be imperfect, and always subject to change and decline.

Then, what should the city do? Should it revert to tradition, in order to stabilize and perpetuate itself? If it does, what does it do with the philosophers? If it banishes the philosophers - who hardly a moment ago were practically banishing the city -, how can the city discover what is good, and thus good for itself? The philosophers may cause problems, but even in causing these problems they enable the city to see what is good for it. Perhaps it is true that pure philosophy, determining all things, is not good politically, but even this cannot be seen without philosophy.

Thus, philosophy enlightens the city, by instructing it in the problems inherent in the rule of philosophy. The greatest of these problems is the effect of philosophy on musical education. Stable music is almost impossible if philosophy rules; but, music which represents that which is and instills true order and harmony is impossible without philosophy. The reason for Socrates' silence on the question of aristocracy becomes evident: the form of the best city is not known. What is now apparent is that neither of the two competing forms - the traditionally just city, or the City of Truth - is simply good.

Then, what is good? But this is not the relevant question. What is? Is it, what is good politically? What is the best form for the city? These questions demand philosophy. The question becomes, how can a city take philosophy in hand and yet not be destroyed? Book VII and its aftermath teaches: not as Socrates suggests. Philosophy cannot simply be put in charge of music. Then, should music command philosophy, and tame it? Perhaps: but will a traditional music permit philosophy to explore adequately and search for the good? Can agreement be reached between them, where philosophy discovers but does not innovate, and music rules but heeds the thought of philosophy concerning the necessary changes that must be made to produce true agreement and harmony? But, doesn't this also present a problem, since it appears that the lesser is ruling the greater?

*   *   *

These questions imply disagreement at the highest level, between the gold philosopher - rulers and the silver Guardian - warriors, the one embodying virtue, the other the ancient establishment. Moderation - that unity of belief about who should rule - either does not exist here, or has been lost. But the city is not composed only of its highest types. As they disagree and contend, the lower orders - the bronze householders and the iron money-makers - are drawn in. Once that unity of opinion about ruling is gone, all believe that their contribution to the city gives them a claim to rule. Disagreement spreads, and faction begins to enter in.

In its broad sweep, Book VIII is a study in the politics of degeneration. Its shows how the loss of wise, virtuous rule in time infects and corrupts all parts of the city. The degeneration is two-fold. The art of rule is lost even as natures ill-made to rule rise to power.

*   *   *

The transformation of the best city begins. True music and genuine moderation slip away. The regime which succeeds the best is a result of a struggle between opposing tendencies, the one favoring and imitating the established order, the other inclined toward possessiveness and the love of money. This mean between aristocracy and oligarchy is called timocracy, the rule of the honor-lovers. Again the city - and the soul - is resolved into three elements rather than four. In timocracy, the spirited element - that middle between reason and desire - becomes independent and rules. Now, spiritedness is no longer sufficiently gentled by music. Love of victory and honor dominate, but the practices of the regime are a compounding of the old austerity and virtue, and the growing love of possessions and pleasure.

Socrates gives only a glimpse of this city, outwardly warlike but secretly money-loving. The spirited Guardians who rule it are no longer restrained from desire by the best men. Why is this? They no longer trust them because, Socrates says, the wise are no longer simple and intent, but mixed. Is it misbreeding that makes them mixed?; or, the decline of music education? Evidently not the latter, since the philosopher-rulers have little if any musical education. Then, does their mixed nature result from improper breeding, either of the wrong partners or at the wrong time? So it seems. This implies that the philosophical natures themselves are always susceptible to sexual desire.

How can they guard against this? Twice Socrates says that the best guardian is the combination of music and argument. Once he says to the spirited Glaucon, stressing there the accompaniment of music by philosophy; once to the more philosophical Adeimantus, stressing the mixing of argument with music here. For the spirited, this blending allows education by persuasion rather than force. But for the virtuous, argument mixed with music dwells within the one possessing it as a savior of virtue throughout life, especially against the love of money.

*   *   *

Thus is Adeimantus propelled back into the discussion after a long silence. He ventures the opinion that the man corresponding to the timocratic regime is much like Glaucon, in his love of victory. Socrates agrees with this, but goes on to point out the difference. The timocratic man is more stubborn and not as musical. He loves to hear speeches but cannot give them. He is brutal with those below him and subservient to those above. His claim to rule is based solely on his hardness, and his prowess in war and hunting. He seems to be like the spirited puppy who is raised with the boot and the lash, and grown hard and tough under their harsh discipline.

But this is too simple an explanation for this human being. For one thing, his love of money must be accounted for. For another, according to Socrates he has not been raised harshly. But neither has he been raised under a good regime. He is the son of a good if easy-going father who has avoided an inferior public life and been indifferent to money-making. The father's behavior prompts a chorus of reaction and criticism from his wife, his household, and the rest of the city. The sensitive son is influenced both by the father, whose arguments strengthen the calculating part, and by the others, who nourish the spirited and desiring parts. Pulled in these opposite directions, the son allows the middle portion to rule, and becomes a high-spirited honor-lover.

Adeimantus is satisfied by this account, but it contains two kinds of puzzles. First, why isn't the timocratic son descended from an aristocratic father who shares in ruling in a good regime? This seems evident: this man in this regime will produce an aristocratic "son", or at least offspring. Second, in an inferior regime why doesn't an aristocratic man who, Socrates says, minds his own business, at least rule his private household well and make his son as good as himself? This depends on what the business of an aristocratic man is. If it is ruling, then he must be in the best regime. The best, it appears, cannot rule in less than the best regime. If it is philosophy, then he does mind his own business: his business is the business of the best man, philosophy. All right: but, why does he marry and create a household? The answer must be, because this is the practice of an inferior regime, and the best man does not break the law.

A third puzzle presents itself: how does an aristocratic man come to exist in an inferior regime? Apparently, genetic miscalculations work both ways. Good regimes may err and produce inferior children, and inferior regimes may produce superior children. The superior man is caught, tragically it seems, between his own good nature and the laws and practices of an inferior city. Alone, neither is strong enough to form his character so that he leads a happy and useful life. It is evident that only the fortunate combination of the best natures with the best practices can produce true moderation. Here, the best man merely follows his strongest, philosophical impulses and leads a life compounded of theoretical happiness and practical unhappiness.

*   *   *

This completes the picture of the timocratic city and timocratic man. Is this Spartan regime stable, a permanent balance between the rule of the best and the rule of desire? According to Socrates, it is not: it degenerates into oligarchy, the rule of the rich. The hidden storehouses of gold undo the timocrats. Apparently they can't keep their hands off it, and soon begin displaying their wealth openly. They compete with one another in getting and spending, and begin to honor money-making rather than victory. In time, they pass laws excluding those without sufficient funds from ruling, and so establish the oligarchic regime.

This regime is full of mistakes. Socrates mentions four or five. It allows the wealthy rather than the able to rule: it sets the rich against the poor: it is too insecure and too cheap to defend itself: it permits the practice of more than a single art by the same man: it allows the alienation of property, and thus breeds poverty and uselessness. It seems to be little more than a city of thieves, a few successful, most unsuccessful. Socrates seems to classify everyone in this city as "drones". The stingless drones become beggars. The drones with stings become professional thieves, and must be forcibly restrained by the rulers. But what are the rulers themselves except drones with stings who are permanently successful and clever enough to have the law on their side?

This city of thieves seems to be the very essence of injustice and the polar opposite of a regime of good Guardians. Adeimantus is suitably impressed, and quite willing to agree that oligarchy is a thoroughly bad regime. Why, then, does Socrates make oligarchy the middle regime, superior not only to tyranny, but also to democracy?

Socrates charges oligarchy with mistakes, which implies purpose and calculation gone somewhat awry. The oligarchs have a single end, wealth. Securing that end requires steady purposefulness and calculation, as well as the control of unnecessary desires in themselves. Thus an oligarchy requires forms - perhaps spurious - of wisdom, courage, and moderation. This argument isolates the fundamental indictment against oligarchy - that it is unjust - and necessitates examination of the relationship between political justice and the art of money-making.

*   *   *

Two questions present themselves here. First, is money-making a genuine art? Evidently, the answer is no, since it produces nothing. Second, is money-making necessary to the city? The answer appears to be, in almost all cases, yes. How is this apparent paradox - that money-making doesn't really exist and yet normally is needed by a city - to be resolved?

Money appears to do two things. First, it provides an object to pursue which is tangible and easily understood. Second, it equates the products of those arts which produce necessary material goods. Both these functions, but especially the latter, bind the city together. Money is not moderation in the true sense, but it is a substitute for moderation. It serves as a dispassionate intermediary which ties together the functionally differentiated parts of the city.

Then, is the oligarchic city just? Well, it is not as unjust as Socrates makes it appear to Adeimantus. It is the substitution of money for the law as a regulator, and the replacement of the things of the soul with the things of the body as a basis for the city. Within these limits, oligarchy has a kind of political justice, <u>as long as money rules in fact</u>. The problem, however, is inherent in the word "oligarchy" itself. Oligarchy is a regime of human beings, the few who are wealthy. It is not simply the dispassionate - and very hard - rule of money. Thus, calculation in an oligarchy is doubly imperfect: it is confined to the material and tangible, and it is tinged with selfish desire.

What is the nature of the oligarchic man? According to Socrates, he is the son of a timocrat who held

high office but then suffered complete ruin at the
hands of his political opponents. The son sees that
his father has lost his very being, and is himself im-
plicated in this loss. He is frightened and dishonored.
He casts spiritedness and the love of honor down from
the ruling place in his soul, replaces it with desire
and the love of money, and begins collecting money
diligently. Calculation and spiritedness become slaves
to acquisitiveness, the one figuring ceaselessly how
to make a profit, the other honoring nothing but money
and its possession.

Socrates asks whether this is the oligarchic man.
Adeimantus replies very formally, saying only that this
man was transformed out of a man like the regime –
timocracy – out of which oligarchy came. Then, is the
genesis of the oligarchic man identical to that of the
oligarchic regime? Oligarchy emerges when the love of
secret gold becomes uncontrollable. The oligarchs are
former timocrats who have become obsessed by the need
to display and honor wealth rather than victory. But
the oligarchic man is the son of a timocrat. This man
continues to love honor and victory, but is defeated
and thus dishonored. Why is he defeated? Socrates
says that sycophants cause his ruin.

What are sycophants? They are public informers
who bring accusations against their fellow citizens.
Two questions emerge: first, in a timocracy who would
have standing to accuse one of the rulers?; second,
what would the accusation be? Speculation is necessary,
since Socrates gives few details. Something along
these lines is plausible. This high office-holder has
an enemy. Who is the enemy? Is it not someone of his
own class, who fears his pure spiritedness because he,
the accuser, is impure? Further, is not his impurity
the possession of secret gold? To bring down the
timocrat, the sycophant tells lies which dishonor him.
The timocrat, not a lover of truth and not adept at
speaking, fails to defend himself successfully. He is
publicly dishonored. Perhaps his punishment is death
or exile – not the loss of money, possibly because this
is not an appropriate penalty in a timocracy but probably because, as a genuine honor-lover, he has none.

His son sees all this, and renounces honor as a
way of life. But, in certain ways, he is his father's
son. He is honest, or at least straightforward. Unlike
the sycophant, who outwardly honors spiritedness but
secretly worships gold, the oligarchic man brings his

devotion to gold completely into the open. He becomes an honest oligarch, not a dishonest timocrat. But, why doesn't he respond to his father's demise by going up, to aristocracy, rather than down, to oligarchy? Why doesn't he become a speaker and a truthseeker? Perhaps for this reason: the way of life of the true timocrat is hard. It is a life of gymnastic rather than music. With his father's fall, the purpose of his life - victory - is renounced, but not the hardness of soul which secured that end. This hardness seeks something equally hard, but more certain, as an end. The oligarch becomes a seeker, collector, and preserver of gold.

The life of the oligarchic man is thoroughly hard. He works hard. He is hard on himself and on others. He admits no softness, satisfying only the necessary desires. His justice is hard: he pays his debts and expects others to pay theirs. But, there is a flaw in this hardness. The purpose of money is exchange, but this man is not certain enough of his being to spend his money freely. But neither is he free from softer desires. Therefore, when the money of those who are quite defenseless - orphans, for example - comes into his hands, he spends that to satisfy those dronish, unnecessary desires which he habitually suppresses by force. An open accumulator, he becomes a secret desir-er. Thus injustice and truly powerful, demanding desire appear through the crack in the oligarch's hardness. He is not, even as an oligarch, a whole man, although his hardness usually wins out.

There is a final aspect to the oligarch's char-acter. His dislike of spending his money make him a peculiar public figure. In peace, he is unwilling to sponsor public contests and civic activities. In war, he is mean and strange. He fears to awaken the unneces-sary desires - corresponding in the city to the many poor - and to call them to an alliance and love of vic-tory. As a result, the oligarchic man loses in contests of honor, just as the oligarchic city loses in war.

Here, the lines between war and peace are very blurred. For the oligarchic man, all of life is a struggle and a competition. Paradoxically, it is a competition he refuses to win, because winning means spending his precious resources for victory. Victory also means admitting other elements into the rule of his soul - and his city - beside the love of gold and the necessary desires. As a consequence, he loses, and remains rich. But, if he is defeated, how does he remain rich? Evidently he, and his city, do what they must to keep their gold. Fearing suppressed internal forces more than defeat, they make their peace with the victor, and keep or increase their gold. This implies that the oligarchic "city" is hardly a city at all. It hardly defends itself as a <u>political</u> regime. Instead, it is a small faction of money-lovers who find it possible to live under any rule as long as that rule enables them to prosper financially.

This points up the difference between timocracy and oligarchy. Under certain circumstances, timocracy is a generous, inclusive, and unified regime. In war, the love of victory can extend to all, victory can be fought for by all, and victory can be shared. In oligarchy, in war or peace, at most only the love of gold can extend to all. It is difficult to struggle together for gold, and impossible to share it. Its fruits could be shared, in public works and activities, but the oligarch is too frightened and stingy to permit this. Timocracy is lost when the principle of the regime is betrayed by greed. But, in oligarchy, the principle is greed, and the result almost that there is hardly a regime to be lost.

*   *   *

Democracy follows oligarchy. It comes into being because the greed of oligarchs is insatiable. Neither their desire for wealth nor wealth itself know any limit. This immoderation in the rulers causes immoderation in the ruled. They are not restrained by law from wasting their own property, and become poor, while the pursuit of wealth by the rich is protected by law, especially the law which enforces contracts. The poor come to hate and plot against the rich. Interestingly, a near reversal occurs in their conditions. The immoderate rich begin to become idle, self-indulgent, and fat; the poor, whose own immoderation has caused them to lose their wealth, by necessity become lean and hard. The poor observe the dissolute condition of the rich, realize that they are vulnerable and, when the occasion arises, overthrow them. Socrates doesn't yet pause to explain how these very hard money-lovers have become so soft as to let themselves be overthrown.

119

Democracy is like a coat of many colors, Socrates says. If, perhaps, aristocracy is white - or gold -, timocracy silver - or red -, and oligarchy grim, gray, and yellow, democracy contains all colors. It is the regime of freedom, and every kind of man and of regime is allowed to exist within it. Many judge it to be the fairest regime. Whether or not it argues that all are equal, it treats all equally. It allows those who wish to rule to do so, whatever kind of men they are; and, those who wish not to rule, likewise to do so, however competent they may be. It has a law, but an infirm one. Those who desire war may have war, and peace, peace. Those who break the law are found guilty, but left unpunished and allowed to go their way. It seems, Socrates says, to be a sweet regime, since it is a regime without rulers, much as oligarchy proved to be rulers without a regime.

Beyond this, Socrates says nothing of democracy. Perhaps only this is puzzling: how does such a permissive regime manage to survive at all? There is this: no one hates this regime. It lays down no single goal, and it demands little if any obedience. It is gentle to a fault. In allowing great diversity, it has the quality of being superficially interesting. Since it is tolerant of change, it manages to maintain that superficial interest. Since it denies no one's desire - except the desire for a different kind of public order - and oppresses no one, it has many lukewarm adherents and few enemies. Since a threat to one expression of freedom threatens all other expressions, democracy is capable of common action in opposition to such threats. Thus, and again in exact opposition to oligarchy, democracy is most a coherent regime in time of common danger.

All of this makes democracy appear a not unlikable regime. It seems to possess freedom in peacetime and cohesion in war. Why then does Socrates rank it below oligarchy? Perhaps one reason is that its lack of prudence and discipline may make war a rather more frequent occurrence than peace. But, beyond this, Socrates the philosopher cannot be nearly as tolerant of democracy as democracy is of him. Democracy is the regime of the rule of every and all desire. Each desire, no matter how noble or ignoble, is accorded equal dignity. Thus Socrates' fundamental principle of rule - that the better should rule the worse - and its underlying principle of logic - that each thing is one thing different in nature and function from each other

thing - are denied by democracy. Although Socrates
does not say so openly - after all, democracy tolerates
Socrates, however prudent or imprudent that may be,
and perhaps Socrates has a certain debt as a result -
by Socrates' lights democracy is unjust, not least because democracy refuses to defend a fixed principle of
justice or, alternatively, confuses justice and freedom. In a democracy, each does not do the one thing
appropriate to them, and better does not rule worse.
By democracy's lights, neither is possible. Thus the
quarrel between Socrates and democracy, although muted,
is fundamental.

Oligarchy, a much harder and less likable regime,
is nevertheless more just by Socratic standards. The
oligarch as money-maker possesses an art, or what appears to be an art. A large part of his money-making
is preserving and increasing the wealth which comes
into his hands, whether his own or others. In this,
there is a kind of guardianship, or at least a reflection of guardianship. In addition, the oligarch does
rule, although in his own interests and those of others
like him. His rule and justice recognize, create, and
exercerbate differences and inequalities. What is
false and partial about this rule is that it is unable
to see likeness as well as difference.

*   *   *

Socrates and Adeimantus look now at the democratic
man. He is not uninteresting. He is the son of an
oligarch, and in childhood is raised to satisfy only
the necessary desires. Socrates defines them as those
which, if satisfied, continue life, and those which
have beneficial consequences. The unnecessary are those
which a good upbringing can eliminate and which bring
either no good or harm. As an example, he cites the
desire of eating simple food for the sake of health and
good condition. As long as this desire is confined to
bread and relish, and the desire for relish is somehow
beneficial - Glaucon raises no questions -, then it is
necessary. This definition of the necessary desires
as inevitable, thrifty, and useful is applied to sex
and the others.

This young man, raised in the necessary desires,
now meets those drones ruled by the unnecessary ones.
They entice and seduce him with every sort of subtle

pleasure, just as a democratic party from another city infiltrates and subverts an oligarchic regime. The youth begins to become ruled by the many democratic desires. Now, his father and his relatives take notice and attempt to support the oligarchic part of him. Factions thus exist in the desiring portion of his soul - the reasoning and spirited parts have long since been starved through neglect -, and each tries to destroy the other, or drive it into exile. Thus his soul comes to be a battlefield of conflicting kinds of desire.

Socrates turns political-military historian and recounts this epic struggle. The battle ebbs and flows, with now one, now the other side in control. But the unnecessary desires are far more numerous, and multiply very rapidly. The necessary desires have only shame as an ally - fear, or memory, seems to have fled -, since the youth is uneducated and the citadel of his soul is unguarded by fair studies and practices, and by true speeches. Thus, the sides prove unequal, and false and boasting speeches seize command of his soul. Once there, they refuse to admit any outside aid, and instead throw out the old, oligarchic Guardians - shame, moderation, and frugality. They then recall from exile the opposite of these qualities, and dress them up in false names - shamelessness become "courage", for example - to make them appear respectable.

Two questions are suggested by this account. First, in what sense is the oligarchic soul moderate? Certainly it is not moderate in its desire to accumulate gold. Neither is it moderate in the best sense, agreeing with true speech that desire should be ruled by wisdom. Evidently, then, this moderation is temperance and discretion regarding bodily pleasures. Second, what rules once the oligarchic Guardians are driven out? Do the various unnecessary desires rule? Are they capable of rule, or merely of seizing temporary control until a stronger desire shoves them aside? Or, does false speech rule in fact, pumping up some desire by flattering it with an honorable name so that it becomes proud to make its brief appearance in the limelight?

It is entirely possible, then, that the lie in the soul makes its first fundamental appearance in the democratic man. He allows himself to be deceived by false speech, not giving things their true names but instead permitting indulgence in many and varied de- sires. These desires become respectable once relieved of the degrading names which characterize them truly. Having become respectable, they can be indulged without shame, and so they are indulged. With this, confusion very likely reigns in the democratic soul, since habitual self-deception reaches a point where right and wrong, necessary and unnecessary desire become indistinguishable.

According to Socrates, however, the democratic man is not completely seized by the lie in the soul. He lacks true speech as a guardian, but he is not ruled completely by false speech. In time, as his passions slacken, and with good luck, some of the necessary desires are readmitted. Henceforth he is ruled in turn by whichever desire - right or wrong, necessary or unnecessary - makes its claim on him. He is now incapable of classifying or ranking the desires. If someone suggests this, the democratic man shakes his head, and says that all desires are equal and must be honored as such. But, at least in his "maturity", he does not permit false speech to elevate evil above good.

The democratic man is disarming, especially as he grows older. The great struggle of his early life has slackened his soul, and made him appear easy-going and open-minded. In truth, good and evil, right and wrong, were never questions for him. To say that he has lost his desire to know these things is to say too much of him. Socrates says that, when the mood is on him, he passes some time idling with philosophy. What he has done is destroyed his power to distinguish between the necessary and the unnecessary. This ability held the oligarchic man within limits. Acceptance of abuse of speech has destroyed these limits for the democratic man. His mild, even moderate appearance is deceptive: he is not very far from the very opposite of good.

But, is the mild, even harmless democratic man really so dangerous, or so close to evil itself? Socrates seems to think so, but why? There are certain puzzles about democracy. Democracy is the regime that contains all regimes. The timocrat, the oligarch, the aristocrat - all these forms are present, but none of them rules; but, the democratic man is ruled by the desire for freedom, or by the succession of varied, passing desires. Practically, then, there is almost no rule in a democracy, except under conditions of extreme necessity when the freedom of the city if threatened. Then, the city acts to save itself and its way of life.

123

This implies that the only desire which the democratic city acknowledges as necessary and ruling is self-preservation.

What of the democratic man? In extremis, is he too ruled by the desire for self-preservation? Is there any element in the democratic city sufficiently author-itative to implant any higher desire in him? If he is ruled by self-preservation, this implies that there may be even less coincidence between the interests of the democratic city and democratic man than there was be-tween the oligarchic man and his city; in other words, that the democratic man may be the least loyal and patriotic yet. What does Socrates say? He and Adei-mantus, continuing their study of decline, now examine how tyranny grows out of democracy.

*   *   *

Socrates launches into a long and vivid description of the practices and attitudes of democracy. Like oligarchy, democracy is destroyed by its lack of moder-ation. It pushes its principle - freedom - too far. The sequence which Socrates describes runs this way: the ruled resent and disobey the rulers; the sons, their fathers; the students, their teachers; the young, the old; the slaves, their masters; the women, the men; the beasts, their owners; finally, everyone, the laws. Solemnly, Adeimantus remembers that he himself has been bumped off the road by donkeys on his way to the coun-try.

All this freedom provokes two kinds of reactions. First and lesser, those in authority try to make them-selves as much as possible like the ones over whom they are supposed to rule. The teachers appear as students, the old try to make themselves young. Opposite to this and greater, the principle of democracy when over-ex-tended provokes a violent reaction to it. Socrates announces this as a probable general law for physical and political nature - one excess provokes the opposite excess. In this case, too much freedom produces too much slavery. But the principle is worth reflecting on further, especially in the case of virtue.

Socrates calls these excesses a disease. But they are the disease in general: there is a specific disease that grows naturally in oligarchy and, even more, in

democracy. It is a political cancer, a class of idle,
extravagant men. They are the drones. The more active
and courageous of them lead, the rest follow. Socrates
remarks that it is this class which the lawgiver must
guard against and, if it does occur, must cut out
quickly and completely. Adeimantus agrees vehemently,
and Socrates suggests that, as political physicians,
they should examine the problem more closely.

                         *   *   *

     Socrates divides the democratic city into three
parts, which he claims correspond to its actual divisions. One part is the class of drones. This class is
small and dishonored in an oligarchy. But democracy
honors all alike, and here this class - held in equal
honor, quite large, idle, and ambitious - becomes involved in politics. The drones with stings speak and
lead, the less potent types gather round in support.
The result is that, for the most part, this class
directs things in a democracy.

     The other two parts of the city are those who are
wealthy, and the relatively poor majority who mind
their own business. Curiously, Socrates remarks here
that when evervone engages in money-making, the most
orderly by nature become richest. Yet this city is
not an oligarchy, but a democracy; why then do all engage in money-making, if the principle of democracy is
freedom?

     In this city, there is little or no true education.
In this situation, the good appears to be freedom or,
possibly, the satisfaction of various kinds of desire.
Money is needed for this. But not everyone engages
equally in the art of money-making. Those who are most
orderly restrain their desires to the necessary and
become more or less pure money-makers. That majority
which is neither very orderly nor very disorderly by
nature becomes partly money-makers, partly seekers of
less than necessary desires. These are the relatively
stable private producers and parents. But those who
are disorderly by nature aren't money-makers at all.
Neither do they have any art, except perhaps some imitation of the art of ruling, especially by false
speech. These are the drones who engage in politics,
and their followers. This is the natural order - the
order determined by nature uneducated - in the city.

                              125

If this is the natural order, why isn't the city an oligarchy? One reason is that money-makers are not in the majority. But, more basically, the money-makers here are not obsessed with making money. They simply are naturally superior men, and, lacking education, their natural superiority manifests itself this way. Still, if they are naturally superior, why don't they rule? Socrates only hints at the reason: their orderliness. Politics, at least in this ordinary city, is not an orderly business. In fact, it seems to be the opposite of orderly, since it attracts the naturally disorderly.

*   *   *

The distaste of the naturally superior men for the disorder of politics has dire consequences. By default, control of the city is relinquished to the drones. They use their control to strip the orderly of their wealth, keeping most of it for themselves, giving a small share to the inactive majority. This action by the drones necessarily draws the orderly into the political arena, to try to defend themselves. But the drones are clever creatures. By reacting as they do, the orderly play into their hands. They are drawn into politics at the wrong time, against their will, and are placed in the most unfavorable light. The drones charge them with being oligarchs, and plotting against the people. Stung by this charge, they behave in ways that give it some truth. This enables the drones to set themselves up as defenders of the people against the dangerous, usurping, anti-democratic oligarchs. A leader comes forward from among them. The roots of tyranny appear.

Thus it is apparent that individual orderliness and hard work and decency cannot save the city. The drones are clever enough to put these qualities in the worst light, and seemingly transform them. These qualities must be brought into public affairs, and rule. But the orderly lack education. They do not even know that the preservation of their own interests - to say nothing of the good of the city - requires that they rule, or at least participate actively. Incapable of understanding the nature of politics and political life, they merely react against it. Their ignorance dooms them, and with them, the city of which they are a part.

*   *   *

Socrates begins with a story about the genesis of
the tyrant. The transformation from leader to tyrant
begins when this man acts out the legend told of the
shrine of Lycaean Zeus in Arcadia. As Socrates tells
it, the legend is that the man who tastes a single bit
of human entrails cut up with those of other victims
must necessarily be transformed into a wolf. Adeimantus knows this legend. Then Socrates asks, isn't this
how a man becomes a tyrant? Having gained control of a
docile mob, doesn't he unjustly bring charges against
a kinsman, try him, murder him, and taste of his blood
with unholy tongue and mouth? And go on to banish and
to kill and to hint at the cancellation of debts and
redistribution of land? Isn't this man fated to be
killed by his enemies, or else to become a tyrant and
be transformed from a human being to a wolf? Quite
necessarily, Adeimantus replies.

Why does Socrates tells his story? Is it to shock
the placid Adeimantus? Why is the tyrant linked with
the Homeric religion? Is there something holy about
the most unholy of acts? Is it that the act is inhuman,
that of a god or a beast, perhaps, but not of a human
being? If oligarchy is a regime containing two cities,
and democracy a city with many regimes, tyranny evidently is beyond the compass of human things.

Once begun, the tyrant's career goes its inevitable
way. He is exiled, and returns stronger than ever.
Fearing his enemies, he requests bodyguards from the
people, and is granted them. He threatens the wealthy:
only the fortunate among then escape with their lives.
He makes extravagant promises to the people, but most
of them go unfulfilled. Instead, he distracts them
with war, and keeps them at their daily business by demanding contributions. He takes pains to eliminate all
good and decent men, including those among his associates who dare to criticize him. As a result, he grows
even more hateful, and fearful for his own life. Trusting no one in the city, he is compelled to import foreign mercenaries, and to free the slaves. The city,
once so free, is now poor, embattled, and fearful.

Why does all this happen? Evidently, Socrates is
aware that his previous explanation - the horror story
about the wolf-man - left something to be desired. He
offers another, which recalls the very beginning of

127

their search for justice. Now, it is the tragic poets,
and particularly Euripides, who are held responsible
for tyranny. They praise the tyrant's life, and themselves as the wise companions of the tyrant. Their
plays travel around to the various cities, drawing
large audiences, and thus inclining the citizens toward
tyranny and democracy. Socrates suggests that the tragic poets, in their wisdom, will pardon he and Adeimantus if they exclude them from their good regime.

Thus Socrates links democracy and tyranny. The
implicit connection is that proposed by Glaucon at the
outset of Book Two. The many have no love of justice,
but instead long for the life of the tyrant. Every
man a tyrant, or so the fantasy of the democrat seems
to run. But this is an easy tyranny. This life has
the pleasure of injustice without paying the price in
effort, danger, and fear. Socrates now shows that its
practical effect is the weakening of resistance to
tyranny, and the subsequent massive visiting of injustice upon the democrats.

*   *   *

In the beginning, Adeimantus says, the tyrant lives
off the sacred money of the city, together with that
expropiated from the wealthy. And what happens, Socrates asks, when this gives out? Then, Adeimantus says,
the tyrant draws his support from his father's property. This cryptic answer is clear to Socrates: the
tyrant will live off those who begat him - the people.
Nothing is more necessary, Adeimantus replies. And
what, Socrates asks, if the people resent that the
tyrant allows their own slaves - now his companions -
to enslave them, rather than providing the freedom
which he once held out to them?; and, like a father
driving a greedy and worthless son from the house, order the tyrant and his companions to leave the city?

Then, by God, Adeimantus replies, the people will
know what a beast they have given birth to and nurtur-
ed, and they will learn that they who would drive out
the tyrant are the weaker attempting to drive out the
the stronger. With this, the cycle of justice begun in
Book One is completed. Justice in a tyranny is nothing
other than Thrasymachus held it to be so long ago:
justice is the advantage and will of the stronger. Now,
the tyrant who has deceived, weakened, and disarmed

the people is stronger. The people, who foolishly gave up decent rule for the promise of freedom and a certain injustice implicit in it, are now weakened in soul and in strength. The tyrant began with the taste of the blood of one kinsman unjustly slain. Grown great on this foul diet, he now turns parricide and enjoys the rivers of blood drawn from those who indulged his first appetite.

With justice reduced to power, being the weaker, they submit. They become the slave of slaves. With this, both the account of the tyrannic city and Book VIII end. There is no more unhappy political situation. But, is it unjust? Socrates speaks of democracy as the enslavement of free men, this probably from the perspective of the democrat. It appears that any rule is obnoxious, and even illogical, to democracy: but the alternative to rule turns out to be enslavement. If rule is unjust, as the democrat sees justice, then is this enslavement just? In democratic practice, is justice necessarily the domination of the weak by the strong? Do the freedom-loving democrats then accept their weakness, and their enslavement? Or, does bitter experience again teach them that it is much worse to suffer injustice than to do it, and rouse them to agree among themselves on rules of justice? Will the tyrant, if he is stronger, permit this? Evidently, something must be said about the tyrant in a personal sense, and the nature of his strength.

THE POLITICS OF MODERATION

CHAPTER NINE

BOOK NINE

Socrates and Adeimantus come at last to the tyrannic man: where he comes from, who he is, what kind of life he has. At once, it is apparent that it is his soul which will be viewed; there will be nothing polished or external about this man. Socrates says that they must look further into the unnecessary desires. While these probably exist in all human beings, in some the laws and the better desires, aided by argument, eliminate or weaken them. It is in the tyrannic man that the unnecessary desires remain numerous and strong.

What, Adeimantus asks, are these desires? In response, Socrates discusses the dreamworld. There are wild and beastly desires that wake up when the decent and prudent parts of the soul have gone to sleep. These desires are for the illicit pleasures of touch. At night, they reign in the immoderate soul. The moderate man behaves differently. He satisfies his desires properly, and soothes the spirited part so that it's not angry. Then, he sets in motion the prudent and calculating part. His soul thus composed, he is least disturbed by the images of lawless desires, and comes closest to grasping the truth.

This is a curious account. Here, Socrates is the pure student of the soul, studying it in that circumstance when it is most completely unconcerned with the body. This is an unusual but very philosophical use of the time when most people are simply resting from their daily labors. Although he speaks of the practice of the moderate and prudent man, what his nocturnal investigations yield are two extremes: one, wild and beastly images of murder and copulation; the other, the apprehension of the truth by the calculating part. Evidently, these are the dream experiences of the tyrannic and philosophic man, respectively.

But Socrates denies at least a portion of this. The wild and lawless desires, he says, are in all of us, and Adeimantus agrees. If this is so - and we have our own dreams to tell us whether it is - then moderation and prudence appear in a somewhat different light. Aware of the lawless parts of himself, the prudent man

prepares himself for sleep - of whatever duration -
less in order to grasp hold of the truth than to leave
his sleep undisturbed by the monsters lurking in the
darker recesses of even the normally decent soul.

*   *   *

As Socrates remarks, these thoughts are somewhat
off their subject, the tyrannic man. They recall the
democratic man: his frugal upbringing, his temptation,
his intercourse with the fiery drones and their pleasures, his partial recovery, and his eventual settle-
ment into a life of easy-going distraction by the
necessary and unnecessary pleasures. It is a life
which is neither praised nor condemned. This man now
has a son, reared in his father's disposition. He un-
dergoes the same temptations, but with a quite different result.

Like his father, the son is introduced to the unnecessary and lawless desires. His father cannot draw
him back to the necessary desires - to a life leading
toward true moderation -, since his own life is a middle one between the necessary and the unnecessary.
Despite this, the father's struggle to save his son
appears to be succeeding. He seems to be on his way
to becoming a democratic man.

Seeing this, the tempters move to gain control of
the youth. What they do is this: they somehow implant
erotic love - Socrates calls it a great winged drone -
in his soul. This love becomes the leader of all the
unnecessary desires. These desires buzz around and
feed eros, making it grow great and planting the sting
of longing in it. Eros - the tyrant in the soul - takes
madness for its armed guard. Together they drive out
or slay any good opinion or necessary desire. In this
way, all moderation is destroyed, and a foreign madness
fills the soul.

What does this eros long for? Socrates is not
explicit, but it is evident what it does not long for:
not the good, as the aristocratic man does; not honor,
the desire of the timocrat; not wealth, the oligarchic
end; not freedom and the various easy-going pleasures,
the democratic life. What then is left to desire?
Perhaps the further account of the tyrannic man's life
will reveal what he longs for.

*   *   *

Before discussing the tyrant's life, Socrates discusses his character further. It is not only eros that
makes the soul tyrannical, but two other conditions.
First, the drunkard also has a somewhat tyrannical
mind. Second, the melancholic man, who Socrates identifies as mad, expects to rule not only over human
beings but gods as well. Must all three of these elements - eros, drunkeness, and melancholia - be present
to produce the tyrant? Socrates seems to suggest this.
This is the precise definition of the tyrannic man.
Thrasymachus remains silent.

But the elements differ greatly among themselves.
Eros is implanted by others; drunkeness, whatever its
deeper cause, results from addiction to liquor; melancholia results from an excess of black bile, a physio-
logical condition. Respectively, the elements are put
in, taken in, and indwelling. Thus there is a third
kind of explanation for tyranny. First, tyranny was
caused by tasting a single morsel of human entrails;
next, by the glorification of that life by the tragic
poets. Now, this explanation roots tyranny as deeply as
the very physiology of the man, and in his habits and
bad outside influences. As well, there is as always
Socrates' general doctrine that certain kinds of
fathers produce certain kinds of sons.

What should be concluded from this? That there
are many causes of tyranny? That tyranny is always a
danger in cities and men, and must always be guarded
against? That the practical problem is less to attain
the good than avoid the bad? That this danger places
a practical limit on the attainments possible as long
as men, families, cities, and souls are constituted as
they are? The tendency of the argument is clear: each
one of us is a potential tyrant. Tyranny is unusual in
its occurrence, but not in its possibility. Perhaps
above all, prudence and moderation must stand guard
against tyranny. The argument implies that they do
and will.

*   *   *

It remains to be seen, however, how right this
argument is. Socrates and Adeimantus discuss the tyran-

nic man's way of life. It is a life dominated by eros.
Socrates presents eros as a desire which is unnecessary, but which breeds and leads other desires. Together, all of these unnecessary desires consume every re-
source the tyrannic man can get his hands on. For the
tyrant as a private man, this culminates when he attacks and enslaves his parents who refuse to support
his way of life.

His career continues. He is mastered by eros, and
stops at nothing to satisfy its demands. From request-
ing, he takes: from taking, he steals: from stealing,
he robs: from robbing, he murders. His once rare dreams
of forbidden pleasures become his everyday reality.
No murder, no food, no act is too terrible for him.
Eros dominates, but a whole host of other desires -
some foreign invaders, some released from within - make
their separate demands upon this man. He is driven to
satisfy each and all. Somehow, the unnecessary has
become compellingly necessary.

What does this man want? What does eros seek? Is
there a clue in the way the unnecessary becomes necessary? It is calculation and prudence that distinguish
the necessary - for life, for a good life - from the
unnecessary. This man has lost the ability to make
this distinction. Now, all desires are necessary. In
other words: he has lost his practical wisdom. It,
the true ruler in the soul, is replaced by eros. If
practical wisdom seeks appropriate goodness by distinguishing the necessary from the unnecessary, then does
eros seek the inappropriate - the inhuman, the evil -
by commanding that all desires, but especially the unnecessary desires, must be satisfied? But these desires
cannot be satisfied: it is the essence of their nature
that feeding them only makes them more hungry.

Then, what does eros seek? Endless growth? The
destruction of all limits? A world in which no thing
is any longer one thing distinct from each separated
thing? But, according to Socrates, this is injustice:
injustice is the opposite of justice, and justice is
each thing being itself and not some other thing.
Then, does eros seek the the injustice which destroys
the individuated character of things, and substitutes
for it a chaos in which each thing is or tries to become all other things? So the argument suggests.

Does the tyrannic man knowingly seek injustice?
Very probably not, the argument indicates. Somehow,

he has destroyed his ability to reason practically. He no longer thinks as a human being thinks. There is a curious integrity about his soul. It is not a whole of parts bound together by moderation, but instead a seeking, pulsing, driving force filled with overpowering eros. Practical wisdom and moderation have been cast out by this throbbing eros. It does not know: it is incapable of true thought: but it seeks the mindlessness of non-differentiation with a terrifyingly sure instinct. This soul is no longer that of a human being, but rather that of an evil, beastly genius, at least at its worst.

How much damage can this man do? According to Socrates, that depends on the circumstances. In a city in which the rest of the people are moderate, this type and the few like him will serve a foreign tyrant or a city at war; if there is general peace, they will stay and become petty thieves or sycophants. In these circumstances, the few tyrannic souls will have few public consequences: they will probably destroy only themselves. But if such souls are numerous, and the rest of the multitude is not moderate, then a tyranny is likely. The tyrannic man most ruled by eros becomes the tyrannic ruler. If the city submits, tyranny - perhaps relatively mild - is established. If it resists, the tyrant imports new comrades, and enslaves the city.

Thus, politically, the tyrant destroys the distinction between "this, our city" and foreign cities. He makes foreigners or slaves citizens, and citizens slaves. More personally as well, he destroys the distinction between friends and enemies. At first, everyone is his friend, and later his flatters and imported mercenaries are; but soon they too are place in the category "slave" or "enemy". The tyrant becomes a man without friends. But is he his own friend? How can he be? Is his soul any longer a whole of parts? Can desire any longer be properly ruled, or spiritedness allied with prudence? Evidently, the hatefulness of the tyrant extends to self-hatefulness. The master of others, he is himself enslaved to eros and injustice.

*   *   *

Socrates does not now take up the deep and interesting question of the nature of enslavement to injustice. Instead, he steps back and speaks again of the

tyrannic man in his private capacity. The tyrant is
the worst man: he comes from the tyrannic man. This
distinction is both unexpected and curious. What is
the difference between the tyrannic man and the tyrant?
Why is it necessary, if at all?

These questions recall the very beginnings of the
sustained argument, in Book II. Appropriately, Glaucon
reenters the discussion: he anticipates the comparison
of the perfectly just and perfectly unjust man. The
fundamental method in the search for justice has been
the comparison of city and soul. Each regime has a
kind of man whose soul corresponds to it. It follows,
then, that there must be a tyrannic soul as well as a
tyrannic city, and that one can consider the tyrannic
man as private as well as public.

There are problems here, however, evident when
the best city and soul are recalled. Each is a whole
of parts, with the philosophical ruler and practical
wisdom, respectively, as ruler. There, it is possible
to understand ruling and being ruled. In the lesser
regimes, rule continues to exist but becomes increas-
ingly uncertain. But the tyrannic soul is ruled by
eros, which is no ruler or a mad ruler. What does eros
"rule"? Everything else? Does it? Doesn't it enslave
everything else? More, doesn't it move beyond enslavement toward destruction, in the city, in distinctions,
in the man? And, what does a city ruled by eros look
like? If eros desires a perverted and destructive
intercourse with bodies, does the tyrannic - erotic -
city desire that kind of intercourse with other cities?

This loss of form threatens to destroy the comparison. Cities and men cannot be compared when they cease
to exist. But at the other extreme from this tyrannic
formlessness is perfect justice. Perfect justice is
also a problem. Strictly, perfect justice also destroys
cities and men, since the parts are so perfectly distinct that they are unrelated to one another and incapable of forming and acting as wholes. The central
position of moderation is again evident: moderation is
that mean between perfect justice and perfect injustice
that makes integrity and activity possible. But is it
at all likely that moderation is a simple mean? Is it
thinkable that moderation could be as close to injustice as to justice?

*   *   *

136

Glaucon's reentry deepens the problem. At the outset, he desired to compare the perfectly just and perfectly unjust man, but to compare their souls only, disregarding all outward appearances. To this end, he made the just man perfectly miserable in body and reputation, and the unjust man perfectly splendid. Now, Socrates has reached the point where perfect justice and perfect injustice are at last becoming apparent. The basis for the comparison of souls is established. But, can he make the just man perfectly miserable in externals? And, can he afford to mitigate the clarity of perfect justice by tempering it with moderation? In a word: How will Socrates order his appeal to Glaucon?

*　　*　　*

Socrates takes this approach. First, he asks Glaucon whether the worst man is also the most miserable? He loads the question a bit by suggesting that the many may well answer, "no". Glaucon takes the bait: yes, the worst is also most miserable. Then, Socrates further prejudices the argument. Doesn't, he asks, the tyrannic man correspond to the tyrannic city? And, regarding virtue and happiness, won't the relation between man and man be that between city and city? Glaucon agrees without question. Socrates continues: regarding virtue, what is the relation between the tyrannic city and the kingly city? Glaucon replies they are opposites, the one the best, the other the worst. It's obvious which is which, Socrates replies.

In effect, the argument is over: Socrates has agreement on premises that lead logically to the conclusion that the tyrannic man is most miserable. Yet he doesn't simply proceed to make the argument. Instead, he suggests another procedure. This procedure doesn't depend on logic, but on insight and experience. Who should judge about virtue and happiness? Isn't it one who can see through the facade of tyrannic pomp? Shouldn't it be one who also has lived with the tyrant, and seen him at home and in public danger? Glaucon agrees. Then, Socrates asks, shall we pretend that we are such men, knowledgeable and able to judge? Certainly, Glaucon replies.

Why introduce the further procedure, rather than rely simply on logic? It assumes that happiness and its opposite can be seen and judged, if a man is clear-

137

sighted in such things. Is this perhaps the equivalent - but of the opposite kind - of the Ring of Gyges? That ring made the body invisible: this ring somehow makes the soul visible. What is this ring? Socrates says only that thought enables one to see into the character of a man. What kind of thought? Well, the thought of a man of judgment and experience; of a man who observes constantly and sees through the trappings of the human drama. Evidently, this quality enables this man to see the things which are, at least for human beings.

*   *   *

Thus equipped, Socrates and Glaucon examine the worst city and worst soul. The discussion flows smoothly, arguing that the tyrannic city and soul are enslaved and miserable. Each is ruled by the most depraved part. Perhaps this is a salutory conclusion, but is it logical? After all, the tyrannic city is ruled by the tyrant. How can the soul of the ruler of an enslaved city itself be enslaved? Whatever the condition of the tyrannic soul, must not the soul of the tyrant be the only and most free thing in this unhappy city? Isn't it still possible, even probable, that the tyrant is the happiest man and lives the best life?

Socrates denies this emphatically, saying that it is not the private tyrannic man but the tyrant who is most wretched. Neither is he content with Glaucon's casual agreement: such a conclusion must be firmly established. At stake is understanding of the greatest thing, the right way of life. Obviously, further argument is needed to prove that the tyrant is the most unhappy man.

*   *   *

They begin again, using the first of three arguments. Consider the condition of individual private men who are rich and rule over many bondsmen. They are, Socrates says, similar to the tyrant, in ruling many. Here, he does not say, "slaves" but uses a word implying that those ruled over have been free men. Don't you know, he asks Glaucon, that these householders are not frightened of their domestics. Glaucon knows, and also knows why: the city as a whole defends these private men.

Socrates goes on. What if, however, some god lifted the householder, together with his property, family, and domestics, out of the city and put them down in a deserted place? Thus, Socrates smoothly identifies tyrannic rule with the household rather than the city. Would the household tyrant then fear destruction by the domestics? In the extreme, replies Glaucon. Would he be compelled to flatter and free some of his servants, even if under no legal obligation to do so? Certainly, or be destroyed. And what if he found himself surrounded by other neighbors, who refuse to accept the mastery of one man by another and who punish anyone who tries to impose it? Then, Glaucon replies, he will be even more threatened, surrounded as he is by enemies.

Isn't this the situation of the tyrant?, asks Socrates, and proceeds to assert that it is. The tyrant is the most unfree man, reduced to hiding in his house like a woman while others travel freely abroad and otherwise enjoy themselves. He reaps a much greater harvest of ills than does the private tyrannic man, when he is compelled by some chance to attempt to rule others, he who in fact is unable to rule himself. Glaucon agrees that the cases of the deserted householder and the tyrant are perfectly similar, and that what Socrates says is most true.

The matter demands a bit more thought than Glaucon appears to give. These questions beg to be considered. What is the nature of the householder's rule? Has he given his bondsmen cause to hate him? And, how did these bondsmen get to be bondsmen? Are they free by nature? In either case, might not they respond non-rebelliously to appropriate rule? And, what of this city? If it is good, does it permit or protect a cruel householder? If it is bad, can it protect a householder, however he treats his servants?

The questions continue, and reach the tyrant. How valid is the comparison between householder and tyrant? Assuming that each possesses an art, is it the same art? But, what became of the art of the tyrant? How did it happen that he is now terrorized by those whom he previously terrorized? Is there an art of tyranny whereby the tyrant rules so cleverly that all his in-

terests are perfectly served? What are his interests?
If he rules so cleverly, must not he serve his own interests by serving some of those over whom he rules?
The question emerges: how, practically, does the art
of the successful tyrant differ from the art of the
good king?

Socrates ignores these obvious questions. His
comparison is based on these assumptions: those over
whom the tyrant rules loathe him. These assumptions may
be true. But, if they are, the question remains: how
can the analogy between tyrannic city and tyrannic soul
be maintained, unless the tyrant in fact rules freely
and as he pleases over the enslaved city? The persistent difficulty remains: the soul of the private tyrannic man does not appear to be identical with the soul
of the tyrant. More: they appear to be reversed. The
tyrannic soul is full of fear: the tyrant causes the
fear, and lords it over the fearful, or so it appears.

Is this Socrates' basic contention, that the
tyrant only appears different, but in truth has a soul
full of fear? If it is, then the art of tyranny is the
art of creating appearances. And, the art of seeing the
things which are, regarding human beings, is that which
sees through appearances and looks clear-eyed into
souls. Perhaps: but what is the soul of the tyrant -
the tyrannic soul - filled with when seen truly? Is it
filled with fear - or, is it filled with eros? And, is
there some mysterious connection between fear and eros?

It comes to this. Tyrant and philosopher are left
facing each other, one possessing the art of creating
appearances, the other the art of seeing the things
which are, souls in their true condition. These men
are beyond practical politics, circumscribed as it is
by the timocratic, oligarchic, and democratic cities.
They create worlds, not cities. The tyrant and the
philosopher are the most just and the most unjust men.
They seem locked together in some eternal, unending
dance, each living to oppose the other, each practicing
his art to the fullest to defeat the art of the other
practiced to its fullest. One seeks the true order,
the other, to perfectly conceal or destroy the true
order, perhaps above all by mimicking that order. In a
curious sense, the work of each is destruction, the
tyrant attempting to destroy human order, the philosopher to destroy the works of the destroyer.

Who is philosopher and who destroyer? It may be that Socrates has more to say on this subject. But this can be said now. That is very, very hard to say. The art of the tyrant is no mean one: his appearances are not without charm and evident reality. Who can recognize which is which? Who can create or discover forms which persuade others of the truth or untruth of their works or the works of the other? Between absolute truth and absolute untruth, Socrates has argued, lies opinion. Opinion is a dim flickering light. Can we do more than hope and pray that it is just strong enough and steady enough to tell the one from the other, or perhaps the direction in which each lies?

Socrates seems to have provided that light for Glaucon. Untroubled by logic, the brave Glaucon is persuaded of the fearfulness of the tyrant. His soul is held to be the seat of all vice. Socrates acts as if Glaucon is one of those clear-eyed soul-seers competent to judge the things which are. He says: rank the cities and souls - kingly, timocratic, oligarchic, democratic, and tyrannic - with respect to happiness! Just that order, says Glaucon, in virtue and vice, happiness and unhappiness. Shall we then triumphantly announce that Ariston's son has proclaimed that the best and most just man is the happiest, and that this man is he who is king of himself?; and, the worst and most unjust the unhappiest, and that he is the tyrant of himself and of the city? Announce it! And shall we add this to the proclamation: that this is so whether or not it escapes the notice of all human beings and gods? Glaucon doesn't hesitate: Add it! Then, says Socrates, we have one proof. Evidently, the flickering light has proved just bright enough.

*   *   *

They proceed to the second proof. The soul is again divided into three forms, and a pleasure associated with each form. Predictably, Glaucon is curious about these pleasures, and Socrates explains. He begins with the desiring part. It desires food, drink, sex, and so forth: but Socrates identifies this form as the money-loving part, since these desires are satisfied by means of money. Glaucon accepts this, but his acceptance is questionable. Isn't the eros of this part much more for the pleasures of touch than for money? Isn't the tyrant defined by the enormity of his

141

eros? Wisely, Socrates diminishes the attractiveness of these pleasures for Glaucon, a man unlikely to be much intrigued by money.

The other two parts are assigned victory-loving and wisdom-loving as their pleasures. Here Socrates makes another small move, associating victory and honor-loving with opinion. Which of these three lives is best? Obviously, this depends upon which of the pleasures is greatest, and each of the partisans claims the honor for that associated with his own pursuit. The speech of the wisdom-lover is noteworthy - Socrates puts his heart into this. He finds the pleasure in knowing the truth constant, and associated somehow with necessity.

How then to judge between pleasures and lives? Socrates suggests that they use as criteria experience, prudence, and argument, and Glaucon agrees. It appears that for the moment they have exhausted the art, or method, of looking directly into souls and observing their order or disorder. Certainly their method here is far more commonplace.

It does not prove to be much of a contest. In experience, the lover of wisdom wins. Only he has tasted of all three of the kinds of pleasures, or so Socrates and Glaucon agree. Just exactly when and how he gains honor and, especially, money is not specified. Of course, all of this vast experience is gained in association with prudence, so the lover of wisdom naturally triumphs there, too. Finally, argument is the peculiar instrument of the philosopher and, since it is, there is no doubt that argument will judge that life best. Without further ado, the philosopher is declared the winner, the warrior runs a rather distant second, and the money-maker brings up the rear, if indeed the poor soul finishes at all.

So, these commonplace criteria yield an apparently very uncommon conclusion. But perhaps this is deceiving. The "philosopher" here does not appear to have very much in common with either the dishonored philosopher of the normal city or the propertyless philosopher-ruler of the City of Truth. The argument indicates that this is a prudent man of wide experience who secures first money and then honor before entering into his sustained pursuit of truth. He follows a balanced, progressive course of life which does not ignore but rather puts in their proper place the more usual human

142

goods. It is very hard to understand this man, or this
model of the philosopher, as identical with the soul-
seer locked in perpetual combat with the tyrant. He is
altogether more moderate, and his victory much less
surprising than it first appeared.

In the light of this argument, how "erotic" is
the philosophical, wisdom-loving portion? There is, it
appears, a natural progression of desires, beginning
with the sensual and that which satisfies the sensual,
proceeding to the honorific, and culminating in the
philosophical. The lack of finality in the earlier
desires indicates their incompleteness. It also suggests that the parts of the soul come into existence,
or more full existence, progressively.

If this is true, several arguments follow. First,
whether or not all three portions are erotic, they are
not simultaneously erotic. They cannot be, because
they do not exist simultaneously, at least at some
stages of human development. Second, it appears that
there is at the beginning, and then again at the cul-
mination of desire, both a unified - or unitary - soul,
and an undifferentiated desire. The early desire is
for sensual pleasure, the final desire for wisdom or
understanding. That final desire is generated by experienced understanding of the imperfection of sensual
and honorific pleasure. Both the early desire and the
final one appear to be for completeness, for union or
communion with some larger whole. Both imply the loss
of a differentiated soul regulated by calculation and
prudence.

The further implication is clear. The mature,
differentiated soul is ruled not by the desire for wisdom but by two things. First, it is ruled by the desire
to maintain differentiation. This means that, substantially, desire is confined to the desiring part and,
to a much lesser extent, to the spirited or honor-loving part. Second, this rational desire to maintain
differentiation is founded on the understanding that
perfect communion - sensually or "ontologically" - is
not possible for human beings. Human wisdom again is
the knowledge that we cannot know completely, and the
understanding that we can be only human. The longing
for perfection may remain, but non-erotic understanding
keeps it in its place. As Socrates says, the criteria
are experience, prudence, and argument.

*   *   *

Two of the three forms of the contention - the
first decided by a curious combination of clear-eyed
soul-seeing and much less bright opinion, the second
by those judges experience, prudence, and argument -
have been concluded and the just, prudent, kingly man
has taken both. A third and greatest form remains.
This form, it appears, will discover the quality and
reality of the pleasures themselves. Glaucon is fascinated, but much in the dark. Socrates proposes that
together they seek enlightenment.

An intricate philosophical argument on the nature
of pleasure begins. Socrates distinguishes three conditions: pleasure, pain, and a state of repose between
them. Pleasure and pain, or the pleasant and the painful, are motions, although presumably somehow distinct
and different from one another. The state of repose
between them is just that, the absence of motion.

The state of repose causes problems. Assume pain,
or painful motion. The cessation of the painful motion
- the existence of the state of repose - will often be
experienced as pleasure, rather than as what it truly
is, the cessation of pain. Similarly, the cessation
of pleasure will be experienced as pain. Curiously,
in each case the absence of motion is experienced as
motion opposite to the original motion, whether it was
pleasant or painful. Very often, pleasure and pain are
experienced - and defined - only in relation to one
another. Whatever is not pleasure, is pain; and whatever not pain, pleasure. We are prone to the condition
of the man who insisted in banging his head against the
wall, because it felt so good when he stopped.

The argument opens the possibility that there will
be no agreement on what is painful and what pleasur-
able, since a man whose daily life is pleasant and one
whose life is painful will call the same condition -
that of repose - painful and pleasant, respectively. To
avoid this, Socrates asks Glaucon to consider pleasures
which do not emerge from previous pains, especially
those of smell. Nothing specific is mentioned, but we
can imagine Glaucon walking by a bakery where his
favorite Attic cakes are being prepared, and breathing
in their delightful aroma.

The pleasures of smell may be pure and painless, but are they of relevance for human beings per se? The pleasure of smells is general to all animals; but the pleasant smells are probably quite specific, and perhaps even particular. But one thing is certain: there is very little pleasure in considering the pleasures of smell. They seem perfectly without consequence for mind or body. Is this perhaps the nature of pure pleasure, divorced from any eros, of understanding, of spirit, of desire? If it is, then pure pleasure has nothing to do with being a human being. Our pleasures, it seems, are only more or less impure, more or less associated or mixed with pains.

What then can be made of Socrates' discussion of the up, the down, and the middle? Presumably the up, down, and middle correspond to pleasure, pain, and repose. Socrates argues that we are prone to the down - the painful - and thus inclined to believe that the middle, or repose, is the heights. He asks Glaucon whether these things exist in nature, and Glaucon holds that they do. But what experiences have human beings with the heights, or with unmixed pleasure? Shall we say that heaven is a giant cookie factory? This does not mean that there are no pure pleasures - beside smell, of course. But it does suggest that we who are inexperienced in the truth are very likely to understand pleasure as relative to pain.

Who, if anyone, is experienced in pure pleasure? Socrates approaches the question this way. He asks, aren't hunger, thirst, and so forth an emptiness of the body's condition, and ignorance and imprudence an emptiness of the soul's? And, doesn't one become full, in body and soul, by taking in nourishment and understanding? Glaucon agrees. Then, what of fullness? Is the truer fullness that of a thing which more is, or less is? Glaucon, familiar with the notion of things which are, replies appropriately.

Then, what more is? Is it the class of things to which food and drink belong, or the class containing knowledge, understanding, and, in sum, all virtue? Socrates helps Glaucon along: is that which is connected with the changing or with the unchanging more that which is? The unchanging. And, isn't the unchanging also connected with knowledge and truth and being? Necessarily. And, in general, don't the things of the

145

body participate less in what is than the things of the
soul? Of course. Then, isn't the soul capable of more
fullness than the body? It follows.

This argument moves toward its conclusion. Socrates continues: if it is pleasant to become full of that
which is naturally appropriate, then that which becomes
full of things which are experiences truer pleasures
more really and truly than that which is filled with
things which less are. In other words: each thing
finds pleasure in filling with the things appropriate
to it, but that which is filled with the true things
finds truer pleasure. The soul, and especially the part
which knows, experiences the truest pleasure because it
is capable of fulfillment with the things which are.
The body, seeking different things, knows lesser pleasures because it desires things which are less real. It
is in perpetual motion between emptiness and temporary
fulfillment, and thus its pleasures are passing. Socrates finishes this argument by comparing the latter life
and its pleasures to the life of cattle.

Glaucon, who unexpectedly finds himself in the
company of pleasure beyond his wildest dreams, applauds
this, and says that Socrates has shown perfectly the
life of the many in this oracle. But what of Socrates'
argument here? How fine is it? There are these considerations. How possible is knowledge of the things
which are, especially in comparison with the relatively
available goods of the body? And, if attaining knowledge is the greatest pleasure, is there an opposite,
corresponding pain of ignorance, and how great must it
be? Then, what of this? If attaining, or having prudence and knowledge is a high and pure pleasure, does
such a fortunate man live in a state of constant pleasure? Is such a condition bearable for a human being?
Is it really more desirable than a state of repose, or
of more gentle pleasure? Finally, what of the area
between the life of the body and the life of the mind?
What are the pleasures of domestic and political life?
How real and attainable are they? To what extent are
they an alternative to the other two?

There is a yet more basic difficulty. Pleasure -
and pain - are motions in the soul. The best condition
of the soul is held to be fulfillment with the things
which are. These things are unchanging: this fact is
held to be the basis of the great - or true - pleasure
which attends being filled with them. But, how is it
that a motion arises from the possession of unchanging

146

things? Is it possible that they can be at once unchanging and impart somehow the motion which is pleasure? Or, is all motion, pleasure included, indicative
of incompletion, so that it ceases upon the possession
of the unchanging things? If so, then the pleasure
supposed to be true and attendant upon intellectual
fulfillment is a shadow painting like all other pleasures.

But Glaucon has been enticed by the supposedly
pure pleasures of intellectual fulfillment and convinced of their reality. Socrates' discussion of the
spirited part appeals to this conviction. By themselves, the pleasures of this part - honor, victory,
high spirits - carry with them the pains of envy, violence, and anger. Here, the pleasures and the pains
seem almost inseparably mixed. But Socrates does not
make this result in a state of repose, or anything like
it: the pleasures of the middle portion, like spiritedness itself, present problems. Neither does he say a
word about the pleasures of music, or their relation to
the motions of spiritedness.

Socrates begins to draw the overall argument on
pleasure to its powerful conclusion. We are shown the
soul of a man who understands pleasure properly. It is
a soul in which practical wisdom rules. In ruling, it
informs and tempers the taking of all other pleasures.
There is a limitation of pleasure to that which is true
because it is necessary, especially necessary to the
specific part. This is the kind of truth of which
pleasure is capable. Socrates does not say whether
there is a pleasure common to the soul as a whole.
But, if there is, very probably it is associated with
that which binds together the soul as a whole. The
truth of pleasure, then, appears to be specific, necessary, and moderate: all else is greater or lesser deception. Thus is the way prepared for the great, con-
cluding image of Book IX.

At last, they are in position to compare the pleasure of the kingly and the tyrannic life. These lives
are, respectively, closest and most distant from philosophy and argument, and from law and order. The true
pleasures, they agree, are those of philosophy: thus
the truly pleasant life is philosophical. Socrates asks
Glaucon if he knows how much more pleasant is the life
of philosophy than of tyranny. No, replies Glaucon, I
don't, but I will if you tell me. Socrates the philosopher proceeds to do just that.

There are, says Socrates, three pleasures, one genuine, two bastard. They are knowing, winning, and accumulating. The slave pleasures of the tyrant are out beyond these. This established, Socrates then places each of the kinds of lives. The tyrant, he says, stands third from the oligarchic man, who knows the pleasures of money-making. The pleasure of the tyrant, then, is removed by three from the pleasure of the oligarch. The oligarch, in turn, is third from the kingly man, and his pleasure likewise removed by three. It follows that the tyrant is removed in pleasure from the kingly man by three times three. So it appears, Glaucon agrees.

Before reaching the higher mathematics of this, a question or two is necessary. First, why does Socrates place the tyrant third from the oligarch? The order here is oligarch - democrat - tyrant. The tyrant seems to be twice removed from the oligarch or, arguably, even once. Then, what of the pleasure of the democratic man? He partakes equally in all pleasures. True, he is not ruled by practical wisdom: his pleasure-taking is random. But, does he not achieve an imitation of moderation, never indulging too much in any one pleasure? Arguably, pleasure is greater when a single principle rules. But, what then of the tyrant, ruled by his mad eros? Finally, what of the middle position of the oligarch, who is both ruled and partaker only of the necessary pleasures? Is he, rather than the democrat, the imitation of the kingly man?

Then, the mathematics of it. Socrates' calculations are fairly obscure, but this much is evident. The oligarch is placed in the middle. His value in pleasure is squared and then cubed to obtain the value of the kingly man, and the square and cube root taken to discover the pleasure of the tyrant. The fact that this doesn't quite yield the ratio 729:1 may indicate that mathematics is not wholly applicable here, or perhaps only that the pleasure of the tyrant is irrational anyway. In any case, Glaucon is extravagantly impressed with the pleasure of being just, and with Socrates' further association of this with the rhythms of the natural order. When Socrates tells him that this victory in pleasure is surpassed in the same ratio by a victory in grace, beauty, and virtue, he is again all but overcome. He does not stop to reflect upon the relative poverty of pleasure.

*   *   *

They have seen the perfectly just, the perfectly
unjust, and the possible. Book IX ends with the question that Book II introduced: is doing injustice profitable to the perfectly unjust man who is able to
appear perfectly just? To respond to one who believes
this, Socrates proposes that they mold in speech an
image of the soul so that he will be able to see exactly what it is that he is saying.

The image is a complex one. The first form is a
colorful beast with a ring of heads of various tame
and savage beasts. The beast is able to change these
heads by making them grow from within itself. A single
form - the beast - is molded from these forms. The second form is a lion, and the third form a human being.
The first of the forms is greatest in size, the second
second, and the human being smallest. Then, these
three forms are somehow joined so that they grow naturally together. Glaucon pronounces this done. Then, an
outer shell, that of a human being, is put in place
round about the three joined forms. Only this external
shell is visible to those unable to see what is inside.
To say the least, this image is forced - especially
the joining of the three internal forms -, but perhaps
Socrates will give an account of this. Glaucon is
willing to accept in speech what is most improbable
otherwise.

What does this image have to do with justice and
injustice? Socrates suggests that they say to one who
praises injustice as advantageous - and condemns justice as not advantageous -, that he affirms nothing
other than that it is profitable to feed and strengthen
the beast and the lion, while starving and weakening
the human being. This man will be told that, in praising injustice, he sets the human being, the lion, and
the beast in opposition, instead of making them
friends.

Then Socrates asks Glaucon, won't the man who
praises justice as profitable affirm the opposite?
That it is necessary to do and say that which strengthens the human being, and enables him to tame or control
the many heads of the beast? Doesn't he also affirm
the necessity of making the lion's nature an ally, and

of caring for all in common, making them friends with
one another and with himself? Glaucon replies, this is
exactly what the praiser of justice means.

Evidently, there is a basic difference between
these two men. The man who praises justice knows what
he is doing: the praiser of injustice does not. The
differences rests on knowledge or ignorance of the
soul. Socrates holds that the praiser of justice knows
the nature of the soul, and thus knows the effect that
the praise of justice has on the soul. Although the
soul is complex, the effect is simple. The human being
without - the external man - becomes one with the internal human being who controls the other, non-human
parts of the soul. Appearance and reality are one: the
evident human being is an actual human being. Justice
is being what you seem to be, being oneself, being a
human being. The image of the soul offered here embodies the fundamental logical truth of justice.

If justice is being in truth what you are naturally intended to be, then injustice is not being what
you appear to be. But the man who praises injustice
does not explicitly praise the strengthening of the
beast or the lion. That strengthening results from the
praise of injustice, but it is inadvertent. Socrates
holds that the praiser of injustice does not know what
he is doing. He is mistaken, and a fool, and self-
destructive, but he is not evil or intentionally unjust. Because he does not understand the nature of
the soul, he does not know what praising injustice does
to it. In his soul, the lion and the beast overwhelm
the human being, and claw and strike at one another for
supremacy: but he does not intend this. His failure is
his inability to understand, practically, the principle
of justice: that justice is each thing being itself,
and not some other thing.

Since this man is ignorant rather than intentionally evil, Socrates suggests that they persuade him of
the folly of praising injustice. The persuasion is an
informal introduction to the nature of the soul, and to
the effects of various excesses and deficiencies on it.
The treatment is unsurprising: it begins and ends with
an endorsement of good laws as conducive to the health
of the soul. Evidently, such laws will not be found
in an oligarchy or a democracy, much less a tyranny.
The persuasion, then, is one which turns a man away
from the norms and practices of inferior regimes for
the good of his soul.

*   *   *

This persuasion addresses the problem of the man who praises injustice. Certainly, it is better for him to esteem and praise justice. But is the praise of justice sufficient? Is it advantageous to be perfectly just? In other words: is the right condition the identity of the external and internal human beings? If it is, what of the lion and the many-headed beast? Can these be expurged from our nature? If they are, how can we preserve our own life and carry on human life? But, if they are not, how can we be just, justice being perfect humanity without animality?

Socrates equivocates on the human being within. He wonders aloud, is this part human, or is it divine? Suffice it to say that it is the best part. It orders the other parts, taming and befriending but not suppressing or destroying them. Then, what of the human being within? Can it be free of lion and beast? The magic of the original image is apparent. Somehow, the three parts grow together naturally. The human animal, physically and psychologically, is a wonderful thing, neither god nor beast. Again, strict justice - which seems to demand suppression or destruction of much of our nature - is softened and made practical by moderation. The best nature is defined by moderation and justice together with prudence. In Socrates' account, moderation is the goal, and prudence or practical wisdom the method of attaining it. But how much do moderation and practical wisdom differ? A closer look is necessary.

The soul is well-ordered when the human being tames and rules the beast, and is assisted by the lion. This arrangement is concord or moderation. In turn, this well-ordered soul rules the body, and governs the acquisition or expenditure of external goods. Here, the "human being" seems to be practical wisdom. He, or it, judges the effect that any change - in the soul, in the body, in external things - will have on the basic harmony of the soul. That harmony is the standard of judgment. It either is moderation or is the human version of moderation. In this argument, the human being in us - practical wisdom - keeps us human - moderate or harmonious of soul. Perhaps the equivalent of the growing together of external and internal human being is the growing together of practical wisdom and moderation.

Thus, this analysis shows justice and moderation
to be much closer together than they appeared in Book
IV, let alone Book VII. Here, justice and moderation
are humanity: they are the maintenance of the form of
the human being as the organizer of the soul. The
human being is very close to practical wisdom: this is
its form in the soul. Justice and moderation - no
longer very distinct - are the result of its action.
Active humanity maintains humanity. The human being
strictly is the just and moderate person, a complex
whole integrated by practical wisdom. Rightly, Glaucon
says of this man that he is truly musical.

An implication or two follow. First, some further
reflection must be given to the closing words of Book
IX. Socrates seems to direct the well-ordered man away
from the politics of his own city toward the divine
politics of his own soul. How sincere is this other-
worldly project, except as a further caution for the
honor-loving Glaucon? The treatment of moderation
implies that it is a natural condition: the normal
healthy soul is moderate. As well, the truly musical
soul of Book IX follows upon the discussion of the inferior regimes and of tyranny. The moderate and musical man - the man who is truly just because his soul is
human - has come to terms with and befriended the beast
within himself. He has maintained his harmony in action, seeking to preserve the natural - the human - in
the midst of expected internal and external disturbances. Is this a counsel of escapism and other-worldli-
ness? True, the inferior regimes depart more or less
from the natural: but how can the natural be known except in contrast with the distortions of it which we
experience in the everyday world and in ourselves? It
appears that what is best for us is seeking and finding
our humanity, in action.

Does this go too far? Is Socrates really so com-
fortable with participation in inferior regimes? Certainly one's bearing must be taken from the regime
within oneself, but where does that come from? Socrates seems to say, that regime is in heaven. But the
parts of the moderate regime to be established exist
naturally. They are as natural to the unjust man as to
the just. What differs, then, is the arrangement of
them. These questions remain, as Books X opens: what
is the divine arrangement which it is just and proper
to imitate? What is the eye which is able to see that
arrangement? Why have some that eye, and are able to
open it and look, and others not?

Together with this, the fundamental question must be raised again: is it more profitable to be just than unjust? Socrates and Glaucon appear to have resolved this. Injustice strengthens the beast within and diminishes the human being. This is the formal proof stated above: injustice is being something other than you appear to be, or not being yourself. Granted this: but, is it disadvantageous or unprofitable not to be yourself? May not being something other than you appear give you the advantage over others? Won't it deceive them, and leave them open to exploitation? If a man is skilled enough to appear a man and yet be a beast, won't he be able to disarm, exploit, and even destroy those who believe in his humanity? Evidently, imitation may be used by injustice. May not injustice imitate justice to take advantage of the unwary? And, if justice, why not the other virtues? Isn't this to the advantage of the imitator? More exactly, isn't it if one disbelieves in the soul and its basis, justice formally, logically understood? And, isn't imitation the basic method of the unjust man, as well as of the just? Deep questions open themselves. Socrates' choice of imitation as the topic to begin the final book is a knowing one.

There is a still more practical aspect to the question of imitation. Throughout Books VIII and IX, Socrates has created a series of images, of cities, of souls, of men. The series concludes with the image of the soul of the human being. This image is of nakedness beyond nakedness, unlike the vivid, immediate images of king and tyrant, oligarch and democrat. To some perhaps very great extent, the young embrace an image of what they would be, and act on it. Is the image of the truly human soul powerfully attractive enough to compete successfully with other clothed and merely naked images? Presented with a specifically human image of the just soul, will one therefore long for it, and act to become it? Or, must all decently effective images be political, and thus imply a justice bounded by the city's wall and the great men of the city's past? What can a Glaucon be led to make of himself, beyond a somewhat more civilized Achilles?

153

THE POLITICS OF MODERATION

CHAPTER TEN

BOOK TEN

As the book opens, Socrates appear to deny the very basis of the investigation. Their city - the inner city, the one based on the divine pattern - is right in not admitting anything which is imitative poetry. All such things maim the thought of those who hear them and do not have knowledge of how things really are as an antidote. Since, however, the city in the soul is itself apparently an imitation, there is obviously more to be said on the subject.

Socrates' ingrained friendship and respect for Homer - the first teacher and leader of the tragic poets - makes him reluctant to oppose him. But truth must be honored above a man, and told. He proposes that they discuss imitation in general, using the usual method and beginning from this point: that there is some one particular form for each of the particular "manys" with the same name. Clearly, this method is hypothetical and thus suspect according to Socrates' own strictest standard of truth. In adopting it, they seem to oppose one tradition to another, rather than ruthlessly attack all traditions using the dialectic. The investigators of imitation seem to be imitators themselves, of themselves.

*   *   *

The discussion begins by heaping custom upon custom. The participants are now many hours into the discussion. Are they not at leisure in Cephalus' well-furnished house, comfortably reclining on couches with tables before them? What could be more natural - or more conventional - than to select couches and tables as examples of "manys" for which there is nevertheless one name and thus presumably one form or idea for each? Thus the inquiry into the nature of imitation begins with two ideas, the idea of couch and the idea of table. Why Socrates makes these remarkable choices will perhaps become clear.

The craftsman who makes the particular couch does so by looking to the idea of it, as does the one who makes the chair, and so on. He does not, Socrates suggests, make the idea itself. Glaucon agrees with this. Curiously, he says nothing of the substitution of chair for table, instead accepting the ideas of separate craftsmen for distinct implements. But is not the idea of "table" - a horizontal rectangular prism supported by four equal vertical columns? - the basic idea behind "couch" and "chair"? Are not the ideas behind the idea fundamentally mathematical, and thus hypothetical? Do not a host of other, difficult questions arise from the "idea" of "table"? On philosophical reflection, doesn't it become utterly problematical what the craftsman does when he makes a table?

One problem must be discussed, since it bears on the question of justice. The formal definition of "table" is reducible to mathematics. Using this definition all but destroys the common sense notion of a table, and does destroy the distinction between tables, couches, and chairs. But one who knows nothing about prisms and cylinders knows well enough what a table is. A table is a piece of furniture used to eat at or place things on. Practically, a table is defined and differentiated by its use, and thus distinguished from similar objects. It is designed by the craftsman for that use. He has in mind the form "table" which best serves the intended purpose.

These things follow. First, definition according to use saves Socrates' contention that there is a distinct form "table", a form "couch", and so on. From the point of view of purpose, these are not reducible to mathematical forms. Second, tables are designed by craftsmen for use by ordinary men, not speculative philosophers or mathematicians. Now, Socrates has carefully avoided "justice" as an example of form. The formal definition of justice is well known by now. But what if justice, like "table", is thought of according to use? Then, justice becomes something designed by craftsmen for the use of ordinary men, to enable them to live together harmoniously according to appropriate rules. This is a much more human and perhaps more useful understanding of justice.

This approach does not completely humanize justice, or make it merely the product of immediate desire or convenience. The craftsman of tables has some idea of table, wherever it comes from. Probably, that idea is compounded of form and function. Likewise, the craftsman of justice must begin with some understanding of

what justice is and what it does. The source of that
understanding is not obvious. As well, that understanding can be refined, tested in practice, and adjusted
according to experience. This understanding of justice
- not purely formal, somewhat more human, looking in
part to use and practice - accords well with the picture of a human being drawn at the end of Book IX. It
also accords well with the notion of learning through a
tradition.

*   *   *

Socrates does not directly raise these points with
Glaucon. Instead, he offers him a glimpse of a far
more interesting craftsman. This craftsman produces
all visible things, both natural and the products of
human art. Glaucon is amazed and distrustful, and then
puzzled when Socrates tells him that he, too, in a certain way, can make all these things. And what way is
that? Well, Socrates says, carry a mirror with you,
and quickly you will make the earth and the sun and
everything else.

Glaucon objects: this man only makes them so that
they appear to be, not so they are in truth. Yes, says
Socrates, and isn't the painter like him? In a certain
sense, doesn't he also make a couch? Yes, Glaucon says,
he makes what appears to be a couch. And what of the
couchmaker? Haven't you said that he doesn't make the
form of the couch, but only a particular couch? And,
if he doesn't, then wouldn't one who says that the
couchmaker makes what completely is say what is not
true? Glaucon replies, so they who concern themselves
with such things would argue. Then, says Socrates,
let's not be surprised if this, too, proves to be a dim
thing when compared with the truth.

At this point, they approach the problem somewhat
differently. Instead of asking, what is imitation,
they ask, who is the imitator? No explanation is given
for this change, but again it humanizes the problem.
Or at least it seems to, since now these three kinds of
couches are mentioned: one which is in nature, made by
a god; the everyday couch made by the carpenter; and
the one which the painter produces. Socrates argues
that the god, whether willfully or by necessity, produces only one couch, that which is or which exists
naturally. The carpenter produces a particular couch,

but he, too, earns the name "craftsman". It is the painter, third from nature, who is denied the name and instead called "imitator".

There is a certain ambiguity about the god's function, however. The couch which he makes exists by nature. But he makes it, and is addressed as "nature-begetter", or something similar. The god appears to be the author of nature. Yet it is strange to say that the couch exists in nature, as a tree does and perhaps even justice does. Does it solve the problem to say that this god-produced couch is one by nature? That there is a single necessary form of "couch"? The implication is that this couch must be as it is: it is the couch which underlies and causes all particular couches. Then, does the god produce this underlying formal reality? Is this what is meant by nature? If it is, then material nature - rocks and trees and so forth - is of relatively little importance. Materials can be found, or made: what is decisive is the existence and discovery of the underlying formal reality. Since it is god-produced, evidently this reality is divine or close to divine.

There are several interesting implications to this argument. First, it is necessary to discover what is and is not a part of this reality. Is, for example, "couch" a true underlying form? If it is, then this reality has a curiously humanized content. It is not merely, or perhaps even essentially mathematical or, so to speak, formally formal, but instead comprised of the forms of our everyday life. Then, consider justice as Socrates has discussed it. Justice is not merely another form like "couch". Justice is the form underlying these forms: it is the form, or power, which makes each what it is and not some other form. Justice appears to be more divine than most forms. On the other hand, trees and perhaps also mathematical figures appear to have little divinity or reality. Reality appears to be full of significance for practical human living.

This argument squares with Socrates' suggestion that the imitator is at the third generation from nature. The various forms themselves are the first generation, produced by the elemental power; the particular objects modelled upon them, the second; and the imitation of those objects, the third. But what of this? Is the maker of tragedy in the same situation? Is he, as Socrates says, third from a king and the truth? Probably, Glaucon replies, and for the moment they leave this intriguing assertion at that.

They return to the painter, and specifically to his art. They agree that he imitates the work of the craftsman, not the thing itself in nature; and, not that work as it is, but only as it looks; and, not as it looks as a whole, but only a part of it. This is the genius of the painter's art: by imitating only a small part of the appearance of a given thing, he is able to produce everything while understanding nothing, and thus able to deceive the unknowing into believing that he knows everything. His art appears to encompass all arts, and produce all things, thus rivaling that of the god who is "nature-begetter".

But what painter claims that he knows all things, and what man believes this? Socrates' target is not painters, but tragedians, beginning with their leader Homer. These are the men who are thought to know all arts, and all human things which have to do with vice and virtue, and the divine things as well. If this is the content of the world of underlying forms - that world as Socrates seems to understand it - then these are the men who are intimate with the world. And, since that world is of the things which are, then these are the men who know, or at least are held by others to know.

There is an interesting formal parallel here. Earlier, Socrates distinguished three levels or degrees of reality: the idea made by the god; the particular object made by the craftsman; and the imitation of the object by the painter. The argument suggested certain difficulties with a formal definition of the idea, but saved the distinct ideas of "couch", "table", and "chair" by considering them in terms of use rather than form. Now, the tragic poet claims to know three kinds of things: all arts; all human things having to do with vice and virtue; and the divine things. Evidently, the divine things corresponds to the nature-begetting god, and the arts to the craftsman who produces particular objects. This leaves all human things virtuous and vicious to correspond to imitation. This implication is in line with others before and after it: virtue and vice are somehow associated with imitation, and perhaps even caused by it.

*   *   *

The inquirers' task now is to test whether common opinion, which believes that Homer and the other tragedians know the things which <u>are</u>, is right or wrong. What is the test? Socrates <u>is</u> not explicit, but at least its purpose is stated: to discover whether the poets really know the things which they talk about so convincingly. How then to determine whether someone knows what he is talking about? What does Socrates suggest? First, he asks, would one who could make both the thing to be imitated and the phantom of it choose to devote himself to making the phantom? Evidently not. Then, wouldn't one who was able to do as well as imitate deeds choose to do, and thus win praise and honor rather than be the one who praises? Of course. These tests hold that knowing is manifested in making or in doing, and that these things are better and more honorable than imitating.

The tests are then applied, but generously, passing over the lesser arts and those concerned with the body. It is the whole of the political art - including its military and ethical parts - which Socrates first questions Homer about. What cities, he asks, have you ruled well or given good laws to, so that you were not third from the truth about virtue - an imitator -, but also second, an active practitioner? Glaucon finds none. And, if you are a wise man like Thales, what deeds of invention did you do? Nothing here. Well, what tradition of private education did you begin, as Pythagoras did? There is even less to say here, since Homer was neglected during his own lifetime. Then, who honored and loved and paid you as a teacher of virtue, as those now in the cities do for Protagoras, Prodicus, and many others? Isn't it true that, rather than cling thusly to you, those alive when you were allowed you and Hesiod to wander about unwanted and unrewarded? Glaucon agrees.

So, Homer fails every application of the test. He is neither a doer nor a maker of anything substantial, nor does he know the truth about anything. He is only a maker of names and phrases, a user of meter and rhythm and harmony who presents everything so colorfully and attractively that he seems to the ignorant or the bemused to know. He is judged to be a painter in words, a deceiver, and an imitator.

Socrates presses his case: he doesn't want to leave things half-said. He returns to the painter. The painter paints the reins and bit, and the smith and leather-worker make them. But, do any of these understand them? Doesn't only the horseman - the user - understand them, and especially their virtue and beauty and rightness? Are not these a function of use, rather than of appearance or even form? Isn't the same true of a flute? Doesn't the flute player alone have knowledge of flutes, and the flute maker, who trusts him, have only right opinion? And, isn't the painter of flutes ignorant of both? Glaucon agrees with all this. Then, we agree that the imitator is ignorant, and playful rather than serious; and that the tragic poets are all imitators in the highest possible degree.

Has Socrates said too much? Has he undercut his own case against the tragedians? He has made the ability to use the standard of knowledge. The poets may not know how to ride horses or play flutes, but by Socrates' own admission they use meter and rhythm and harmony. If they use these things successfully, must not they know them? Their words may be lacking in knowledge, and even insane, but don't they have great and powerful knowledge of music? Doesn't Socrates argue that music is the cause of gentleness and harmony of soul? The poets may not understand philosophically the nature of soul, as Socrates does, especially that a very high kind of justice causes its parts at least to be. But Socrates has caused the nature of knowing to shift from form to use. Knowledge of forms in now less ruling than ability to use. In other words, the harmonization of the soul by music is higher than knowledge of the individual forms, or even knowledge of the cause of the forms. Evidently, the ability to make or to do is more truly knowledge than abstract knowledge is. Thus, in principle, the poets as musicians rule the soul. The question then becomes, not should they rule - since there can be no human soul at least without music - but the more narrow one: do the poets know enough about the effects of music on the soul to rule well?

With this, the case for philosophy seems to have undone itself. But has it? To rule well is to use music well, so that a harmonious soul will be formed. The harmonious soul is the moderate soul. This is knowledge of the highest kind, beyond even knowledge of justice and its power. But, does the tragic poet have this knowledge? Does he have anything other than a god-given gift to make music? If moderation is the greatest good, and moderation is caused by music, then knowledge of how to use music moderately is the highest kind of knowledge. But, is that possible without knowing what moderation is? And, who is it who knows moderation?

Socrates again suggests that imitation is third from the truth. How true is this in the light of moderation? The flute player may know a good flute, but that flute is useless without something to play. The musicmaker - the poet - uses the flute player. Let's place him above the flute player, and place beneath the flute player the maker and painter of flutes. Evidently, all "imitators" are not equal: the poet is far above the painter. Now, who stands above the poet? Shall we say, the one concerned with ordering souls? And who is this? The creator of political order, the law-giver? In the dialogue, these are Socrates and the brothers, who decide which poets to admit and which to exclude. Does the law-giver then rule?; or, is he also used?

This seems to turn upon which part of the soul rules. The order of precedence among philosopher, poet, and law-giver is not clear, although the question is prejudiced in the dialogue by the fact that Socrates is a philosopher playing a legislator. This can be said: if moderation rules, then the part of the soul which is or contains moderation rules. Does this part belong to poet, philosopher, or legislator? Ah, but the question is wrong. As we well know - as Socrates has so often said or implied - moderation belongs not to a part but to the whole. This question is better: which person represents the soul as a whole? Or, in terms of imitation: if the harmonious soul imitates moderation, then which man - philosopher, law-giver, poet - imitates the harmonious soul?

True, Socrates still speaks ill of imitation, or at least of certain forms of it. But it is becoming obvious that there is a right order of use; or, to put it otherwise, that each thing in a chain of reality or being imitates - or is a more evident manifestation of - the thing directly above it which is more real. It seems that there is proper imitation and improper imitation, almost true and false imitation. True imitation seems to be . . . but perhaps Socrates' discussion of how imitation acts on the soul will help here.

* * *

Socrates begins with an obvious fact: we don't always see things as they are. Sometimes naturally, sometimes through human artifice, our eyes are deceived, and deceive us in turn. To guard against this, various kinds of measurements have been devised by, Socrates argues, the calculating part of the soul. But the fact is that what appears to us is often out of accord with the measurements. Socrates then invokes his first principle from Book IV: it is impossible for the same thing to opine contraries about the same things at the same time. Thus, there must be two parts of the soul involved, one trusting measurement and one trusting appearances. And, the part trusting measurement is the best part, while that opposed to it is ordinary. This latter part, trusting appearances, is the part which imitation keeps company with. It sees appearances, and is far from truth and prudence. Glaucon agrees with the argument.

This is a curious argument. It associates imitation with appearances, but fails to distinguish between the appearances given in nature and the appearances produced by the painter. Evidently, either may deceive, when judged by the standard of measurement. All that is established is the sight, and the part of the soul associated with sight, may deceive or be deceived. But measurement depends in part upon sight. The possibility of deception thus exists there as well. In fact, trusting measurement is trusting the sight and the agreement of many taken many times over: it is trusting careful and refined common sense. It is accurate to call this prudence; but how accurate is it to call it truth?

Socrates then asks, does this also apply to the imitation connected with hearing, called poetry? He says nothing of hearing per se. Is poetry serious, like measurement and calculation, or ordinary like painting? Glaucon is ready to associate painting and poetry, but Socrates goes directly to the very kind of thinking with which poetry's imitation keeps company. He gives this very precise definition of the art of imitation: that which imitates human beings doing forced or voluntary actions, and as a result of the actions thinking themselves to have fared well or badly, and in all of this feeling either grief or joy. Doing, thinking, feeling - tragic poetry may be high or

low, but it appears to be comprehensive. Now, the concern is not visual appearances - things seen - but
actions, opinions, experiences - things done, things
thought, things felt. The tragic poet imitates these
things, which are the stuff of distinctively human
life. He presents a world. The question is, is it
the real world, or a good imitation of it? Are the
things which the poet presents things which should be
imitated by his listeners? Or, should they go elsewhere
for actions, opinions, and feelings to imitate?

*   *   *

Socrates begins by recalling a previous agreement.
They have agreed that a human being is not always -
perhaps not usually - at one with himself. This recalls the familiar argument, that the soul has parts,
and that those parts often disagree about which should
control the whole soul, and thus the body and person.
In other words, the human soul is often not moderate,
acting rightly as one. The question may well be put:
are the poets teachers of moderation? Presumably
Socrates will now in one way or another answer that
question.

*   *   *

Take, for example, a seemly man whose fate it is to
lose a son, or something equally dear. Being seemly,
he'll bear the loss better than most, of course feeling
the pain of the loss, but acting in a measured way in
the face of the pain. In the presence of others,
especially, he'll withstand the pain and present a
noble face; but when alone he'll perhaps succumb to it,
and say and do shameful things. In Glaucon's opinion,
this behavior is quite normal, but certainly doubts
have been raised about whether the man's composure is
genuine.

Socrates now asks, isn't it logic and law which
tell him to withstand the pain, while emotion draws him
toward it? Glaucon agrees. Socrates again invokes his
first principle: the presence of different tendencies
toward the same thing at the same time indicates the
existence of two different elements. One element
listens to the law. The law speaks again, as it did in

Book VII. Then, it told the philosopher that he is
obliged to become involved with the human things. Now,
it says that what is most becoming is to be as calm as
possible in misfortune, for these reasons: the good and
the bad in such matters are not clear; taking them hard
is of no use to you; none of the human things are worth
great seriousness; and being in pain hinders the arriv-
al of that which can aid one. Evidently, the law does
not always say the same things, but varies its advice
and command according to the situation.

The law suggests that the best medicine here is deliberation. One must accept what has happened and make
the best of things in the way which logic indicates.
What is not indicated is dwelling on one's misfortune,
and in that way keeping the wound open. The best part
of the soul is willing to accept this advice; but there
is another part which seems to be in love with pain and
suffering, and which can't get enough of crying and
complaining. It wishes to make much of what has befal-
len the sufferer.

Here is where the imitative poet comes in. The
calm, prudent, orderly portion of the soul, being one
with itself, doesn't lend itself to imitation, Socrates
says, or at least its imitation isn't very interesting
to a popular audience. On the other hand, the crying,
complaining, self-pitying portion can be imitated in
many ways which are interesting to the many. It is
this part, and this audience, which the imitative poet
fixes on.

At last the poet is justly placed in the company of
the painter. Two points of similarity are found: first,
both make things which are ordinary by the standard of
truth; second, both are associated with a part of the
soul which is on the same level and not with the best
part. Thus, in the soul, prudence and orderliness are
associated with calculation and measurement, and emotion and self-pity with the belief in appearances. The
poet imitates emotion, and the painter appearances.
Emotions and appearances are many, and very far from
being true or lasting.

These are similarities, but the poet and painter
differ also. The one works with sounds - words and
music -, the other with sights. The poet's range is
far more comprehensive. He imitates deeds, thoughts,
and speeches, as well as emotions. The painter is restricted to presenting appearances. Socrates points

toward a basic difference. The poet affects the soul, causing a part of it - the emotional part - to be strengthened and overwhelm the calculating part. He calls the stuff of this part phantoms, but how is it that phantoms far removed from the truth are able to rule that which is more real? The painter also deals in phantoms, but these phantoms are images. They may be seen by any soul possessing sight. But the phantoms of the poet - words and rhythms which arouse emotions - affect the distinctively human soul. Not only do the imitations of poet and painter affect the soul differently: it is not at all clear that they affect the same portion of the soul.

Why then does Socrates lead Glaucon to believe that they do? Is there a clue in the fact that Socrates - philosopher turned law-giver - wishes to banish the imitative poet from his city? Wisely, Socrates associates himself with the law, and associates logic and the law with the better, orderly portion of the soul. But is it clear that Socrates, who deals in words, is concerned with a different portion of the soul than the poets are? After all, both deal in words, and words affect and perhaps create the distinctively human soul. Socrates and the poets, according to this argument, are competing for the same portion of the soul. Socrates believes that the poets' words are not true - are unreal and misleading - and that they triumph perhaps because they appeal to the many. But is this the real reason? Might not the genuine cause of the poets' triumph be that they possess rhythm and harmony - their god-given gifts - and philosophy does not? Or, to ask another question, who - poet or philosopher - is more capable of making the distinctively human soul - the heart of the soul - moderate?

But wait! Socrates has not yet finished his indictment. He returns to the seemly man, and charges that imitation maims even him. For the most part, he is able to keep his emotions in check when sorrow befalls him personally. But when he hears Homer or some other tragic poet imitating great suffering, he enjoys this. He suffers along with the hero as though he himself were in the situation, and praises the poet for his art. Glaucon finds this inconsistency unreasonable, but Socrates says that it is not, and proceeds to explain.

There is a part in each of us - Socrates calls it the lamenting part - which by nature desires to weep

and wail and suffer. There is another part, the laughing part, and another, the lusty part, and in fact a
whole host of parts, one for each of the desires and
pleasures and pains. Each of these parts, or all of
them together, are governed by our better nature, that
part of us which is one and constant and orderly, or
tries to be. The seemly man controls his emotions in
personal suffering, but his governing part is incompletely educated by argument or habit. It relaxes its
guard when watching someone else suffering or laughing
at bawdy jokes or indulging in sexual pleasure or
anger. The poets, through their imitations, provide
these opportunities for relaxation and indulgence.
The man who believes that it is shameful for him to act
in these ways may not, if imperfectly educated, object
to watching others and enjoying their deeds and sufferings. He does not condemn the poet, because he doesn't
understand the nature of his own soul, and thus the
effect that this seemingly harmless vicarious indulgence has in strengthening the least noble portions of
himself. In time, Socrates implies, prudence - or what
has seemed to be prudence - is weakened, and the seemly
man's indulgence in the pleasures of observing imitation becomes direct indulgence.

But, direct indulgence in what? In imitation or in
action? This question defines the relationship between
imitation and the soul. There is a certain reality to
the portions of the soul which are not noble. They
cannot be denied completely, nor indulged completely.
In the less than perfectly educated soul, excessive
denial - itself modelled on false imitation - leads to
excessive indulgence, first in the observation of imitation, then in imitation itself. But, if there were
no imitation, would these actions never occur? Would
we never laugh or cry or love? How could this be, if
there is reality to those parts of the soul? In a certain sense, the actions - necessary actions - would
occur, but not as they occur when they are modelled on
imitation. Modelled on imitation, they become heroic,
not merely necessary. Socrates' case for banishing the
poets is not that the portion of the soul which they
appeal to is unreal. On the contrary: it now seems to
make up at least half the soul. Rather, it is that the
poets, in making heroic what is merely necessary, cause
that portion to be something it is not, namely inflated
beyond its natural significance and apparently noble.

But, are the philosophers immune to this criticism?
Haven't they puffed up the calculating portions of the

soul until it too appeared to be the whole? Isn't the seemly man - the man who only seems - susceptible to imitation precisely because he has repressed his natural emotions in a vain attempt to appear noble? He too imitates, but what he believes to be nobility - some measured calm - which is not his. There is no more reality in the imitation of excessive dispassion than in the heroic exaggeration of the passions by the poet. Both are unreal, and dangerous, because they make too much - or the whole - of what is only a part.

Then, finally, what of imitation? Is any of it true, or good for the soul? Socrates is willing to admit this much: hymns to gods and praise of good men. Is this imitation? It does not seem so. There are no just or moderate grounds for having men imitate gods. What of the imitation of good men? Perhaps this turns on a further question: do good men have quantities which can be imitated without being truly possessed? Or, is a good man one who is exactly what he seems to be, no more and no less, who also is that which is completely and truly human? True, this is very formal, which raises this further question: can good or right form, everywhere and always, even be merely imitated?

*   *   *

The last word on the poets has not yet been said. Socrates explains their expulsion from the city. If lyric and epic poetry are allowed to remain, then pleasure and pain will be kings in the city instead of law and the argument which seems best in the opinion of the community in each case. In short, emotion rather than law and common sense would then rule. Socrates is most judicious here, or is ambiguous the word? Logic, he says, has dictated the poet's expulsion; but logic is made to appear almost identical with the law and common sense. He is careful, as law-giver, not to identify himself completely with the philosopher's position. Wisely, the old quarrel between poetry and philosophy is laid at poetry's doorstep. It appears that the "soul" of the city which rules - and excludes - includes all the reasonable elements. Philosophical argument, law, common sense - all these are allied against passionate poetry.

Poetry's expulsion is not final. It will be allowed to return if it satisfies this curious condition:

it must make an apology for itself, as the philosophical law-giver has made his apology for expelling it.
Poetry must show that it is not only charming and pleasant, but beneficial to regimes and human beings. It is
permitted to make its apology in lyrics or some other
meter, while its non-poetic supporters can provide a
defense in plain language. The good city is open to
poetry, if poetry is willing and able to become more or
less logical and prudential, perhaps by reflecting upon
its effect on the soul. How logical and prudential is
not yet clear, except to say that Homer and the other
tragedians have not passed the test. The extremes seem
to be these: on the one hand, poetry may simply give
some account of how it is beneficial; on the other,
poetry must show that it is a serious thing grasping
the truth. If it cannot do something like these, then
Socrates and Glaucon as law-givers will steel themselves against its charms by chanting the argument they
have used to expel it.

The struggle, Socrates emphasizes, is a serious
one. Exactly which struggle does he have in mind here?
That between philosophy and poetry, or that between the
opinion that justice is advantageous and the opposite
opinion which praises injustice? Or, has Socrates
succeeded in showing that these apparently distinct
struggles are finally one? That poetry causes the
opinion that injustice is advantageous by feeding the
part of the soul which is not the human being but the
beast, while philosophy which seeks to know the soul is
allied with the opinion that justice is advantageous,
indeed necessary? And, if he has done this, has he
shown how the struggle can be ended, and the antagon-
ists reconciled? At any rate, Glaucon is persuaded of
the seriousness of it; but Socrates has yet another
surprise for him. It is this: the greatest rewards
for virtue have not yet been considered. Glaucon is
astonished. What inconceivable greatness can this be,
if it is greater than the wonders they have already
spoken about?

*   *   *

Socrates' wonder is this: the soul is immortal.
Glaucon finds this wonderful. Here is a thing which is
for all time. Socrates finds this easy to say. To
him, it is obvious that the soul is immortal. It would
be unjust to speak of it as other than immortal. He

169

doesn't find this at all wonderful. But Glaucon cannot bring himself to say this. He obviously does not believe that the soul is immortal. He may be persuaded that justice is better than injustice, that only the just man is at one with himself. But he has never seen the logical connection between the belief in justice and a belief in the immortality of the soul. The fellow law-givers are somewhat out of accord.

What is the logical connection? Granted that justice is the power which makes each thing itself and not something else. It makes the human being a human being, and not a beast. But, it also makes the couch a couch, and not a table. Yet, does anyone assert that a couch is immortal? Why then should anyone believe that an individual human soul is immortal? Evidently, Socrates' argument must find something strikingly different between a soul and every other thing.

*   *   *

He asks Glaucon, do you call something bad and something good?; the bad, that which corrupts and destroys, the good, that which preserves and benefits? I do, Glaucon replies. And, is there something good and bad for each thing? Socrates gives five examples of bad things, things which destroy other specific things: ophthalmia, sickness, blight, rot, rust. If a thing escapes its own evil, Socrates asserts, then it remains uncorrupted, since neither what is good nor what is neutral destroys. And, if we find something whose evil can harm but not destroy it, then won't we know that for a thing of this nature there is no destruction?

So it seems, Glaucon replies. But it does not seem so. Two things are left unmentioned that destroy, but not specifically: time and chance. Are not all things subject to time and chance? Isn't the soul, to which Socrates now turns? The soul, they establish, has things which make it bad - injustice, licentiousness, cowardice, and lack of learning. Do these, or any one of them, destroy the soul? Socrates compels Glaucon to approach this question very carefully. Each thing, they have agreed, is destroyed by the one evil specific to it - or it is not destroyed at all. According to this logic, a body cannot be destroyed by an evil incident to a soul, nor a soul by an evil incident to a body. Thus, no body could ever be destroyed by injustice, and no soul by cancer. Explicitly, Socrates argues the analogy, that no body is ever destroyed by badness of food, but that if badness of food introduces badness of body into the body, then the body is destroyed by its own vice, disease.

Then, does injustice destroy the soul, as cancer evidently destroys the body? Glaucon answers that it does not. This too seems evident: men are unjust, yet they do not die from their injustice, although they may be put to death for it. On the contrary, Glaucon says: not only does the unjust man not die from his injustice, but he is made very lively, indeed sleepless, by it. Injustice does not kill the soul, and they have agreed that the diseases of the body kill only the body. The soul, then, does not die from its own specific evil, and cannot die from any other evil. It is indestructible, according to the argument.

They do not consider here whether the virtues of each part of the soul are corrupted or destroyed by the opposing vices. Evidently, moderation is destroyed by licentiousness, courage by cowardice, and wisdom by lack of learning. But, if vice destroys virtue, does it also destroy the portion of the soul in which vice or virtue resides? Is, for example, the spirited portion destroyed by cowardice, or the moderation of the whole soul - indeed, the very (integrated) soul itself - by immoderation? Socrates, so far from answering these questions, does not even raise them. He seems to be content with the argument that injustice, while it may corrupt the soul, nevertheless does not destroy it. But his argument about the status of the parts suggests that there may be a relationship between the moderation of the soul and its immortality. This is an amazing and wonderful argument, since a first glance suggests that moderation is much more closely associated with the distinctively human soul, while the immortal soul would seem to be associated with pure justice or, perhaps, pure logos.

*   *   *

The argument leaves the soul immortal, and also leaves body and soul radically separated. They seem to have nothing whatever to do with one another. Nothing that a soul does can harm a body, and no matter what befalls a body the soul is unaffected. The implications of the argument are sweeping. Human responsibility and human beings themselves are destroyed. The unjust man is put to death unjustly, since no action of the soul can destroy the body. In principle, the world of this argument is one of disembodied souls, and of bodies perfectly unaffected, or at least uncorrupted by other than internal mechanical causes.

It is curious that Socrates makes this argument. Much of the dialogue, and especially the last two books, have been spend integrating the distinct parts of the soul into a human soul, which is the motive principle of a human being. Moderation is the integrating agent. Now, with a single argument based upon a single principle all of that work is undone. The principle is this: a thing is affected only by the vice or virtue which is specific to it, and nothing else. How different is this from the principle of justice itself? Justice makes everything what it is: the new principle - to the extent to which it is new - unmakes everything according to its specific and distinct evil. It seems to be the power that is the mirror image of justice but opposed to justice. Is it not injustice, the principle of lonely and isolated destruction? Just as justice and moderation associate to form the distinctively human soul in its good form, so perhaps injustice and immoderation join to destroy it.

What exactly is destroyed here, and what exactly does the destroying? The soul, Socrates has lead Glaucon to believe, is no simple thing. It is composed of parts based on the power of justice, with the parts integrated by moderation. Injustice, they have agreed, cannot destroy the soul. But the distinctively human soul is, in a sense, destroyed by justice. Strict justice of the parts without the integrating effect of moderation destroys the integrated human soul. Yet there is another form of justice - justice of and for human beings - which saves and preserves the soul: this is the justice which is good for human beings. It is the power which makes human beings what they are, beings moved by an integrated moderate soul. From the human point of view, strict justice is injustice - a form-destroying power - for human beings.

Then, which is more real, the power which is strict, logic-perfect justice, or the form of the human being? Is this not another great wonderful mystery?: everything depends on justice for its existence, yet the strictest justice destroys anything which, like the human soul, is a composite, a whole of parts. It seems that no world - at least no world which we can know and participate in - is possible either without justice or with the strictest justice.

Socrates now begins to tell Glaucon of these things. They have been looking at the human soul as human beings. In this condition, Socrates says, it is mixed with the body and with other evils. What they see, then, is not pure soul. Pure soul can be seen only by reasoning. Reasoning sees its beauty and the forms of justice and injustice more clearly. To begin to know the unencumbered soul, the seeker must look to its love of wisdom and what that love seeks and would become were it free to do so. Then the truth of the soul, and especially whether it has a single or many forms, would be known.

*   *   *

The long argument approaches its end. Have they proved that justice is best for the soul, strict justice for pure soul, justice in human form for the human soul? Yes: if soul is to be soul, whatever form it takes, it must be just. Glaucon is persuaded of this fundamental, undeniable truth. He is not philosophically curious, longing to see and know pure soul, whether it is pure justice, perfectly itself, or whether it too must associate with something which is other. Evidently, Glaucon is happy with human justice. Perhaps Socrates knew this all along. At any rate, when Socrates asks him if he will give back what he borrowed - the reputation among gods and human beings that justice wins for its possession - he does so willingly. One by one, he pays his debts. The gods know, love, and reward the just man, if not in life, then in death, and give the unjust man his just due also.

And what of human beings? Isn't this the way it is with them? In time aren't they able to distinguish the just from the unjust? Doesn't the clever unjust man start well and leap ahead, but then falter and fall by the wayside? And, won't the just man, as time passes, pull ahead in the race, and win whatever rewards and honors he wishes? Finally, won't it be the unjust, not the just, who are ridiculed and whipped and destroyed? So Socrates will say on behalf of the just man, just

as Glaucon once spoke for the unjust. But now Glaucon
agrees with Socrates, since what he says is just.
Everyone else is silent.

Socrates has delivered the apology for justice.
Only at the end does he mention the honors it brings,
and then only because it is just to do so. No doubt,
he has persuaded his audience. They now believe that
justice is good, as well as advantageous, and injustice
bad. That they do not know is of no matter to them,
and perhaps not to Socrates either. He has done his
work, nay his duty. Has he not paid his debt to justice? But perhaps he is not certain. He has spoke of
human rewards. Now, he will tell his attentive listeners of far greater ones.

*   *   *

Socrates tells them a story. It concerns a man
named Er, whose name in Greek closely resembles two
other words: eros, or passionate love, and hero. Socrates calls him a strong man. Er meets his end in war.
His body is found in a remarkably well-preserved condition, and is about to be burned on a funeral pyre. But,
just at that point, Er comes back to life, and tells
what he has seen in the other world.

This is Er's tale. His soul left his body, and
travelled with many other souls to a certain holy
place. In that place, there were two opening in the
heavens. Between the openings sat two judges: these
judged the souls. The just were told to continue up
and to the right, and the unjust down and to the left.
Signs of their judgements were attached to each soul,
in front of the just, behind the unjust. Er himself
was told to observe things, and to act as a messenger
to human beings. Why he in particular was chosen, and
whether he was just or unjust, Socrates does not say.

The souls, having been judged, went up or down.
Souls also came out of the other two openings, some
from earth, some from heaven. The earthly souls were
full of dirt and dust, the heavenly ones pure. Evidently, Er's description was no more complete than
that. He leaves something to be desired as an observer
of souls; but perhaps souls find nothing remarkable
about the appearance of other souls. However that may
be, Er's soldierly account continues as follows. The

arriving souls, worn from their journey, gathered in a
meadow and set up camp there. Acquaintances greeted
one another, and souls from heaven asked about the
earthly journey, and those from the earth about the
heavenly. Weeping and wailing, the earthly souls told
of their travails, while the heavenly ones spoke of
the beautiful sights they had seen and experiences they
had had. Each journey, Socrates remarks, takes a thousand years, so evidently souls don't wear out in that
time, although they may be the worse for wear.

Basically, the souls said this. Each unjust deed
is punished ten times over, and each just deed rewarded
ten times over. Since the journey above or below lasts
a thousand years, each deed in a human life, just or
unjust, is rewarded or punished once every hundred
years. But more is said about bad deeds and their punishment than good deeds and their reward. Er also spoke
about those who lived only a short time, but said nothing worth repeating.

The account makes it clear either that the same
soul may have done both good and bad deeds, or that bad
deeds differ from one another in their badness. In any
case, not all of the earthly souls are able to escape
the earth even after a thousand years of punishment.
One soul inquired about a certain tyrant of Pamphylia,
Er's country. This tyrant had murdered his father and
brother and done other unholy deeds. The soul who had
seen this tyrant responded, and told of his fate. He
neared the exit in company with some others, mostly
tyrants but a few private men of great fault. As they
approached, the mouth - of the underground passage -
roared and would not let them pass. They were incur-
able, or at least had not paid a sufficient penalty.
Fierce and fiery men waited at the exit. They took
some of these evil men back, but they seized the Pam-
phylian tyrant and others, bound them, threw them down,
and stripped off their skin. Is it the case that the
most evil souls are doomed to retain their bodies?
Well, the skinned tyrant and his companions were dragged down the rough road like wool being carded on
thorns. Their fate, and the reasons for it were ex-
plained to those who watched. They were thrown into
Tartarus, the infernal region beneath Hades.

What about the rewards? Socrates reports that Er
said this. The earthly souls were full of all sorts
of fears, but the greatest was that the mouth would
roar and refuse to permit them to leave. This fear, if

realized, seems to lead to despair that one is doomed
forever to punishment. The rewards are the counterparts of these. What, then, are the counterparts - or
antistrophes - of fear and despair? Confidence and
hope. The earthly soul will mourn, the heavenly one
sing. Evidently, the heavenly soul is truly musical
and harmonious. If this is so, then happiness for a
soul is not the sight of the good - what the philosopher of Book VII longs for -, but the condition of being musical. As well, the heavenly soul, like the
truly human soul, would be a whole of parts rather than
simple intelligence. Socrates does not make these
things explicit, but this can be said: there is a
divine as well as a human case to be made for moderation. Perhaps there is less divergence, or even no
divergence, between divine moderation and human moderation. This did not seem to be true for justice.

But, if all this is true, why does Socrates - or
Er - mention the beauty of the sights? Do the just
souls who pass their time in heaven see any sights and,
if they do, which ones? According to Er's report, they
said they did: is it possible that just, heavenly,
musical souls say things which are not so? Or is it
that there is some problem here with language? What
does a soul mean when it speaks of "seeing"? No doubt,
these souls, so pure, are clear-eyed. If any souls
could "see", they could. And yet, how would they speak
of what they saw? What words, what language, correspond to the beauty of the vision?

What follows from these things is not completely
surprising. The collection of souls stayed seven days
encamped on the plain, and on the eighth continued
their journey. Four days out - the eleventh day after
Er was killed - they arrived at a place from which this
wonderful sight was seen: a column of light like a
rainbow, but purer and brighter, binding together heaven and earth. After a day's journey they arrived at
the middle of it. From there they could see that this
light held together the outer surface, as the structur-
al members bind the hull of a ship. It appears from
the account the lesser members branch off the central
column of light, like frames from the keel of a ship.

From the extremities of the column stretch the
spindle of Necessity. The spindle rests in the lap of
Necessity and turns the outer spheres, which are equivalent to the whorls or round weights of a spindle.
The stem and hook of the spindle are of adamant, and

the whorls a mixture of that and other, softer metals.
The whole cosmos, then, is composed of parts ranging
from pure light to the hardest metal.

There is not a single whorl, as on an ordinary
spindle, but eight whorls, each fitted inside the other
like bowls. From above they are seen as concentric
circles, and from the side as a single whorl. The
circles formed vary in breadth, with the outer whorl
forming the broadest; the sixth, second; the fourth,
third; the eighth, fourth; the seventh, fifth; the
fifth, sixth; the third, seventh; and the second,
eighth. The relative sizes are not given. The colors
vary as well. The outer circle is multicolored; the
second, yellowish; the third, white; the fourth, red;
the fifth also yellowish; the sixth, less white; the
seventh, brightest; and the eighth, innermost whorl, a
reflection of the seventh's brightness. The direction
and speed of rotation also varies. The outer whorl
follow the motion of the whole spindle, but the seven
inner whorls rotate gently in the opposite direction.
The speed of the outer whorls is not given, but probably it is very fast. Of the seven inner whorls, their
speed decreases from the center out, with the seventh,
sixth, and fifth rotating at the same speed, and the
fourth, third, and second progressively slower. What
this looks like in motion is not easy to say. But,
whether from above or from the side, it is a pageant of
whirling color.

But is it more than color. It is also music. A
siren sits on each circle, singing a single note. All
eight heard together produce a single harmony. Around
this whirling harmony of color and sound at equal dis-
tances - thus, in a triangle - sit three others. They
are the daughters of Necessity, the Fates: Lachesis,
who sings of what has been; Clotho, of what is; Atropos, of what will be. They sing in accord with the
sirens' harmony. They are dressed in white with wreaths
on their heads. Clotho - the present - turns the outer
sphere with her right hand, but not continuously; Atropos - the future - the inner whorls with her left; but
Lachesis - the past - puts one hand to each, in turn.
Perhaps the outer whorl, associated with what is, does
not turn so fast after all; but it does not stay still.

Thus, Necessity and the Fates control the spindle -
the cosmos - as a whole. Apparently Er only observed,
and asked no questions. Were things always this way?
Is the Cosmos immortal? Is it unchanging? What about

177

the forms? How if at all do they figure in things?
What of justice? Is it the power that makes the cosmos
what it is? Then, why does it seem that there is motion
everywhere? Is this consistent with changelessness?
What is the relationship between cosmos and soul? Is
the one a visible, physical representation of the
other? And, what of moderation ... but perhaps some
answers will be suggested as Er continues.

*   *   *

The arriving souls went straight to Lachesis. She
evidently looms very large in the order of things. She
did not speak herself, but instead used a certain prophet. First he arranged the souls in ranks, and took
lots and patterns of lives from Lachesis' lap. Then,
going upon a high platform, he delivered this speech
for Lachesis, maiden daughter of Necessity:

Souls that live for a day, now begins another
death-bearing cycle for the mortal race. A
demon will not cast lots for you, but you will
choose a demon. Let him to whom the first
lot falls first choose a life to which he will
be bound by necessity. Virtue has no master:
he who honors or dishonors her, that one will
have more or less of her. The blame belongs
to the one choosing. God is blameless.

Having said this, the prophet cast the lots among
them. Each one, except Er, picked up the lot which lay
next to him, and thus received a number. Then, the
patterns of lives were set before them. There were
very many, more than enough, and of all kinds: lives of
all animals, and all sorts of human lives. There were
tyrannies, some life-long, others short and bitter.
There were lives of men noted for various things: form
and beauty, strength and athletic prowess, birth and
ancestors. There were also unnoticed lives. There
was the same variety of lives for women. The ordering
of the soul was not included, since that is necessarily
determined by the life chosen. But all other things
were included, mixed with one another and with wealth
and poverty, sickness and health, and the middle conditions as well.

Socrates now intercedes with advice for Glaucon. This - the choosing of a life - is the greatest concern of a human being. To make a good choice, he must discover who will help him develop the knowledge and capacity to tell a good life from a bad one, and the effects of lives, and parts of lives, on the soul. He must become an expert on the soul. He will learn to call the better life that which helps make the soul more just, and the worse that which produces injustice in it. He will retain this belief in death as in life, and thus not be misled by wealth and power when the time of choosing comes. When it does, he will choose a moderate life, not one of excesses, since that life is happiest for human beings.

Socrates advises, seek and study that by which you may know who knows, especially who knows the good life from the bad; who knows the just from the unjust; who knows the nature of the soul; who knows and practices moderation. What place does the wonderful sight of the cosmos and its various parts have here? Need one know that the eighth circle rotates faster than the fifth? Learning itself is but one of many things that must be considered in choosing the parts and mixture of a life. Then, what is the study which teaches who will give a man the power and knowledge to know what must be known to live justly and moderately? This study seems to comprehend all human things. Then, can it be philosophy, which seeks to know that which is? Must not the appropriate study for living well be political science? And, must not the man sought be the political scientist?

Does this mean that philosophy is denigrated? Perhaps, but perhaps it is only put in its place. Think back to the apparent competition between the philosopher, the law-giver, and the poet. Is it not true that, of these, the law-giver is closest to the political scientist in the full meaning of the term? And, has Socrates not spent much time now suggesting that the soul is composed of two parts, not three - the one part, calculating and desiring to learn, the other passionate and emotional? Does not the philosopher deal with the first, and the poet the second? And, is not the good for human beings moderation, and moderation the integration of the soul? Then, according to this argument, the law-giver is he who knows and teaches moderation, and in so doing unites and harmonizes the soul. In so doing, if he does well, he resolves the old quarrel between philosopher and poet, who now love or at least understand one another.

This is from the human point of view. We must choose a life, and we wish happiness. But what of eternity, and the immortality of the soul? What of the things which are, and the part of the soul which seeks to know them? Granted that these are only a part of human existence, are they not in themselves much greater than the whole of human existence? But how can a part be greater than the whole? Somehow the soul, in its greatness, comprehends the things which are but is not limited to them, and in its totality, mortal and immortal, surpasses even the immortal. Perhaps the truly human life is lived in the light of the eternal, but not blinded from seeing necessity by it.

*   *   *

Er reported that the prophet also said this: "for every man, if he chooses intelligently and lives seriously, there is a lovable life, not a bad one. Let the one choosing first not be careless, nor the last discouraged." Then they chose, in the order that fate had determined.

Fate played a role in the selections. Those who chose first had the opportunity to select the best lives. Evidently, some of them did. But others did not. The drawer of the first lot acted hastily, and chose a tyranny, without noticing that it necessitated that he eat his own children, among other horrors. Yet he had not been a bad man previously, but a good one. He had just returned from heaven. Then, why did he choose so foolishly? There were two reasons. First, his past goodness was based on habit and not on philosophy. This implies that his goodness was not truly his but was due more to the chance of living under good laws and good parents. Yet, had he not previously chosen to live under good laws? Perhaps the second reason will shed some light here. It is that his choice was determined by folly and gluttony, not by careful reflection. Where did these vices come from? After all, here was a heavenly soul. Were these vices retained in his soul despite his previous good life and his journey through heaven? In fact, did he choose to live under good laws because he knew of the weakness of his soul? Yet now that weakness ruled. Why?

The answer is evident. This soul had forgotten the consequences of its vices, since it hadn't been punished for them recently, but rather had been rewarded for its immediately past sound choice. On the other hand, the earthly souls now tended to choose well. Their pains were fresh in memory, and they were careful to choose a life that would bring them rewards and not further punishments. Thus, as Er reports, most souls simply exchanged conditions, the heavenly ones choosing bad lives, the earthly souls good ones. These choices, then, were determined by the memory or lack of memory of pain, and the apparently not very strong logical - or memorable - ability to connect wrongdoing with punishment. Only the souls who philosophized well during their embodied existence could, with a little good fortune, expect to be happy always and everywhere.

There is a problem here. Has a soul which philosophizes healthily during its embodied existence chosen to live the life of a philosopher? Is that choice made at the point of reentry into embodied existence? Reflection on the condition of all souls will help here. It appears that it is lives, not souls, which vary in goodness. All souls contain every potential, for good or evil. The life chosen brings out some and not others of these potentials. How then do some souls make good and others bad choices of lives? If all disembodied souls are identical, why don't all choose the same life? Two reasons are given: first, fate - the lives available; second, memory of immediately past suffering or non-suffering. All right: but where does philosophy enter in? Are certain souls philosophical, regardless of fate or immediate past? Do they choose the philosophical life and, if they do, why?

Er's account makes it appear that philosophy occurs only in this embodied life. In other words, it appears that a life may be philosophical, but not a soul. Then, it is not philosophy or philosophizing that selects a life at the point of choice. It must be some other capacity, one which seeks not knowledge of the things which are, but rather human happiness. Here, as in the normal reversal of good and bad lives, is another ironic reversal. The philosophical life seeks knowledge of the things which are: the soul which selects the philosophical life seeks human happiness: but the philosophical life looks always beyond human happiness.

Then, is the condition of souls merely ironic, always seeking the opposite of what it has, and always

losing what it has in attempting to gain what it wants?
Perhaps, but perhaps not. Er, or Socrates, speaks of
philosophizing not well - that is, with technical precision or excellence -, but in a healthy way. What
does this mean? Does it mean that one who philosophizes lives a life looking always beyond human existence? Or, does it mean that philosophy leads to a
healthy understanding of what human happiness is, and
how it is to be obtained? Can it be that philosophy
properly understood leads us to understand that the
strictly just life and the moderate life are one?

It appears, then, that one who philosophizes
healthily does not live the life of a philosopher.
What life does he live? What is the just and moderate
life? Most of the souls chose new lives in reaction to
the character of their former lives. Their character
had brought them sufferings which they now wished to
avoid. More or less thought went into the choices.
Some merely chose an apparently opposite life. Interestingly, musical animals, for example swans, chose
human lives. Why was this? Again, the question of
whether there are certain types of souls - here, musical - arises. Evidently, the soul which has been musical believes that a human life is better than an animal
life. But probably the human life chosen is not that
of a musician, since Orpheus in angry reaction to his
life chose to become a swan. It appears that this
soul, once musical, chooses to become a human being
pure and simple. Perhaps the soul which makes music
makes the same choice as the soul which philosophizes.

This sheds some light on the most interesting
choice. Odysseus' soul chose last. It had, Er reports,
been cured of its love of honor by the memory of its
great labors. Now, it looked long and hard for the
life it would choose. Finally, it found that of an
private man who minds his own business, lying there
neglected by the others. Happily, it chose this life,
and said that even had it picked first the choice would
have been the same. So, if the wily, experienced, no
longer ambitious Odysseus is a good guide, the best
life is that of a normal human being. This man, it
seems, minds the business - practices the art - of being a human being.

*   *   *

182

The process of beginning again nears its end. Having chosen, the souls now went to the three Fates: first Lachesis, who assigned a demon to each as a guardian of their particular life; next, lead by the demon, to Clotho, to pass under her hand as she turned the whorl, thus confirming the destiny drawn and chosen; then, to Atropos, who spun the threads of their destiny to make them unalterable. Finally, without turning around, they passed under Necessity's throne. From there, all together passed through the great heat of the barren plain of Lethe, and camped next to the river of Forgetfulness.

Now all were hot and tired, and had to drink some of the water. But not all drank equally. Some, saved by prudence, drank the right amount, but others drank too much. Er reports that he was prevented from drinking, but that each other soul as it drank forgot everything. But how reliable is Er on the subject? If some souls drank more, must not some souls forget more completely than others what happened to them, and what they chose before this present life? Er does not say why prudence saves some souls, and not others, by giving them an abiding sense of the proper measure. Is prudence only in some souls, or have their chosen lives already begun, even before birth? Is this prudence, which mitigates the necessary forgetfulness, a necessary part of certain lives? In any case, it seems that prudence permits right remembering and right forgetting.

In sum, the tale suggests, these are the elements which make possible a good choice: philosophy, when it concerns itself with the proper things; music, when it seeks to make being musical a part, not the whole of life; memory, which remembers not perfectly but in the proper way and amount; prudence, which restrains but never tries to eliminate the necessary desires. Each of these points in the direction of appropriateness and due measure and moderation.

*   *   *

Thus the dialogue ends, and the cycle begins again, with birth. The souls, having drunk, some enough, some too much, none too little, now sleep. At midnight, there is thunder and an earthquake. Like shooting stars, the souls are carried from their forgetful sleep

183

to their births, each by a different route. This is Er's tale. It could, Socrates says, save us, if we believe it. But if we believe him, we will hold the soul to be immortal. We will keep to the upper road, and practice justice with prudence. We will be friends to ourselves and to the gods, and receive the rewards for our virtue. If we do this, then here in this life and on the thousand year journey, we will fare well.

CHAPTER ELEVEN

CONCLUSION

There is no Book XI. Er's tale ends the Republic. But in a philosophical dialogue - a dialectical testing of opinion -, a final statement invites comment, on itself and on its relationship to what preceeds it.

Er's tale is the third great myth or parable of the dialogue, following the Noble Lie at the end of Book III which founds the just city, and the early Book VII account of the philosopher's ascent from the cave. It is a cosmic tale, following first a particular political one and then a generally human one. Each, implicitly, is a critique or corrective of the one preceeding it. The human tale puts the political one in perspective and shows its limits, and the cosmic tale places the human one in its larger setting. Perhaps this is a sufficient discussion of the truth of the tales. Whether or not they are strictly true, each is more true because each comprehends the earlier and shows what it is silent and thus unknowing about.

Thus, the brighter light which Er sheds on the whole is anticipated by the dimmer lights which the progressively more inclusive parts shed on one another. The Noble Lie is the first example of this. It may seem to be utterly dark, but let's remember that there is a fire in the cave which does shed some light on human things. The Noble Lie or myth of the metals is preceeded by Socrates' first city, the City of Necessity. It reveals the City of Necessity - the anarchist vision - to be a fond dream. Human beings, it shows, are not precisely differentiated by nature into every and all necessary arts. Human society does not simply fall into place naturally. A more comprehensive art - the art of politics - is required to fit, adjust, and reconcile human beings to their places in the political whole. The human city is a complex blending of nature and education which employs political rhetoric to bind the whole together. Moderation in its political form is manifest in this rhetoric.

The Noble Lie is the foundation of the just city. In it, human beings are defined by political justice. They are no more or less than the practice of an art necessary to the city. As before, the city is a compo-

185

site of necessary arts, but now the arts are hierarchically arranged and acquired more by education than by nature. The city is just because the artisans are never self-serving or, in other words, because no one practices the art of money-making except to benefit the whole city. Political power exists, but is perfectly separated from material wealth, and in fact, inversely related to it. The problem of political order is solved by this combination of justice and moderation. The city is a happy, self-sufficient whole.

Erotic desire disrupts this whole at the outset of Book V. It does so by compelling discussion of things better left undiscussed, at least from the political point of view, and thus destroying moderation. The relationship between eros and philosophy is elusive. How much Polemarchus and Thrasymachus are moved by erotic desire, and how much by philosophical curiosity is unclear. But Socrates implicitly acknowledges the connection, in what follows, by representing knowing as seeing. In any case, until Book V, it appears that the just city and just man are perfectly compatible provided, first, wisdom is understood as practical not philosophical and, second, moderation is maintained.

The emergence of the philosopher - the best, self-sufficient man - destroys the city. The philosopher has perfectly channelled eros into desire for knowledge of his own soul. He is, so to speak, auto-erotic. That this is so raises questions about his justice absolutely, to say nothing of his political justice. But his quest for knowledge takes him beyond the city, in mind if not in body. He compels the city to see that its myths and practices are based on opinion, not knowledge. He also compels the best young to consider whether justice, even in the human sense, means being a human being pure and simple rather than a citizen of some particular city. His enlightened relegation of political life to the dim, dark cave demands a replacement of practical by philosophical wisdom, and leads to the intellectual education set forth in the rest of Book VII.

The argument of Book VII suggests that it is very doubtful that intellectual education enables the philosopher to know the things which are. It is more likely that what the dialectic, properly practiced, teaches him in his own ignorance. But there is no doubt that perfect knowledge is the goal of intellectual education superficially understood. The perfection of the soul is equated with the development of pure mind. This <u>eros</u>, or transformation of <u>eros</u>, carries the philosopher far beyond the city. Even if the best city, speaking through its laws, persuades the philosopher to pay his debts and share in rule, that return is against his developed inclination. Left to himself, the philosopher would strive to become pure mind. Because his musical education is neglected, he lacks moderation. What practical wisdom he has is literally forced upon him.

Explicitly, the philosopher's incompleteness as a human being - his lack of harmony and integrity - causes the best city to fall. Implicitly, that same absence of moderation and harmony calls into question in principle the standing of the city of philosopher - rulers as best. In any case, the journey through imperfect regimes in Books VIII and IX reveals that justice for a human being is being a human being - that is, a being defined by an integrated moderate soul. This journey ends with the powerful image of the soul in which wild, hungry desire is tamed and befriended by practical wisdom. With this, the scene is set for the final, cosmic myth. This myth is told to place in perspective and thus correct the political and human stories which have preceeded it. Being as it is from beyond the grave, it is the corrective to any understanding of human life as seen from the perspective of human beings no matter how philosophical.

*   *   *

Er's tale is an account of the whole, of each thing that exists placed in relationship to each other thing, not at one moment but at all moments. Souls are a part of this, although the whole may also somehow be equivalent to the soul or the soul writ large, far larger than the city. The whole is the final object of knowledge for the philosopher, and as such that knowledge is the good absolutely for the philosopher absolutely. Whether it can be known, and by whom, and how - all this need not concern us greatly now. Our concern is the practical concern, the human good, understood in the light of even a very dim and imperfect knowledge of the whole.

The human good is the right or best life. This is Socrates' abiding concern throughout the dialogue,

187

and his ability to make Adeimantus and, especially, Glaucon share that concern is the motive force of the Republic. They ask: how should we live? Should we be just, and what does it mean to be just? What life should we choose, and to what extent is a choice of lives within our power? Er's tale answers these questions, not with perfect exactness, but with sufficient precision for practical purposes. These answers can best be understood when discussed against the background of the other kinds of answers suggested earlier in the dialogue.

*   *   *

The first possible answer is, the natural life or the life according to necessity. This answer is explicit or implied at three points in the dialogue: first, in the City of Necessity; then, in the discussion of the first two waves, when men and women are allocated places in the city according to their distinctive individual natures; finally, in the passages at the end of Book VI discussing that thought which moves beyond hypotheses according to a necessary logic. Although the applications differ somewhat, the essence of each instance is simple inevitability. Persons or things or thought will do or be what they cannot help but be. The proper life is that lived in awareness of some awesome superior power which regulates the whole and informs each part of it in determinate fashion. The necessary and proper choice is to succumb to that power and allow your self, your form, and your life to be shaped and directed by it. No other regulating power is needed, in the soul, in the city, in thought. Necessity determines all: wisdom is knowing this and not attempting to oppose it.

It's hard not to see the very close family resemblance between necessity and justice as Book IV defines it. Necessity is the great power which determines all things: justice either is that power or its result, each thing being itself. There is a certain reassurance in believing this, since it takes care of everything, and frees us from all human responsibility. But it is also hard not to see the explicit or implicit absence or rejection of moderation in each of the three instances. In the City of Necessity, there is no unifying element which binds together the various natural artisans. Predictably, the least intrusion of desire destroys this city. In Book V's treatment of the communistic Guardians, moderation and discretion must be overturned to permit these revelations. The consequence of this development is unholy, racial warfare. Finally, in the discussion of pure, unregulated logic, thought moves irresponsibly beyond opinion and creates a philosopher who is unmusical and immoderate and a city which fails in computing some intricate scientific calculations and thus destroys itself. That dependence upon hypotheses which limited the soul in its Book IV trial, and again in its Book X critique of the poets, is noticably lacking here.

What then of necessity, or of the very strict justice which compels each thing to be what it must be? How great are these powers? Er does not make this clear. Certainly they figure in his tale. Necessity is a great, primal power which somehow moves and controls the cosmos as a whole. Evidently, the cosmos could not be other than it is. To that extent, it is perfectly necessary. But that the whole is necessary does not seem to mean that the fate of each part within it is completely determined. Souls have fates, but these fates are chosen and only then, once chosen, do they become necessary. There is an area of choice, although exactly where and what it is, is not yet clear.

*   *   *

It seems, then, that souls are fated to do what they do: to lead the lives which they lead and experience the working out of those lives. This is a change from the merely necessary view. Now, human beings are not predetermined by necessity or justice or art, but instead individuated by fate. They must accomplish their fate, but their fate is their own. This is a view of the tragic poets. It is tragic because the individual - Agamemnon or Achilles or Antigone - cannot help but do what they do. They are not shaped by a great, impersonal, and fundamentally beneficient power like necessity or justice. Instead, they cannot help but lead the lives and perform the acts and undergo the sufferings which are their fate. They are in the hands of a power, but that power is only their own dimly understood and perversely destructive self. Er adds to this the thought that fates are bound up with certain kinds of lives. The self - the completely personal soul - and a given way of life blend together and be-

189

THE POLITICS OF MODERATION

come one thing: your fate. The tyrant is the classic
man ruled by fate; that is, by his own unreflective
self.

This view is pessimistic. A person is doomed,
senses his doom, and yet is unable to do more than act
out that doom. But there is more than pessimism here.
A fate is one's own. One exists as an individual, with
a self if not a soul. No longer is a human being formed by a primal necessity or justice which is not only
irresistible but also unknown and unknowable. Now, it
is a relatively short step from the fatalism of the
tragedian to the measured optimism of the philosopher.
That step is the movement from the dim, destructive
self to the understood, differentiated soul. One frees
oneself from fate, at least partially, by understanding
that what formerly was apprehended - if it was understood at all - as the entire, unlikable self is truly
only a portion of the soul. That portion is lament-
able, and consequently loves to lament, as Socrates
notes. But it is only a portion. There is hope, because there is more.

*   *   *

Necessity and fate, then, are put in their place
by the science of the soul. The whole view of the soul
accepts each of the earlier views, incorporates each,
and goes beyond them. This is represented in Er's tale
by the decisive place of choice which, while limited,
is prior to the fatalism implicit in a given life and
the binding of the soul to that life by Fate and Necessity. Necessity as a primal force is present in the
soul in the distinctive, irreducible charcter of each
of its parts. Fate is most obviously present in the
parts of the soul most mingled with the body: its personal history, its passions, and its desires. Choice
is choice. But what in the soul should choice be
equated with? Certainly not with the familial and historical background and the passions: these are closest
to a person's individual fate. Then, with spiritedness? This is not likely. One is spirited or not, by
nature. Then, with pure logical reasoning? Again, not
likely. As seen above, pure logic seems close to pure
necessity.

Where, then, do we find choice, and what image of
the soul is required by a human reality in which choice

is primary? The image of the soul presented in Book IV
is somewhat useful here. This image corresponded to
the just city, which by now has been revealed and revealed again to be much less than the whole truth. But
questions about that image are raised. First, should
spiritedness, if it is a distinct portion of the soul,
be seen as natural and necessary, or as the fate of a
particular individual? Beyond this, what of the ruling
portion of the soul? Is it practical wisdom, as it appears in Book IV, or philosophical wisdom, as at least
a superficial reading of Book VII would indicate? If
it is practical wisdom, then possibly choice can be
located here, since it is the essence of practical wisdom to decide about matters that are not completely
determined by some other force or factor. As well, if
the ruling portion is practical wisdom, some further
light is shed both backward, to the question of the
best city, and forward, to that of the best life. Concerning political matters, the correspondence between
the just, moderate city of Books II through IV and the
final, most comprehensive account in Book X is further
reason to disbelieve in the goodness of a city ruled
by reluctant philosophers. Concerning the best life,
this relationship between choice and practical wisdom
suggests that the best life will not be completely
private.

                    *   *   *

     Is a final picture of the soul now possible? There
seem to be three elements, corresponding to the three
basic powers; Necessity, Fate, and Choice. To the elements and powers may be added the lives, Philosopher,
Tyrant - which appears to have some Poet in it - and
Legislator. But first let's present the soul itself,
and then worry about the lives.

     Where in the soul is necessity found? Well, each
part is necessarily what it is, so necessity informs
each part, or at least seems to. Then, as Glaucon remarks in Book V, there is both a geometric and an erotic necessity. Let's say that these necessities are
those of pure logical thought and pure erotic desire,
respectively. If we think of the soul as hierarchically arranged, these would probably be placed at the top
and the bottom. But it is becoming less reasonable to

think that way, so let's say that these logical and erotic necessities are extremes. They are both very unlike and very like one another.

Now, what of fate? Does it have a place in the soul? Perhaps not, in a pure model of a pure soul. But the poets contend that every soul is individual, implying that there is no science of the soul, only fates of individuals. This is a dark enough teaching, but there is some truth here. All human souls are of bodies, families, regimes, times, and places. Perhaps the purest logic is untouched by fate - and perhaps it is not. However that may be, one's particular psychic and physical makeup is influenced - strongly influenced - by the contingencies of one's particular existence. The poets would say, determined by fate, but Er's tale argues that they exaggerate. It does appear that the less one studies the soul, the more fate - acting through its various typical agencies - is a decisive power. This implies that fate is most strongly represented in powerful but unexamined desires and ambitions, and is least effective in cool, reflective but practical reasoning.

This leaves choice. But before we place, or discover, choice in the soul, there is the question of spiritedness. Spiritedness has always been suspect, even as early as Book V. Toward the end of the dialogue, it is placed in the lower portion of the soul with desire. Spiritedness is the characteristic of the original Guardian, the friend of friends and foe of foes. Later, it is represented by the nature of the lion, a beast noble perhaps, but certainly dangerous. Now, is it to be excluded from the soul altogether? Is there to be no life, the warrior? What of Er? He dies, and returns to tell the tale of the cosmos. Is the warrior who sees something like the truth about the whole - its beauty and its harmony - then forever after unable to return to his city and fight blindly against other cities? Er is carefully chosen. He is the Guardian of Book III who, while insusceptible to philosophy, nevertheless is transformed from a man of unquestioning political loyalty to something less violent. Does a blending together of spiritedness and a glimpse of the things greater than the city occur, tempering both spiritedness and the pure theoretical impulse? Or, is the quality of spiritedness transformed by a wonderful account of the whole? Poetry and philosophy and rhetoric blend in Er's tale to transform spiritedness into something much more reflective.

Thus, it seems, does spiritedness pass over into some other quality or element in the soul. Here, it appears, must be the locus of choice, here in this middle portion of the soul which once was spiritedness but which now has been tempered by the knowledge of a world greater than politics. Perhaps it can be called practical wisdom, but it is no longer the practical wisdom of Book IV. There, practical wisdom was limited always by thought of the city's good; and there, spiritedness existed only as a discrete, quasi-beastial portion or the soul or, at most, as an ally of political prudence. Now, the soul has been both better differentiated and better integrated. Philosophical wisdom has been separated from prudence, and its anti-political tendencies made clear. Spiritedness has been tempered and humanized by an understanding of the whole. As before, the middle portion is decisive. But now, the middle portion sees. It has some knowledge: it is not blind anger or spirit. It sees beyond the city, and knows something of the whole, and of souls as simply human.

Here, it appears, is the locus of choice, in something like a blending of practical wisdom and spiritedness when that blending is further tempered and humanized by knowledge of the human soul and the cosmic whole. Why is it choice, or the home of choice? Well, it is not simply necessary, as logic and eros are. For that matter, it is not simple, made up as it is of some philosophical wisdom and some spiritedness and some political prudence. In its blended nature, it suggests its close affinity to moderation. It is a portion of the soul - whatever its name is - which, in its own compounded nature, suggests the moderation characteristic of the well-integrated soul as a whole. It is, as it were, the soul of the soul.

A backward glance helps to bring choice into clearer view. In Book IV, justice was the virtue which remained after the others had been discovered. Socrates never explicitly categorizes the virtues into kinds or classes; but in Book VII he remarks that all of the virtues except exercising prudence are somewhat close to those of the body, and are placed in a person by habit and exercise. Justice, then, is the one remaining of what will come to be called the moral virtues. In Book VI, the good itself, and knowledge of it, was what remained after all the other objects of knowledge had been considered. Again to use language which, while not Socratic, is accurate nevertheless, knowledge of the good itself is the residual intellectual virtue.

193

Now, choice - which may be the blending together of moral and intellectual virtue - is the thing remaining in the soul after each thing which must be what it is has been located. The distinctions between Necessity and Fate are minimal here: each determines some portion of the soul in a way which precludes choice. Choice can operate only where specific or particular psychological predetermination is absent or - in the case of particular causal factors - incompletely effective. How large is this area? In a person whose behavior is caused entirely by logical or erotic necessity, or by the happenings of his childhood, choice is non-existent. But this person is scarcely human; instead, he is an automaton controlled by external forces. According to Er's tale no one of us is like that. Each is able to make fundamental choices. For each, significant - the most significant - kinds of action are left undetermined. To this extent, we are free.

Does this mean that we can choose whatever we wish? Or, is there right choice, choice somehow in harmony with the nature of things? Perhaps it is helpful here to recall that evidently the portion of the soul which chooses is what once was pure spiritedness, now refined by prudence and some philosophical wisdom. This suggests that right choice will retain evidence of its original spiritedness, but now be more lofty and thoughtful. The classical term for this kind of choosing is magnanimity, greatness of soul. Choice will be of the best actions, thought, and objects which are consistent with one's humanity. Necessity will be acknowledged, and acquiesed in, but the overriding necessity will be the realization of one's full humanity. This kind of choosing harmonizes with the whole by leading a man to assume his rightful and appropriate place in the whole.

*   *   *

Two questions remain. First, is it possible to reconcile this greatness of soul with moderation? Are they not naturally at odds, even enemies with one another? Second, what is the place of politics in the right life? Er says that Odysseus, who appears to be the best man, is cured by his sufferings of his former desire for honor, and now chooses the life of a private man who minds his own business. Is this his choice, a life apart from politics? If it is, what sort of life

194

does he lead? These questions cannot be answered fully: it will be enough to suggest some arguments in agreement with the thesis of the Republic as a whole.

*   *   *

The business of a man, Book IV teaches, is the well-being of his soul. The basis of that well-being is that each portion of the soul does its own work properly: the perfection of it is the integration of the soul by moderation into a harmonious whole - the human being. To accomplish this task, two circumstances are evidently necessary: leisure to contemplate and work on one's soul, and a regime which permits that leisure instead of twisting and distorting the soul away from its full humanity. Here is the first suggestion that the perfection of the soul is the result of some agreeable compound of the public and the private.

In these favored circumstances, the well-ordered soul is brought to completion. This man adjusts and tunes the strings of his soul until each is itself, and then combines the notes of each into the harmony of the whole soul. He is musical and moderate and in accord with the cosmos as a whole. That this soul occurs is rare perhaps, but certainly not impossible. All - all! - it requires is leisure and sound material and a regime which protects privacy and the very best instruction and no untoward influences. Assuming these, in time we have our new Odysseus, the private man who minds his own business well.

Is his journey then over? So far from being over, it is hardly half begun. The origins of the crucial middle portion of the soul are in spiritedness. This is the part which is the heart of moderation, and which chooses. It may for a moment be happy with its success in becoming itself, musical and moderate. But it cannot forget - it must remember - that it began as fierce indifference to its own selfish interests. The impulse to greatness which sees and moves beyond itself remains alive in this soul. It wishes to extend the harmony which it has discovered beyond itself: its greatness is the greatness which desires true moderation for all, or for many, or at least for some few other than itself. No sooner is the private task completed than the public project - and the public problem - presents itself.

195

Thus does this soul, which once wished for no more - no more! - than private happiness find posed for itself its characteristic problem: the politics of moderation. This problem is as easy to formulate as it is hard to solve: how may moderation be extended to the public realm, so that it may be shared in by many, without losing that indispensible privacy which made the best and truest moderation possible in the first place? Socrates has, in Book V, demonstrated once and for all that the regime which loses its sense of moderation and destroys all privacy in the name of perfect justice is the most hellish thing on earth. The truly moderate soul may avoid this trap, but its magnanimity seeks for ways to make its own goodness public. What these ways are is, of course, the substance of the political science of moderation.

*   *   *

What is this political science? What way of life leads to possession of it? How may it be put into public practice? The questions take us beyond the bounds of the Republic. The Republic poses the questions and problems of the politics and political science of moderation. It defines them, as it were, negatively. But that healthy and lasting integration of the public and the private is not set forth in the Republic. Neither the too-public Guardian nor the too-private philosopher lives the moderate and integrated life. Each is too just, a finding which would be ironic were not the incompleteness of justice pure and simple known. Guardian and Philosopher are too much a complex human being reduced to one single element of a fully human person. True moderation eludes each of them, to say nothing of the simply passionate Poet - Tyrant.

But, what of the Philosopher - Ruler of Book VII? Is he not properly integrated, the living embodiment of genuine moderation? We know by now that he is not. For one thing, his political activity is undertaken only given barely-cloaked compulsion. There is little here of the gentleness of moderation or of the public spiritedness which underlies magnanimity. For another, his isolation from and superiority to ordinary humanity is unjustified given Socrates' implicit argument here, and explicit argument elsewhere, about the status of human wisdom. This suggests that the proper life will not be so far removed from that of the normal human being; and, conversely, that the normal human being will share more fully in the simply good life. Third, this person is unmusical: there is nothing of the poet about him and, whatever the dangers of <u>eros</u>, no human being is complete without its influence.

Then, is the <u>Republic</u> simply negative, an extended lesson in what the politics of moderation is not? Those politics cannot be identified with any one of the cities or models of man explicitly presented in it, although the dialogue moves toward them with its closing consideration of the integrated human being and with Er's tale. But there is more to the dialogue than its explicit parts, or the relationship of the parts, or the implication of that relationship. There is <u>form</u>. After all - and all is very much here -, the <u>Republic</u> is a dialogue, of a certain kind. In closing, confronted with the problem of the politics of moderation, let's reflect for a moment or two on this most fundamental fact.

                    *   *   *

     First, a few simple facts, facts which now take on new meaning. Socrates, a philosopher in company with a bright young man, Glaucon, is overtaken by some other young men, and more or less coerced into changing his plans. He is taken to the private home of a wealthy, conventionally religious man, and begins a discussion about justice. In the course of that discussion, Socrates and the best of the young men, Glaucon and Adeimantus, turn into legislators and construct a number of different "cities-in-speech". This construction is accompanied by three memorable myths invented by the Philosopher-Legislator. Toward the end of the dialogue, the rudiments of a political science are set forth, this shortly after presenting a plan for higher intellectual education.

     The dialogue is inconclusive, except to say that one who would be happy must make the right choices in the right way. But the <u>form</u> suggests certain conclusions. The right life is <u>of</u> the nature of a conversation. In that conversation, one person is not limited to one role, although most tend to play one or a very few. The leading role - Socrates' - incorporates and blends additional elements of humanity as it proceeds. Socrates' role is authoritative: he lays down the law for others: he keeps them in line: he provokes and silences them. But he does this in conversation with them. His authority is that of wisdom and prudence and rhetoric and poetry. He allows them to enter in, and guides them into compelling him to take charge and create structures - intellectual structures, political structures - which they occupy, and which occupy them, for a short time, and which they then discard or modify.

The structures which they create are provisional, temporary, experimental. None are perfect; in the dialogue, every participant is willing to try the structures, and willing to let them go. No one is, so to speak, pre-occupied: each can choose, to grasp, to relinquish. That is, all but one: Cephalus. He cannot. He is too old, too fearful, too opinionated, too propertied. But Cephalus is the indispensible condition of the dialogue, and its resultant playfulness about intellectual and political forms and structures. Cephalus is wealthy, and his wealth builds the protected house of privacy and freedom within which they dwell and discuss. This house is open to Socrates, and well-disposed toward him. It, together with a temporary freedom fron _eros_, is the basis of the philosophical playfulness and political experimentation.

That playfulness and that experimentation are possible, in the event, because everyone behaves well. For almost all, this politeness and decency is due to their good, careful upbringing. For Socrates, it is due to his exceptional powers of self-control. For Thrasymachus - a basically primitive and naturally violent man - it is due to Socrates' quiet but evident strength coupled with Thrasymachus' barely educated but nonetheless effective sense of his own interests.

Thus, the open community rests on these bases: wealth, privacy, tolerance, a good moral upbringing, subdued but evident strength, and an accurate sense of one's own interests. In themselves, none of these elements is or insures good living. Even taken together, and coupled with the spark of philosophy, they do not insure it. But, they make the search for good living possible, as long as the search does not, in its eagerness, heedlessly cast them aside. As the dialogue shows, the most important element - these various factors drawn together - is moderation. If it is lost, all else disintegrates.

*   *   *

The form of the dialogue suggests certain conclusions about form. This is not double-talk: it does show that form is a complex thing. The various intellectual and political forms are provisional. They are playful and interesting. One need not be committed to any one of them beyond its obvious suggestiveness and usefulness. Any given one is dispensible: new forms of this sort are easy to invent. The theoretical mind readily spins them off, criticizes them, and moves on to new theoretical constructs.

More than this: it is dangerous to take these forms seriously as other than provisional theoretical constructs. They may serve some immediate purpose. But their utility is limited by the precise circumstances which gave rise to them. In the dialogue, the intellectual and political forms serve to educate the brothers, and others in the audience. But Socrates' commitment to them is only insofar as they serve that particular purpose. They are not intended to be transposed to other circumstances, or erected into permanent intellectual and political structures which then measure all others. They are theoretical: they are products of the relatively free-floating human mind temporarily divorced from normal human reality. Both their origin and their purpose suggests that they are permissible and useful if not grimly believed in and adhered to, and dangerous - very dangerous - if more than this is made of them. The consequences of attempting to practice openly the very strictest definition of justice - a definition itself entirely hypothetical - is only the best example of this.

There is another understanding of form implicit in the dialogue. It is good human form. It is behaving and speaking and thinking as a fully human being would. This form is the product of good natural material properly shaped by gymnastic and music. In direct contrast to the theoretical mind, one who embodies it is precisely limited in speech and action by one's humanity. It is not antagonistic to theory, but this form knows theory for what it is: a superhuman force which characteristically forgets about both the circumstantial and the permanent facts of human existence. To give names to this form, it is the best manners coupled with the practical wisdom whose task it is to remember and be substantially guided by those facts.

*   *   *

Where does this leave us? With the search for the right political form, a form which will produce the right human character? This is the explicit quest of the Republic. It is a search for forms. The dialogue seems to teach that forms are decisive, and that human life, always so disordered, will be put right when, and only when, the right political form is discovered and put into practice. The dialogue is a search fueled and fired by the longing for true form. Yet that final form - of city, of soul - is elusive. The best form of the Republic - the just city - aims at good character, but fails to satisfy the erotic curiosity which expresses the highest and lowest aspects of our nature. This curiosity - this longing to know, the highest and the lowest things - seems to defy and defeat moderation.

But does it? Is moderation doomed to war against eros and philosophy, a victory resulting in lifeless forms, a defeat in the wreckage of all normal and decent human existence? If not warfare, is there not at least an inevitable tension here, a tension which at best can be preserved and result in a way of life which is a compromise or balance between opposing forces? Neither of these outcomes reflects the belief - the opinion - which shapes and moves the dialogue. That belief is a belief in harmony, in the incorporation of eros into the truly moderate soul, the soul which becomes human because it seeks beyond the human and thus knows the human for what it is, and chooses it, and loves it, and expresses it in the only forms which retain meaning: beautiful speech and beautiful action.

INDEXES

I. General Index

Search for, xviii, 6,
   11, 37-38, 41, 44-45,
   128, 136
Traditional, xx

Knowledge, xix-xxi, 38-
   39, 46, 67, 70, 81-82,
   85, 88, 90, 92-94, 96,
   100, 102, 107-108, 137,
   143, 145-146, 155, 161-
   162, 179, 181, 186-187,
   193

Law, 6, 29, 36, 46, 59,
   71, 92-93, 99-100, 104,
   108, 110-111, 114-116,
   119-120, 124, 131, 147,
   150, 160, 164-166, 168,
   180, 187, 197
   Of Identity, 45-46, 48-
   49
   Of Reaction, 124
Leisure, 1, 17-19, 195
Lie, (see also, Deceit),
   20-22, 76
   Noble, ix, 31-32, 35,
   79, 89, 92-93, 108,
   185
   In Soul (see Soul)
Life, Lives, xxv-xxvii,
   1, 3, 32, 35, 50, 52,
   63, 89, 92-93, 104,
   106, 109, 115, 118,
   121, 128, 131-132, 134,
   138, 142-144, 146-148,
   151, 158, 164, 174,
   178-180, 182-183, 187,
   191-192, 194, 196-198,
   200
   Choice of, xxiv-xxv,
   12, 18, 178-182, 184,
   188-189
   Philosophical, xiii,
   105
   Political, xv-xviii,
   xx, xxiii, 6-7, 32-
   33, 79, 93-94, 98,
   106, 114, 126, 146,
   186

Light, 50-51, 68, 82, 87-
   92, 94, 100, 106-107,
   141, 144, 177, 180, 185
Line, Divided, 83-84, 87-
   88, 90
Lion, 149-151, 192
Logic, (see Logos)
Logos, (see also Speech),
   xviii, xx, 4, 11, 14,
   43, 46, 55, 82, 84-85,
   90, 93, 97, 104-106,
   109, 113, 120, 131,
   133, 137, 141-144, 146-
   147, 150, 158-159, 163-
   171, 179, 181, 188-196
Luxury, 12, 14-16, 18,
   41, 64
Lyric Poetry, (see Poe-
   try)

Magnanimity, 194-196
Marriage, 36, 60-61
Mathematics, (see Form,
   Mathematical; Geometry;
   Measurement)
Material, Matter, 17, 19,
   28, 45, 61, 87, 89,
   116, 158, 174-175, 177,
   195, 199
Mean, 30, 47, 77, 114,
   136, 145, 148, 178,
   183, 193, 195, 200
Measurement, 148, 156,
   163, 165
Medicine, 8, 29, 46
Melancholia, 133
Memory, 30, 79, 81, 90,
   122, 181-183
Method, x-xi, xix-xx, 38,
   44-46, 48, 86, 103,
   142, 153, 155
Middle, (see Mean)
Model, 21-22, 25-26, 28,
   52, 78, 94, 143, 167,
   197

III. Index of Names

213